"In today's world, everyone will have fifteen minutes of fame and spend six months as a consultant. This book does a great job of bringing a business sense to professionals in the difficult position of creating a business where they, themselves, are the product. It is practical, compassionate, and a good alternative to an M.B.A."

—Peter Block, author, *Flawless Consulting*

"Have I got a book for you! Take a look at *The Business of Consulting* by Elaine Biech. The title notwithstanding, this is really a guide for anyone trying to start a one-person business on a limited budget."

—Anne Fisher, *Fortune Magazine*

"Why would anyone consider consulting without devouring this book? A great blend of solid information on consulting A to Z: the operational issues, the business and emotional risks, the personal discipline required, along with the tremendous payoffs of the profession! Applying the start-up thinking alone should increase first-year revenues four-fold."

—Dianna Booher, Speaker Hall of Fame, Booher Consultants, Inc., and author,
Communicate with Confidence and *Speak with Confidence*

"Elaine Biech has written about consulting from every angle! In this book, she offers her perspective on the business side of our work. If you are succeeding with your work but struggling with your business, Elaine can help."

—Geoff Bellman, author, *The Consultant's Calling* and *Getting Things Done When You Are Not In Charge*

"Elaine Biech has built an impeccable reputation as a savvy, practical, and no-nonsense consultant. This important update to her classic will help you jump-start your consulting business."

—Pete Weaver, senior vice president, DDI

"Elaine Biech shows you what to do to get into the consulting business and stay in it successfully. You will not find a better written, more practical guide on all aspects of the business of consulting. The second edition of *The Business of Consulting* adds a wealth of new material that any consultant will appreciate."

—Mel Silberman, author and president, Active Training

"*The Business of Consulting* is from one of the best minds in this business. Elaine Biech is *the* most astute businesswoman in the consulting world today. She speaks the language, knows the acronyms, has seen it done in all environments both in and out of the U.S., and has helped shape organizations everywhere. Elaine has been that one person that is inside my personal inner circle in everything I've done for the last ten years. When you want the hard work done, call her."

—RADM (ret.) JB Godwin III, vice president, Athena Technologies, Inc.

"Bravo Elaine! You do a wonderful job of laying out the pros and cons of the consulting life. Elaine knows her stuff and delivers with humor, compassion, and deep understanding. If only Elaine had written this book twenty-five years ago when I started. It certainly would have made life simpler and moved my consulting career along much faster! Still, after all these years, I continue to learn from Elaine."

—Beverly Kaye, founder and CEO, Career Systems International, and author, *Up Is Not the Only Way*

"Elaine Biech just made a great book much better. The first edition of this book is quickly becoming a classic in its field, and the second edition is even more valuable. It contains many useful, productive tools and examples and a CD that is extremely helpful. The use of technology is invaluable in today's consulting activities. I recommend that you read the first chapter and then scan the rest of the book and read the last chapter. Then, if you still want to be a consultant, use it as a how-to guide to manage, grow, and sustain a consulting practice."

—Jack J. Phillips, chairman, ROI Institute, Inc., and coauthor, *Show Me the Money*

"Hesitating about whether this is the *right* book for you? This is the *only* book you will ever need in order to start, maintain, or grow your consulting business. Elaine uses her years of experience—plus updated info and practical advice—to guide anyone contemplating or already in this profession. Get the book now and save yourself time and money—you won't regret it."

—Ann Herrmann-Nehdi, CEO, Herrmann International: The Whole Brain Company

"*The Business of Consulting* is a must-read for anyone in consulting—new or experienced! It is overflowing with practical insights and how-to tips that help you through the multiple business management challenges faced in the consulting world. Buy it • Read it • Apply it."

— Richard Chang, author and CEO, Richard Chang Associates, Inc.

"Despite the fact that I have greater access to information than I have ever had before, my most trusted resource when it comes to my professional life is *The Business of Consulting*. Elaine Biech has captured, organized, and articulated the heart of the matter when it comes to consulting. This edition provides an expanded blend of practical insights along with a realistic optimism about how to succeed. *The Business of Consulting* is my go-to resource."

— Pamela J. Schmidt, executive director, ISA, The Association of Learning Providers

"This updated edition is packed with tips and techniques to help you establish yourself as a consulting professional."

— Pat Cataldo, associate dean for executive education, Penn State University

"In more than thirty year's work with professional consultants, I have never worked with one I respect and value more than Elaine Biech. She is visionary, experienced, balanced, practical, and above all, responsible. She exemplifies . . . the best of what is meant by 'trusted advisor.'"

— Michael P. Sullivan, retired U.S. Navy Admiral

"This incredible resource is the voice of reality! *The Business of Consulting* is different from most books in that Elaine condenses years of her own wisdom, learned through trial and error, and freely shares it in this practical guide for all practicing and new consultants. And she does so while pointing out the possible pitfalls in the process. A true window into what it takes to be successful."

— Linda Growney, director, Organization Capability, CUNA Mutual Group

"*The Business of Consulting* abounds with the same business acumen that Elaine used when she worked with our senior leadership team. Every consultant should apply her principled practices to guarantee satisfied customers."

— John E. Gherty, former president and CEO, Land O'Lakes, Inc.

"Elaine and her team did an outstanding job coaching our Region through our Quality Management journey. Her approach to consulting is refreshing and right-on for today's and tomorrow's business needs. Read her book. She shares all her secrets!"

— Gail Hammack, former regional vice president, McDonald's Corporation

"If you are thinking about quitting your job and going into consulting, be sure to read this book first! It is a practical guide to help you decide what to do and how to do it. And if you are already a full- or part-time consultant, you'll find many ideas for improving your success."

— Dr. Donald L. Kirkpatrick, former national ASTD president,
1997 inductee into *Training Magazine*'s Hall of Fame

"Elaine is a true leader in the field of consulting and training. She willingly shares her knowledge through leading seminars, developing resources like *The Business of Consulting,* and serving as a resource to support up-and-coming leaders in the field. Having had the good fortune to be Elaine's student, I know you will find this book an easy read and a complete resource, whether you are just embarking on your consulting journey or growing your skills as a seasoned consultant."

— Barbara Schoenleber, business sales leader and former manager of training and development, Schreiber Foods

"So you think you want to be a consultant . . . and so do thousands of others. So how do you set yourself apart? You read *The Business of Consulting* and let Elaine Biech talk you through the steps. If the devil is in the details, then the details and easy-to-follow steps are in this book, and they will keep you on the path to success."

— L. A. Burke, operational strategic planner, U.S. Customs and Border Protection

"Thinking of starting your own consulting business? This book will give you the road map, tips, and wisdom you'll need as you step out. Benefit from the guidance of a pro who's 'been there, done that.'"

— Jean Lamkin, corporate training director, Landmark Communications, Inc.

Consulting Colleagues

"I wish I had this book when I started my consulting practice. Elaine has all the answers it took me years to learn! Even now, I use her pearls of wisdom—the pull quotes—during my annual planning session as a 'tune-up' to make sure I cover the basics of the business—and to bring new consultants up to speed."

—Kristin Arnold, president, Quality Process Consultants, Inc.

"It's all here! Elaine Biech has provided a comprehensive resource to make a consulting practice a viable operation. She provides insight and forms to plan, market, and grow a consulting business as well as guidance about how to make money in the profession. Real-life stories document her examples and advice. *The Business of Consulting* is a wise investment for any consultant."

—Jean Barbazette, president, The Training Clinic, and author,
The Trainer's Journey to Competence and *Training Needs Assessment*

"After reading Elaine's book you will see clearly if a consulting career is right for you. The book gives you all the hints a professional mentor can give. Don't miss one of them. All my German consultant-trainees make excellent use of Elaine's inside knowledge."

—Björn Fiedler, founder, Fiedler and Partners, Germany

"The most effective negotiators know there are no magic tricks; they master the basics and continually refresh their skills and strategies. As the CEO of a negotiation training and consulting firm serving clients worldwide, I, too, return to master the basics of this business. Elaine Biech's updated *The Business of Consulting* refreshed and refined my approach, leaving Watershed Associates a stronger firm for the rest of the 21st century."

—Tom Wood, president, Watershed Associates, Inc., and author, *Best Negotiating Practices*® Series

"Elaine has done it again—she's improved an already great product! The e-Ideas provide great resources that make it easy to find data. I used this book to help my son-in-law start his own business—which is not even consulting. Elaine's style of writing is clear, concise, and easy to understand."

—Kathy Talton, program manager, Precise Systems, Inc.

"Elaine Biech has done it again! She has taken an excellent book and made it better. In the second edition, Elaine shares her expert knowledge of consulting as well as the secrets that enable a good consultant to become a great consultant. She provides 'a star to steer by.' She offers advice on client relationships, ethics, work-life balance, and fifty e-Ideas for using technology to build a successful consulting practice. This book is one that every consultant will want to read, whether they've been in the business for one week or several decades."

—Sharon Y. Rhodes, adjunct faculty member, College of Southern Maryland

"*The Business of Consulting* is an essential guide to the nuts and bolts of consulting. Elaine Biech proves again to be the consultant's consultant."

—Jack Osburn, senior acquisition analyst, CRM Associates, Inc.

"The first edition served to decipher the practice of consulting and expose the benefits and risks of entering the world of consulting. Taking the input of real practitioners, Elaine has now further enhanced this no-nonsense, practical guide that is one of a kind in our universe. In this edition, her magic continues to unfold the many facets of the consulting business, making this book a must-read for any person seeking to either enter, grow, or enhance their experiences in the profession. Even seasoned veterans of the industry—whose egos may prevent them from admitting that they really don't know everything—will benefit from this edition."

—Stephen K. Merman, principal, Organization Consulting Group, former national president, ASTD

"*The Business of Consulting* is an absolute treasure—and so is Elaine Biech! After fourteen years of by-the-seat-of-my-pants consulting, I can now fill in the gaps, polish what I've been doing well, and improve on those things that have always gotten in the way. Elaine's writing style is both practical and conversational. Reading her book is like sitting in her living room and chatting with her over coffee about the business of consulting. This book is a must-have resource if you have ever dreamed of creating or expanding your own consulting business!"

—Sharon Bowman, author, *The Ten-Minute Trainer*

"There is a substantial gap between possessing subject matter expertise and possessing the skills to convey and apply that expertise in a way that adds value for clients. Then, once across the gap, there is need for a well-charted course to negotiate the challenges of simply doing business successfully. Elaine Biech has bridged that gap again with an even more reliable crossing to the realm of integrated expertise and consultant skills, and then provided the essential roadmap for reaching our business goals. This is my go-to book."

— Joseph G. Wojtecki, Jr., senior fellow and business manager, Center for Risk Communication

"We've been in the consulting business for more than twenty years and we've learned something new from practically every page of *The Business of Consulting*. Elaine has done a terrific job of crystallizing the basics of what consulting is and what you need to know to translate your consulting dreams into a reality. Hands down, buying this book is the best investment in the future of your business that you'll ever make."

— Jeffrey and Linda Russell, codirectors of Russell Consulting, and authors, *Change Basics*

"Elaine lives what she writes. She is a highly organized, ethical, and caring human being who is determined to share her success with others. In *The Business of Consulting*, Elaine outlines her own business savvy, practice, and ethics for the benefit of her readers. What could be more compelling?"

— Edie West, consultant and author

"An essential read and invaluable resource! Elaine provides a wealth of practical, relevant information to help you achieve greater success as a consultant. I reference this book for inspiration and guidance on a regular basis."

— Linda Revelle, president, Revelle Management Training Associates

"When it comes to starting up your own consulting business, Elaine wrote the book—literally! Quitting your corporate job and going out on your own is both exciting and scary. To make the transition, I needed a first-class how-to book. *The Business of Consulting* is that book."

— Richard D'Loss, president, Rubicon Aviation Training and Consulting, Inc.

"Don't start a business without it! *The Business of Consulting* is full of insightful tips and exercises to get you from intellectual comprehension to practical application. Sage advice + actionable ideas - inflated guru ego = a must-have tool for any consultant."

— Halelly Azulay, president, TalentGrow

"What if you could sit across the table and learn the secrets of consulting from one of the best in the field? My business partner and I did just that by meeting Elaine before we established our new business! Consider this book your meeting with Elaine."

— Dr. Suzanne Adele Schmidt, cofounder, Renewal Resources L.L.C.

"An incredible mentor, Elaine is intelligent, articulate, and full of great ideas for marketing your business. My business was at a standstill when I met Elaine. She gave me tons of great marketing ideas and got me going."

— Marla Maeder, Maeder Design

"Elaine has that rare gift of translating her ideas into easy-to-understand writing. Buy and read her book if you seriously want to develop a dynamite consulting career."

— Karen S. Ostrov, psychologist and owner, KONECT

"In *The Business of Consulting*, Elaine Biech has written the consummate how-to book for consultants in any field. It is a must-read for new and experienced consultants alike!"

— Barbara Pate Glacel, author, *Light Bulbs for Leaders*

"I treasure every opportunity to learn from Elaine Biech. She is a teaching pro. *The Business of Consulting* offers wisdom that can only contribute to your success as a consultant."

— Garland Skinner, retired U.S. Navy Captain

About This Book

Why is this topic important?

Individuals often become consultants without realizing all the ramifications that accompany starting this new venture. They are joining the ranks of the entrepreneur and must instantly address a multitude of details required to start a business—everything from selecting a name and obtaining necessary licenses to financing and promoting the new business. The crucial start-up days may be frenetic and fraught with questions. Or, even worse, the new consultant may not even know what questions to ask, such as those related to income tax or legal structures. This book is a guide to ensure that every new consultant knows at the minimum what questions to ask and how to find the answers.

What can you achieve with this book?

The Business of Consulting, Second Edition, provides a road map to aspiring consultants. It offers guidance and wisdom from one consultant who has been down this road. The CD-ROM provides financial documents, decision-making tools, and self-evaluation questionnaires to guide you on the journey. The candid and practical approach of this book echoes the first edition, but with updated content and new references. With *The Business of Consulting* as a mentor, new consultants will have the tools at hand to:

- Identify the pros and cons of starting a consulting practice.
- Determine what to charge clients.
- Set up a professional business practice.
- Select a business model, name, and location.
- Establish a start-up business and marketing plan.
- Manage record keeping, cash flow, and other critical financial issues.
- Maintain an ethical, professional business.

How is this book organized?

The book is divided into eleven chapters. These chapters are ordered in a logical sequence from concept to creation of a new consulting practice. Each chapter takes the reader through a progression of business decisions that must be made when starting a new business—and in particular a consulting business—such as:

- Is this the right profession for me?
- How much should I charge?
- How do I write a business plan?
- What should I consider to market a consulting business?
- How do I ensure the business is solvent?
- How can I build client relationships?

Spread throughout the logically sequenced chapters are tips and techniques from the voice of experience. And sprinkled among the practical advice are almost sixty e-Ideas—technology tips to assist the new consultant in laying a solid foundation, finding resources to build the business, and identifying tools to save time and remain on the cutting edge of the profession.

About Pfeiffer

Pfeiffer serves the professional development and hands-on resource needs of training and human resource practitioners and gives them products to do their jobs better. We deliver proven ideas and solutions from experts in HR development and HR management, and we offer effective and customizable tools to improve workplace performance. From novice to seasoned professional, Pfeiffer is the source you can trust to make yourself and your organization more successful.

Essential Knowledge Pfeiffer produces insightful, practical, and comprehensive materials on topics that matter the most to training and HR professionals. Our Essential Knowledge resources translate the expertise of seasoned professionals into practical, how-to guidance on critical workplace issues and problems. These resources are supported by case studies, worksheets, and job aids and are frequently supplemented with CD-ROMs, Web sites, and other means of making the content easier to read, understand, and use.

Essential Tools Pfeiffer's Essential Tools resources save time and expense by offering proven, ready-to-use materials—including exercises, activities, games, instruments, and assessments—for use during a training or team-learning event. These resources are frequently offered in looseleaf or CD-ROM format to facilitate copying and customization of the material.

Pfeiffer also recognizes the remarkable power of new technologies in expanding the reach and effectiveness of training. While e-hype has often created whizbang solutions in search of a problem, we are dedicated to bringing convenience and enhancements to proven training solutions. All our e-tools comply with rigorous functionality standards. The most appropriate technology wrapped around essential content yields the perfect solution for today's on-the-go trainers and human resource professionals.

www.pfeiffer.com

Essential resources for training and HR professionals

The Business of Consulting

THE BASICS AND BEYOND

SECOND EDITION

elaine biech

Foreword by Jim Kouzes

BICENTENNIAL
1807
WILEY
2007
BICENTENNIAL

John Wiley & Sons, Inc.

Library of Congress Cataloging-in-Publication Data

Biech, Elaine.
   The business of consulting: the basics and beyond/Elaine Biech.—2nd ed.
      p. cm.
   Includes bibliographical references and index.
   ISBN 978-0-7879-9464-8 (cloth)
   1. Consulting firms—Management. 2. Business consultants. I. Title.
   HD69.C6B534 2007
   001—dc22   2007002780

Acquiring Editor: Matthew Davis   Editor: Michele D. Jones
Director of Development: Kathleen Dolan Davies   Manufacturing Supervisor: Becky Carreño
Developmental Editor: Susan Rachmeler   Editorial Assistant: Julie Rodriguez
Production Editors: Nina Kreiden and Rachel Anderson

Printed in the United States of America
Printing   10   9   8   7   6   5   4   3   2

CONTENTS

LIST OF EXHIBITS ON THE CD-ROM

For Shane and Thad,

the best consulting projects

a mom ever had

FOREWORD

I will always remember Johnny Smith. Johnny was my very first supervisor in my very first full-time, salary-paying job.

I had returned from two years in the Peace Corps and was fortunate to find work in a consulting firm that had landed a contract from the U.S. Office of Economic Opportunity. I was part of a team that traveled from city to city in the southwestern United States to conduct training programs, facilitate team-building sessions, and consult on organizational issues to newly formed Community Action Agencies. Our group was made up of mostly young, inexperienced, but highly motivated behavioral scientists who wanted to change the world. It was a perfect kind of job for us, but without Johnny most likely we would have gone broke.

Johnny was a Texas Instruments manager who had decided to take on the temporary assignment of leading this small band of do-gooders. He, too, wanted to do good, but from his years at Texas Instruments, he also knew that to be of service we had to stay in business. Johnny brought a discipline to our merry band that was absolutely essential to our survival.

I vividly remember one consulting gig in Dallas, Texas. We had a meeting with the director of an agency to talk about the goals and roles for the assignment, and the director was called out for a few minutes. Johnny said to us, "This guy is very organized." I asked, "How do you know that?" He said, "See all those file folders lined up neatly on the credenza behind his desk? That's how." And, he was right about that. The guy and the agency *were* very organized. Johnny paid attention to detail. He was all about the little things that, when you added them up, either made something work or caused it to fail. I also remember what a stickler he was for filling out expense reports and submitting invoices. He used to say things like, "You'll get my thanks when you fill in the blanks." Corny, but it worked.

Johnny Smith would have adored Elaine Biech. He'd have wanted her on our team. And, had it been available back in 1969, I am certain that Johnny would have handed every one of my colleagues and me a copy of *The Business of Consulting*. It's the kind of straightforward, no-nonsense book that he would have wholeheartedly embraced.

But since Johnny isn't around to give you that advice, permit me to give it instead. If you are just starting out in consulting, or if you are at a place where you're growing but not making enough money, you must study this book. The truth is *The Business of Consulting* is vital to your success. You can be knowledgeable and great at what you do, but if you do not know how to run your business, if you do not understand what you are getting yourself into as an entrepreneur, you will be out of business quickly.

Just take a look at what you'll find in *The Business of Consulting*. In Chapter One Elaine asks, and helps you answer, the question, "What are you getting yourself into?" The chapter helps you come to grips with the myths and realities of the business and asks you to seriously consider whether or not consulting is right for you. Chapter Two is about the talents and tolerances you'll need to succeed in the profession. Chapter Three discusses money—what you think you'll need to earn, how much you should charge, and how to make ethical pricing decisions.

Chapters Four, Five, and Six focus on starting . . . and staying in business and the cost of doing business. These are the meat and potatoes chapters about running the operational, marketing, and financial sides of your practice. Need to write a business plan? It's here. Need a marketing plan? This book has guidelines for developing one. Need to calculate your cash flow or deal with bad debts? It's all inside. Elaine offers wise counsel on these and more.

Chapter Seven addresses clients. From the first meeting to maintaining the relationship after the project has been completed, Elaine coaches you on how to create value for your customer. Chapter Eight describes the pains—sometimes welcome, sometimes not—of growth. One of the most vexing issues you will have to deal with during the life of your firm is how to manage it as it matures, adds people (and costs), and becomes more than just a hobby for one person. Elaine talks to you about the advantages and disadvantages of key aspects of growth.

Elaine and I also share a passion for ethics. Elaine is adamant about how we conduct ourselves in business, and Chapters Nine and Ten are calls to action. As Elaine puts it, "Your reputation as a consultant will be created by thousands of actions, but may be lost by only one." She reminds us that it is imperative that we act as role models for how business should be conducted. We always have to practice what we preach. All this takes continuous professional learning and personal growth.

In the closing Chapter Eleven, Elaine poses the question, "Do you *still* want to be a consultant?" She helps you answer it by giving you a peek into her own daily life as a consultant, a dose of reality for anyone daring to answer "yes" to the question. Of course, we all know what Elaine's answer is, because it's the profession she chose for herself. She's not a journalist who just writes about it; she lives it every day. She's a role model for the advice she gives others, and she's personally helped over 100 people start consulting practices with the information in this book.

And you can understand why so many people benefit from her wise counsel. *The Business of Consulting* is complete and easy to use. The advice can be put into practice immediately. No theory here. Just real-world example and proven tactics to grow, maintain, or build a successful consulting practice. Elaine does not hold back; you don't need to read between the lines. She is straightforward and candid and she shares all that she knows openly. This is a compilation of all the lessons she's learned about running a consulting practice during her twenty-five years of being in the trade. There are over fifty checklists, tables, forms, and other useful tools. It's all between these pages, but as an added bonus there are forms available on the accompanying CD-ROM that can be easily personalized. And in this second edition of her book, Elaine offers e-Ideas that are meant to help you tap into all the resources beyond the book. These "tech tips" are designed to help you use technology to save time and money, tap into ever-changing information, identify resources to build the business, and identify tools to keep you on the cutting edge of what you do.

But there's something else that you need to know about Elaine, something that comes through when you read the book and especially when you talk with her in person. Elaine loves what she does, loves a challenge, and loves her clients. And, as you will understand when you read this book, these are perhaps the only three reasons why you should get into consulting in the first place.

The spirit of this book is best captured in a comment that Elaine sent to me when we were first corresponding about her new edition of *The Business of Consulting*. I asked her to tell me what she most wanted others to know about her book, and one of the things she said to me was, "I feel I owe so much to the industry and to people who have helped me along the way. This book is one way for me to give back to the world that has given me so much." That's quintessential Elaine. It's why those of us who are privileged to know her and work with her so highly respect her and the work she does. This book is Elaine's gift of experience to our field, and I invite you to open it with great glee, read it with delight, and use it to help grow and sustain your business.

March 2007   Jim Kouzes
                                                 Coauthor of *The Leadership Challenge*

PREFACE

Winter 1987

Dear Peter,

For the last year I have been working harder but making less money. I have searched the library for a book, an article—anything that will provide me with a benchmark against which to compare my business. I want to know what the average consulting firm spends on marketing. How can I determine how much my employees should be billing? What is considered a good profit margin in "the business of consulting"? I will call you next week to find out whether you can recommend a book. Thank you.

Elaine

Peter Block read my note. When I called him, he said, "I'm going to do much more than recommend a book. I want you to pull all your records together, such as your expenses for this year, your taxes from last year, your income summaries for the past three years, and your projected cash flow and income for the next year. After you have everything together, call me back. Plan to talk to me for two hours! And by the way, there isn't a book to read about this stuff!"

I couldn't believe my ears! Peter Block was going to consult with me on my consulting business! We had a great conversation. He provided me with sound business advice—you might say it was "flawless consulting"!

Peter's advice encouraged me to examine marketing dollars wisely, study business numbers and data carefully, and explore the advantages and disadvantages of hiring employees and forming partnerships. This second edition of *The Business of Consulting* covers the same topics and is written in the same spirit—giving you sound advice and practical suggestions.

For example, Chapter Five, ". . . And Staying in Business," provides 113 marketing ideas to ensure that you spend your marketing dollars wisely.

Chapter Six, "The Cost of Doing Business," describes forms and processes that I use to ensure that all the data I need for making decisions are always at my fingertips.

And Chapter Eight, "Growing Pains," will help you weigh the advantages and disadvantages of hiring employees, creating a partnership, and otherwise growing your business.

Peter's mentoring helped me make better business decisions for my consulting company, ebb associates inc. Being a successful consultant (like Peter) means that you not only provide excellent advice for your clients' businesses but also implement excellent advice for your own business.

The Business of Consulting, Second Edition, has been written for several kinds of people: the individual who is considering a consulting profession and wonders how to start; the new consultant who may have mastered consulting and now realizes that there is also a business to run; and the experienced consultant who is continuing a lifelong learning journey and is looking for a few practical tips.

IN THE SECOND EDITION

This edition has been updated, renewed, and enhanced. Resources and recommendations are updated to reflect the current world of business. Some of the examples are renewed to present the changes that have occurred in my career and my life. The book has been enhanced with examples and additional content. More than fifty *e-Ideas* have been added. These technology-based tips will help you better utilize the technology resources around you and add content and information beyond *The Business of Consulting.*

Consulting is a most rewarding career. You are no doubt a very fine consultant, but being good at consulting is not enough to keep you profitable. You also must manage your business.

This book focuses on the business side of consulting: how to develop a business plan, market your business, charge for your services, build a client relationship, grow the business, ensure your continued professional growth, and, of course, make money in the profession. To assist you, all the forms presented in the book have been put on a CD-ROM. Pop the CD in your computer, personalize the forms with your company name, and print them out to project cash flow, plan marketing campaigns, track your time, or identify your aptitude for starting a business.

My goal in writing this book was to give you as many practical tools and sound ideas as possible. I learned most of them through trial and error. Perhaps this book will prevent you from making some of the same errors.

The Business of Consulting is written in the first person—singular and plural. Although I'm the author of the book, the employees of ebb associates inc have played a big part in shaping the content, and it isn't right to use "I" when "we" did it.

ACKNOWLEDGMENTS

Many wise and wonderful people were the authors of *The Business of Consulting*. It is a delight to thank everyone who "wrote" this book:

- Consultants who led the way and taught me all that I know: Geoff Bellman, Ken and Margie Blanchard, Peter Block, Warner Burke, Richard Chang, Marlys Hanson, Ann Herrmann-Nehdi, Mat Juechter, Bev Kaye, Don Kirkpatrick, Jim Kouzes, Pat McLagan, Julie O'Mara, Bob Pike, Dana Gaines and Jim Robinson, Mel Silberman, Thiagi, and Jack Zenger.

- Matt Davis, editor, for pushing me to complete this second edition.

- Cedric Crocker, publisher, for continuing to provide me with challenging and exciting opportunities.

- Kathleen Dolan Davies, editor and friend, for trusting me with your deadline.

- Susan Rachmeler, developmental editor, for cheerfully accepting yet another of my books—you make me look great!

- Nina Kreiden, production editor, who gives every book special treatment.

- Brian Grimm, marketing manager, who will ensure that *The Business of Consulting* reaches every aspiring consultant.

- Lorraine Kohart, my assistant, who entered content and enhanced its meaning.

- Dan Greene, for keeping the world at bay while I wrote.

- Mentors and friends who believe in what I do: Kristin Arnold, L. A. Burke, Vicki Chvala, Linda Growney, Maggie Hutchison, Shirley Krsinich, Robin Lucas, Mindy Meads, Celia Rocks, Pam Schmidt, Marianne Scott, Judye Talbot, Kathy Talton, and Renee Yuengling.

- Clients, for allowing me to practice the business of consulting with you.

- And especially Peter Block, for responding to a plea for help in 1987 with flawless consulting.

March 2007

elaine biech
ebb associates inc
Norfolk, Virginia

The Business of Consulting

So You Want to Be a Consultant

A person who never made a mistake never tried anything new.

Albert Einstein

Have you ever admired consultants who zip into your company, capture everyone's attention, accomplish in days what you've been struggling with for months, and waltz out with a big check?

Ever thought you might like to be a part of that glamorous profession? This book will help you determine whether you have what it takes to be a consultant, as well as whether the consulting profession offers what you desire as an individual.

WHAT IS CONSULTING?

Consulting is the process by which an individual or firm assists a client to achieve a stated outcome. The assistance can come in the form of information, recommendations, or actual hands-on work. A consultant is a specialist within a professional area who completes the work necessary to achieve the client's desired outcome.

Whether companies need help downsizing, installing a new computer system, building an executive team, or breaking into the Chinese market, they can call a consultant to assist with the effort. The organization requesting the assistance is usually called the *client*. The term can refer to the entire organization or to the person who actually made the call.

Consulting is not a descriptor that identifies a profession in itself. Unlike doctors or accountants, highly skilled consultants come from very different backgrounds. A qualifying adjective is required to identify the form of service or the area of expertise—for example, management consultant, engineering consultant, or performance consultant. Although consulting is not a profession by definition, it is often referred to as "the consulting profession." For the sake of convention, I will refer to the "profession" in this book.

The actual work of a consultant can vary quite a bit, depending on the area of expertise offered. Every consultant must be a subject-matter expert in some area. The expertise might be in the form of general content, such as management development, organization development, leadership, or family business. Expertise might be in a specific profession, such as computers, security, writing, or marketing. Expertise might also be in the form of how the consultant delivers services, such as facilitation, training, strategic planning, or team building.

Even after you determine an area of expertise, you will want to select the actual work method you wish to use. For example, if you decide to focus on the training and workplace performance field, you could develop and deliver your own material or subcontract material development to another person while you deliver it. You could develop material for others, or you could deliver others' materials. You could even be certified to deliver others' courses, especially for the large training supplier firms.

If you are a generalist, such as a management consultant, you will need to determine whether you will focus on a specific industry, such as manufacturing, banking, aerospace, or one of hundreds of other industries.

FOUR WAYS TO GET STARTED

Taking risks. Embracing ambiguity. Practicing flexibility. Balancing both process and people issues. Managing multiple responsibilities. Tolerating extensive travel. Communicating effectively. Learning continually. Proving your worth again and again. Does this describe you? If you responded with a resounding "Yes!" consulting may be an ideal career move for you.

Let's assume that you've decided consulting is right for you. What opportunities exist? Think about your ultimate goal. Do you want to be a partner in one of the "Big Four"? Will you eventually own your own firm? Do you think you will always want to consult as a sole practitioner? Do you want to teach part-time at a small university and consult on the side? There are at least four ways you can enter the field: as an employee, as a subcontractor, as a part-time consultant, or as a self-employed independent consultant.

As an Employee

Numerous employment opportunities exist for you. You could join a large national consulting firm or a small firm. Another alternative would be to partner with someone in an even smaller firm.

Large Firm. If you have just graduated from college, this is your best bet. You will need to get experience. As an employee in a large firm you will be an extra pair of hands on large projects—a great way to get experience. The summer 2006 Salary Survey of the National Association of Colleges and Employers (NACE) lists consulting as one of the fifteen highest-paying jobs. The average salary offer for undergraduates was $50,657, with some starting offers as high as $65,000.

e-Idea

NACE publishes a quarterly Salary Survey Report of offers to new college graduates in seventy disciplines at the bachelor's degree level. The data are compiled from college and university career services offices across the United States. If you are a recent or soon-to-be graduate, check for the most recent report for starting consultant salaries, among others, at www.naceweb.org.

If you stay in school longer, the rewards are greater. According to WetFeet (2006), a leading career research firm and top career website, M.B.A.s from top schools can expect to be offered a base salary of $100,000 to $130,000 as new consultants with some firms. In addition, about 75 percent of all consultants are eligible for bonus awards on top of their salary. Recognize that high starting salaries and the demand for consultants have led to strong competition for talent.

As a consultant for a large national firm, you would be able to focus solely on delivering consulting services and generating business. Someone else would complete tax forms, hire secretarial support, and pay the rent. You would have instant name recognition and a clear career path. Although this may sound advantageous at first blush, the greatest drawback is that you might become so comfortable with your job that you would never experience the world of the independent consultant. These jobs also generally come with a great deal of pressure. Usually you are expected to generate (sell) a certain amount of consulting services. A great deal of travel is another drawback.

If you choose this route, learn more about these large firms, who they are, and what they do. I've identified several arbitrary segments. The same firm may be represented in more than one of these segments:

- The "Big Four" international accounting firms also offer professional services. They handle the vast majority of audits for publicly traded and private companies. Members of the Big Four are PricewaterhouseCoopers, Deloitte Touche Tohmatsu, Ernst & Young, and KPMG.

- Large national strategy firms, such as Accenture, Booz Allen Hamilton, the Boston Consulting Group, or McKinsey & Co., provide strategic or operational advice to top executive officers in Fortune 500 companies.

- Boutique strategy firms that specialize in a specific industry or along a functional line, such as Cornerstone Research (litigation support) or the Gartner Group (high-tech research), are smaller, and many have excellent reputations.

- Firms that focus on human resources issues, such as change management, design of compensation systems, mergers, or employee satisfaction surveys, include the Hay Group, Hewitt Associates, and Watson Wyatt & Company.

- Technology firms that design, implement, and manage information and computer systems are involved in time-intensive work that requires large teams and usually takes place behind the scenes. These firms are less prestigious, but offer more opportunities for undergraduates. A sample of firms includes EDS, HP Technology, Oracle, SAP, and Synopsis. Note that it is not always necessary to have a technology degree, as many of the jobs in these firms require other skills.

e-Idea

Go to www.WetFeet.com to learn more about the current outlook of the industry and profiles of some of the top consulting companies. Next go to the websites of these companies to learn more about them, the kind of consulting they conduct, and what to expect.

Small Firm. As a consultant in a small, local firm, you would experience similar advantages to those of a large, national firm. One added benefit might be that you would probably experience a wider variety of tasks and be given more responsibility sooner. If you want to travel, a drawback may be that you are often limited to working with businesses in your locality. Although your salary would be only half what it could be with one of the Big Four, you would have less pressure, more opportunity for a variety of projects, and more involvement in the entire consulting process.

Find these companies by location. Check the chapter of your local industry-specific association in the city where you live. Don't depend on the Yellow Pages. Many small firms do not find value in advertising that way. Your local librarian or Chamber of Commerce can help you also. Ask for a listing of local businesses broken down by industry.

Partnership. As a partner with one or more other consultants who are already in the business, you would be able to share the burden of expenses, marketing, and the workload. The biggest drawback is the potential for conflict around communication, decision making, unbalanced work loads, and numerous other business and personal preferences.

How do you find a partnership? Well, more often than not, they find you. You may be able to join a partnership that is already formed (expect to buy in with cash or reduced pay for a specified time period) or identify other individuals who, like you, want to get into the consulting profession. Read more about partnerships in Chapters Four and Eight.

As a Subcontractor

Rather than becoming an employee, you could subcontract with a firm. Many businesses and consulting firms are looking for subcontractors who will fill in the gaps left as a result of downsizing or launching new initiatives. As a subcontractor you may have a less secure position, but you will have flexibility while gaining rich experience and developing a sense of the market. The work will most likely not be full-time, but this allows you time to develop your own business.

Who might hire you? You could consider the larger companies listed previously. They will most likely want you to dedicate time to one specific project. The scope will be larger and more full-time. If you like the idea of being a training consultant, consider some of the leading training suppliers, such as AchieveGlobal, AMA, DDI, Franklin Covey, Herrmann International, and the Ken Blanchard Companies.

As a Part-Time Consultant

If you're not ready to take the plunge, you could consult part-time while keeping your present job. Some people use their vacation time and weekends to conduct small projects—with their employers' approval, of course. For example, if your specialty is team building or facilitating decision-making meetings, you might be able to do weekend retreats for boards of nonprofit organizations. Consulting is natural part-time work for college and university professors. If you are in the teaching profession, you have summers and vacation days that you can dedicate to part-time experiences. Part-time work will not give you the full flavor of what it would be like to be solely dependent on consulting as a career, but it will give you an idea of whether you like the work.

As a Self-Employed Independent Consultant

You could also start your own consulting practice. As an independent consultant, you would have an opportunity to make all the decisions, do what you wanted when you wanted, and receive all the recognition. The drawback, of course, is that you would assume all the risk, be responsible for all expenses, and have no one at your level readily available with whom to discuss business plans and concerns.

The focus of this book is on this final way of breaking into the field—becoming an independent consultant who opens his or her own business. If you have decided this is the route you will take, you can still begin slowly. One way would be to obtain experience as an employee in one of the national or local consulting firms mentioned earlier, or to work part-time as described in the third option or take work with you when you leave your present employer. Chapter Four provides more detail about how you can do this effectively while starting your own business.

e-Idea

Looking for a consulting job? Check the Web for job listings. Here's a quick rundown of several sites. Check www.WetFeet.com; the site lists consulting jobs by state, company, city, and even pay. Jobs can be sorted by categories as well. The day I checked, 3,973 consulting jobs had been posted in the previous thirty days. Other sites for consultants include www.Top-Consultant.com, www.consultingmag.com, and www.amcf.org. At least four sites—www.TheLadders.com, www.Netshare.com, www. 6FigureJobs.com, and www.ExecuNet.com—post only jobs with annual base salaries of $100,000 or more. You may have to pay a monthly membership fee to access some of the data. Although the last four do not focus on consulting, a fair number of consulting jobs are posted there because of the salary.

WHY CONSULTING NOW?

According to WetFeet, consulting grew most rapidly, at double digit rates, from the mid-1970s until 2000. When the economy weakened, consulting declined as well—especially in those large firms mentioned earlier. Revenues shrank in 2001, stayed flat in 2002, and grew about 3 percent in 2003. An independent consultant can take advantage of slower rates in a way that the large firms cannot. As a small entity, a consultant has the opportunity to design the future. As an independent consultant, you can make changes faster than a large firm with thirty thousand employees. If organizations no longer need your expertise to nurture innovation, but need someone to help them plan for their high retirement rate, you can make that switch. Wayne Gretzky, the hockey player, is famous for claiming that his success was due to skating to where the puck "is going to be." Consultants too can skate to where the work is going to be. During a downturn, many consultants stick with doing only what they know, as opposed to offering what clients need. This negates one of a consultant's greatest strengths.

Since 2005, growth has been healthy, though few believe that the rate will mirror the growth rate in the last century. Annual growth estimates are at about 8 percent through the first decade of this millennium. As a consultant, you can economy-proof your business by providing services to at least a couple of industries that are rarely affected by the economy, such as health care, pharmaceuticals, and pet products. As compared to other industries, consulting continues to be one of the fastest-growing professional areas.

Turbulent times have increased how often consultants are used to help organizations make their way through the processes of implementing technology, going global, improving processes, applying lean principles, and negotiating mergers. Consulting projects continue to increase in dollar amount and duration. It is not uncommon for large-scale projects to cost more than $50 million over a five-year period. As Charles Stein (1994) of the *Boston Globe* states, "Once upon a time, consultants were like dinner guests: They came for a brief visit, gave advice, and went home. Now they are like guests who come for dinner, move into the spare bedroom, and stay for a year or two."

Business Trends

Two trends in the business world continue to carry tremendous implications for consulting. First is the trend toward outsourcing more and more services. Corporations will continue to hire more temporary professionals to assist when needed, as opposed to adding highly paid permanent staff. Consultants temporarily provide the "people power" to complete the work at the time it needs to be completed.

As baby boomers continue to retire at a faster rate than new people enter the workforce, corporations will continue to experience gaps and to struggle to fill positions. Consultants meet the need for people in areas as diverse as sales, engineering, health care, information technology, and accounting.

The second trend is that rapid changes occurring in the world make it almost impossible for the members of the executive team to remain knowledgeable about their industry, remain focused on their customers, stay ahead of their competition, and know instantly what to do when these factors collide in a negative way. Consultants offer the knowledge, information, data, and systems to solve the puzzle. They fill in the blanks. When the task is complete, they are on their way.

Several other trends have persisted such that they are perhaps not so much trends as a way of life. As I mentioned earlier, consulting engagements continue to be longer and larger. Other ongoing conditions that affect consulting include the continuing increase in the rate of change; a heightened concern for the security of intellectual property and the safety of the workforce; limited preparation to adequately address an increasingly diverse workforce; a higher ethical bar; the global economy; the continuing development of technology efficiencies, which create heavier workloads that are expected to be completed immediately; and employees believing they are on call 24/7.

"Talent management"—the buzzword of the times—focuses on the recruiting, retention, and rewarding of members of the workforce. Although it is focused mostly on the work that the human resources department is supposed to do, it often encompasses training, dealing with diversity issues, and other aspects of people needs.

Across industries, health care is one of the faster-growing areas. Health care payment and delivery systems have been changing, which has generated a high demand for consultants to help health care organizations adapt to new conditions through alliances, innovation, access strategies, and quality improvement. IT requirements continue to increase the demand for consultants. Other fast-growing industries for consulting include telecommunications, the Internet, the environmental field, and finance. Service industries and government agencies continue to implement lean principles. So even if you practiced your lean Six Sigma skills in manufacturing, there is still more to be done in other areas. Nonprofit and government organizations also continue to use more consultants.

Consulting Trends

Trends also exist in the kind of work that consultants are doing. Coaching continues to be on the rise. Whereas at one time having a coach was a sign that something was wrong with an executive, now the opposite is true: employees think something is wrong if an executive does *not* have a coach!

Some consultants have become contingency workers. These consultants work full-time for months for a single employer, collecting hourly wages but no benefits from an outside staffing agency. They are paid well while they are working, but the work is mostly short term. Companies benefit with lower costs and the flexibility of easy layoffs.

That's the demand side. What about the supply side? The same organizations that are cutting permanent staff to keep payroll down are providing a steady supply of people who need jobs and find that they can do consulting. In fact, many people cut from their jobs today may be placed in the same company as temporary employees next week.

Why this shuffling of the same bodies? Consultants are often more cost-effective for the organization, which can hire the skill it needs on an as-needed basis rather than train and educate staff for skills that may not be used again. Consultants can usually complete projects faster as well.

e-Idea

Kennedy Consulting is a firm that will help you stay abreast of the trends, such as fast-growing industries or demand for specific consulting skills. Check its website at www.Kennedyinformation.com or its magazine at www.consultingmag.com.

Client Perspective

Clients need consultants for a variety of reasons. Several are listed here:

- *Expertise.* The skills necessary for the growing and changing needs of an organization are not available inside the organization. Therefore organizations turn to consultants to complete projects or solve problems.
- *Relief from time constraints.* Even when the skills are available in the organization, staff members may not have the time to complete special projects or research. A consultant can be a part of the organization just long enough to complete what needs to be done.
- *Experience.* Certain professions are experiencing a shortage of trained employees. Consultants can fill in until demand is met by training or hiring new employees.
- *Staffing flexibility.* Consultants can be brought in for the short term to complete a project. When the work is completed, the organization can terminate the relationship easily and quickly without severance pay or other obligations.
- *Objective outside opinions.* Consultants usually provide fresh perspectives. Outsiders can look at a problem in a new, unbiased way.
- *New ideas.* Consultants bring with them ideas from other firms and industries. This cross-pollination is a surefire way to tap into many resources. Staff members may be too close to the problem to see a new solution.
- *Speed and efficiency.* Hiring a consultant who has experienced the same type of project in the past may be faster and more cost-effective than bringing staff members up to speed.

- *Assessment.* A consultant can provide an objective assessment, define the problem, and make recommendations.

- *Resolution.* In the case of a merger or other change of organizational structure, an outside consultant can act as an independent mediator to resolve differences.

- *Compliance.* An organization may not have enough time and may lack the expertise to comply with legal expectations. Hiring a consultant shows that an effort is being made to correct the problem.

Consultant Perspective

I frequently speak at conferences on the topic of becoming a consultant. The title I use is "So You Want to Be a Consultant." I always ask, "Why do you want to be a consultant?" The responses I receive are many and varied. Perhaps you'll relate to several of the following:

- *Own boss.* I want to be my own boss. It has always been a dream of mine. I will no longer need to take orders from anyone else.

- *No set schedule.* I want to be free from daily routine. I am bored with corporate life. I've worked all my life. I've been a good employee. Perhaps it's just this midlife thing, but I feel financially secure, and I want more than just a paycheck. I want something outside of the routine.

- *Greater opportunities.* I see more opportunities now than ever. There seems to be a growing need in every company. I see consultants in our company every week.

- *Do my own "thing."* I have skills that I believe others will pay me for. I have a lot of experience and expertise, and I'd like to set my own agenda, rather than follow someone else's.

- *Technology.* Technology has made it easier to create a fully operating office quickly.

- *Easy start-up.* I think it's a business that I can afford to start. I already have a computer, and I can work out of my home office. The relatively low-cost start-up makes it possible for me to own a business. Most other businesses I checked into required over $100,000 to open.

- *Freedom.* I want to work in my pajamas if I choose. This is as good a reason as any. Besides, there is a new prestige in working out of your home. At one time the consultant working from home was seen as less than professional. This is no longer true.

- *More money.* Consultants appear to make big bucks, and I want to get in on it. I'm working for a company that does not have a retirement plan. I sat down with the numbers, and I believe I can spend my last ten years in the workforce doing something I like and putting money away for my retirement.

- *Out of work.* I don't have a choice; I was downsized out of a job. Actually I'm beginning to think I'm lucky. I don't think I would have made the move on my own. I think I can make just as good a living as a consultant.

- *Greater good.* I want to make a difference. I'm not even concerned that I might not make the salary I am presently making. There is something greater calling me. I want to make a difference in the world and work with nonprofit organizations that will appreciate what I bring.

- *Security.* Corporate America isn't safe anymore. I want financial security, and I can think of no better way to ensure that than to take matters into my own hands.

- *Creativity.* I want to have the opportunity to be creative. I've always wanted to try something new, but in my job I am frequently told that it can't be done. I want to find out for myself.

- *Travel.* This may be a frivolous reason, but I want to travel. I know it may get old after a while, but I'll deal with that when the time comes.

- *Challenge.* I need a greater challenge, but it isn't going to occur where I am now. There is virtually no room for promotions, and I could be doing the same thing for the next six years with very little professional or personal growth.

- *Self-preservation.* I need to look out for myself. I'm in an industry that is fraught with mergers and acquisitions. I need to take care of myself and what I want out of life.

- *Location.* I want to live where I choose. The way I look at it, as long as I'm near an airport, I will be able to reach my clients.

CareerJournal.com, a website sponsored by the *Wall Street Journal,* posted its best careers in 2006. Management consultants and analysts were one of the top eight selected. CareerJournal teamed with polling company Harris Interactive to survey U.S. adults to identify the characteristics that are most common in the jobs of highly satisfied career-focused people. The four attributes cited most included intellectual stimulation, high job security, high level of control and freedom, and extensive direct contact with customers or clients. As you can see, consulting rates high on all four of these aspects.

e-Idea

Check www.careerjournal.com for other information about the consulting profession.

Why did I join the ranks of the independent consultants over twenty-five years ago? The four aspects identified in the CareerJournal research are all important to me in my career. In addition, I have always said that it was because I am a lousy employee. I do not like to be told what to do; I like to march to the toot of my own saxophone; I like a challenge, and I like to take risks; I like to work directly with clients; I am a self-starter and a hard worker, but I want to work during the hours I choose, not on someone else's time clock; I want to express my creativity; and I prefer to control my own destiny.

What about you? Have you explored why you are considering a move into the consulting profession?

MYTHS ABOUT CONSULTING

There are some common myths about the field that never seem to die out. Let's look at them—and the realities behind them.

Myth 1: "Consultants charge over $1,000 per day; therefore, I will become rich consulting." Let's take a realistic look at this myth. It may seem like a huge sum of money for a day's work, but let's examine what that $1,000 covers. Let's imagine that you are the consultant. If you work an eight-hour day, you would make $125 per hour. However, as a consultant you are now an entrepreneur, and it is more than likely that you are putting in a twelve-hour day. That brings your hourly rate down to $83.

Of course it's not possible to bill for 365 days per year. Take out weekends. Remove holidays and a two-week vacation (remember, there's no *paid* vacation). We can conservatively reduce your hourly rate by 8 percent. That brings it down to $76 per hour. Still not bad.

As a consultant you will not be able to consult five days every week. You will need to use one day for preparation, one day for marketing, and one day to take care of administrative jobs, such as taxes, billing, research, and professional development. So now one day's billing covers four days of your time. That's 25 percent of $76 an hour, or $19 per hour.

Murphy's Law states that all your clients will select the same two days in September for their off-site meetings, and the rest of the month you will catch up on reading your *Fast Company* and *Harvard Business Review*. This won't happen just once each year. It may happen several times. Further, you can bet on December as a notorious downtime because of the holidays. No one wants you then. I've often wondered what really happens that month. Does no one work? Do employees turn into elves? When you add December to another bad month, you can expect to turn down 25 percent of all work because your clients' desired dates do not match your available dates. So deduct another 25 percent from the hourly fee. You are now down to $14 per hour.

You must cover all your own taxes. There is no employer to share the burden. As a consultant, you will find that quarters take on a whole new meaning. You will not think of the football score, but of the check you must write to pay your quarterly taxes. In rough numbers, let's say that you will pay 33 percent in various taxes. That leaves you with just a bit over $9 per hour.

You are on your own, so you must pay for your own benefits, such as health and life insurance and retirement. A very conservative estimate for this is $1.50 per hour. In addition you will have business expenses—copying costs, telephone calls, stationery, postage. These expenses will accumulate fast! They may add up to $2 for every billable hour. Now what does that leave you?

Looks like you're down to $5.50 per hour. Oh, and you wanted to purchase a laptop computer? On $5.50 per hour?!? That job at McDonald's is looking mighty good right now!

Actually it's not that bad. Although I've exaggerated the realities of consulting and there are a number of calculation flaws in the example, you nevertheless need to be fully aware of everything that goes into a consulting fee. A daily fee at $1,000 or more sounds great. Yet when you consider expenses and nonbillable hours, a large chunk of that $1,000 disappears quickly.

External consultants may make a six-figure income. Then again, some consultants have trouble making any income. Some consultants make less than $50,000 a year doing the same thing as others who gross over $500,000. Statistics that identify the average consultant salaries vary considerably from source to source. It appears that consulting, more than any other profession, embodies the spirit of entrepreneurship. Free enterprise is alive and well! You can make good money as a consultant. The potential is there. Realizing that potential depends on what you want out of your career. How well you do depends on how hard you want to work.

Myth 2: "External consulting means I will be able to avoid all the politics and paperwork that drive me crazy in my present internal job." The politics at your present job can keep you from being productive and effective. Perhaps politics is a game you have seen your boss play. As an external consultant, you may be able to escape the politics of your present organization, but get ready to be involved in the politics of not one but ten or seventeen or thirty-three organizations, depending on the number of clients you have. As a consultant, you will have many bosses rather than just one. You will need to be acutely aware of their needs and shortfalls, and you may need to make some difficult decisions to ensure that you remain on the job.

The big difference is that instead of dealing with the same politics all week long, you will be able to go home at night knowing that you will have a fresh set to work around or through (depending on your project) later in the week.

No paperwork? You will most likely have *more* paperwork. Not only will you have more, but unless you are starting out with an administrative assistant, you will not have anyone to whom you can delegate some of the work. Some of your paperwork will have a higher degree of importance. As an employee, you may have been able to turn your expense report in late and then beg the bookkeeping department to slip it into the stack anyway. But if you file your quarterly taxes late, the IRS is not likely to slip it into the on-time stack.

You must track hours and work so that you know what to charge clients. You must bill your clients in a timely manner to avoid cash-flow problems. You must determine how you will track invoices to ensure that your clients are paying you. You must track all expenses to avoid paying more income taxes than you should. You must track and file all paperwork so that you can locate it for your attorney and accountant and banker when they request information.

Not only will you not be able to avoid politics and paperwork, but they will be multiplied as you open your consulting business. If you don't take care of your paperwork, you will be out of business faster than you got in it.

Myth 3: "I will be seen as an expert in my area." You are probably seen as an expert in the job you now hold. People turn to you for answers; you are respected by your colleagues and praised by your bosses (some of them, anyway!). Enjoy that while you can. You will be required to build that reputation with every new client relationship. You are about to face a never-ending task of proving yourself.

Starting your business goes far beyond opening an office and listing yourself in the Yellow Pages. You will build your business one client at a time. You will build your expertise one project at a time.

---

*You will build your business
one client at a time.*

Myth 4: "Having my own consulting practice means more free time." If you are looking forward to getting up at noon and being out on the golf course several times each week, you are in for a big disappointment. Being a consultant means that you will become a business owner—an entrepreneur. Like most entrepreneurs, you will spend sixty to eighty hours each week that first year getting your business up and running. You will be marketing your services and networking with everyone you know.

You will be working for others, most likely businesspeople who go to work early, have tight deadlines, and experience huge pressures. You will be there to work as a partner with them to meet the deadlines and to relieve some of their pressures. You may need to work nights and weekends to meet a client's critical deadline. All the while, you may be wondering when you are going to find the time to complete the marketing you must do to ensure that you will have another project waiting for you after this one is completed.

Myth 5: "Consulting is a respected profession." I thought I had chosen a respected profession. I was shocked the first time I was called a "beltway bandit"—the term assigned to consulting firms in and around the Washington, D.C., beltway.

Since then, I've been called a pest because I followed up too often with a client. I've also been called a con man, which really bothered me even though the client couldn't tell he had the wrong gender! Jokes about consultants abound.

Some of the negativity is deserved. There are many charlatans in our business. Unfortunately, the profession lacks legal standards or legitimate certification. It is very easy to go into the consulting business. Go to your local printer and have a business card printed. You are magically transformed into a consultant before the ink is dry.

Often people who are temporarily out of work drift into consulting to pick up a few bucks. They are in the field long enough to make a mess and devalue the role of the consultant. One out of every twenty projects I accept requires me to build the reputation of the consulting profession in one of two ways: I may need to clean up a mess created by a wannabe consultant who lacked organization development knowledge, or I may find myself fighting a battle of trust due to poor ethics or overcharging by a consultant who worked with the client organization previously.

Myth 6: "It's easy to break into the consulting field. All I need to do is print some business cards." This is actually true. It is easy to break in to the business. *Staying* in is what's hard. You did want to make a living, too, didn't you?

Initially you will need to spend at least 50 percent of your time marketing your services. You will need to establish business systems; set up your computers and printers to do all the things you want them to do; and create tracking systems for money, clients, paper flow, projects, and a dozen other things identified throughout this book. You may feel exhausted, and we haven't even mentioned providing services to your clients.

Myth 7: "Deciding to grow my practice is an easy decision. Everyone wants to grow a business." You would think the business of consulting would become easier over time. Unfortunately it does not. If you are good, you will have more work than you can handle. At some point you will question whether to grow your business and how to do it. Should you produce products? Take on a partner? Create a firm? Or stay solo?

This is not an easy decision. It requires risk taking and capital. The pressure will be on you to grow. You must remember that there are many ways to grow without adding people to your payroll.

The responses to these myths were not meant to disillusion you. They were meant to ensure that you had both sides of the story. So let's explore what *is* great about consulting.

REWARDS AND REALITIES OF CONSULTING

I've listed some of the rewards and realities of consulting in the following paragraphs. Take them to heart as you make your decision about starting your own consulting business.

Rewards

Consulting can be one of the most rewarding yet challenging careers out there. Imagine sitting at a desk looking out at the scene you have chosen. Imagine waking up every day knowing that you are going to do what you have chosen to do that day. Imagine not fighting rush-hour traffic day after day. Imagine being able to select the projects you want. Imagine working with the people you want to work with. Imagine doing what you are best at and what you enjoy most. Imagine challenging yourself and living up to your potential. Imagine being paid well to do what you love. Imagine working your own hours. Imagine feeling the satisfaction of being a part of a project that you believe in. Imagine completing projects successfully and being genuinely appreciated. Imagine being able to make a difference. Imagine working in locations that you have selected. Imagine taking the day off without asking permission. Imagine getting up in the morning and not going to work . . . but going to play! These are the rewards of consulting.

Realities: First-Year Lessons Learned

What's the first year like? Three new consultants offer you some of their thoughts about the realities of the field. Perhaps their first years' lessons will remind you of things you need to do.

Consultant Number 1. My first year was a real surprise. I had been on the purchasing end of consulting for so many years as the director of training that I was sure I knew all there was to know. So when our company offered an early retirement package, I took it. The consultants I had worked with were top-notch. They had made the job look so easy! I laugh now about all that I didn't know. For example, I never thought about how consultants completed all they had to do! Giving up my weekends those first months was a real shock! And I had no idea about how business was generated. I didn't know I'd have to sell! It certainly was good that the company provided a generous severance package. I used all of it and a portion of my savings to get started. Otherwise I would have starved!

Consultant Number 2.   Starving wasn't my problem! I gained ten pounds my first six months as a consultant! I had no idea working out of my home would be so difficult. There were so many distractions—the lawn needed mowing, the laundry needed folding, the walk needed sweeping, the dishes needed washing, the floor needed scrubbing, the garage needed cleaning. And the refrigerator was the worst distraction! I seemed to open it every time I passed it. I had to work hard at time management and separating my business from my home. I had to make a few investments I didn't think of initially. I needed more filing cabinets and bookshelves than I thought. I had to purchase a different phone the first week—one with a mute button to silence the dog when I couldn't. I had to establish a way to track who I called, what they said, and when I needed to call them again. Fifty-three pink telephone slips floating all around the office was not a model of organization! Now I share an office area with two other people. We share the cost of a copy machine and a part-time typist and receptionist. I need the social interaction that this arrangement gives me. I need to work away from my home. I just feel more professional.

Consultant Number 3.   I wish I had contacted my accountant before I started my business. I just didn't think of it. I knew I was in trouble on April 3rd when he asked me how much I had paid in quarterly taxes. In fact, I wish I had taken at least six months to plan for my transition. I took a one-year lease on an office space that I rarely used. I thought I needed to be in the middle of things to be in business. My work focus has changed from what I thought it would be. I thought I would be regularly dispensing advice to CEOs. Instead, I find myself doing more and more writing. I have the wrong software, but every time I think about installing something better, I realize that none of the files will transfer. I know that if I continue to do the kind of work I am doing, I will need to make the change. The longer I wait, the worse it gets! I just don't have the time to do it now.

What lessons are in store for you as you enter the world of the consultant?

JUST WHAT ARE YOU GETTING YOURSELF INTO?

As you can see, there are many pros and cons in the consulting field. The number one reason consultants love their jobs is the intellectual stimulation. Two key reasons consultants dislike their jobs are the long hours and the travel. Trying to decide whether to go it on your own can be confusing. Just as you would with any major decision, you will want to conduct your own research. You will want to discover whether consulting is a profession you want to pursue.

One of the best ways to do that is to talk to other consultants. Explore your concerns and confirm your hopes by interviewing people in the profession. Most of us enjoy talking shop, especially if we work alone. As professionals we owe it to those entering the field to share our knowledge and insight. But what should you ask someone who has been in the business? Exhibit 1.1 provides a list of questions you can use to interview consultants. Also spend time thinking about the various

---

 Exhibit 1.1. A Dozen Questions to Ask a Consultant.

1. How long have you been a consultant?
2. How did you start?
3. Why did you decide to become a consultant?
4. How would you describe your consulting practice?
5. How have you structured your business, and what are the advantages and drawbacks of that structure?
6. What do you do for clients?
7. What is a typical project like?
8. What is a typical day like?
9. What marketing activities do you conduct?
10. What is the greatest challenge for you as a consultant?
11. What would you miss the most if you quit consulting?
12. What should I have asked that I did not?

---

ideas explored in this chapter and develop your own questions. How will a change affect your career path? How will it affect your personal life? Take your time in making a decision. Do your homework.

Exhibit 1.2 challenges you with several aspects of becoming an external consultant. Read the statements, checking all with which you agree.

💿 Exhibit 1.2. Are You a Match for the Profession?

Quick Quiz

- ❑ I am willing to work sixty to eighty hours a week to achieve success.
- ❑ I love risk; I thrive on risk.
- ❑ I have a thick skin; being called a pest, "beltway bandit," or con man does not bother me.
- ❑ I am good at understanding and interpreting the big picture.
- ❑ I pay attention to details.
- ❑ I am an excellent communicator.
- ❑ I am a good writer.
- ❑ I like to sell myself.
- ❑ I can balance logic with intuition and the big picture with details.
- ❑ I know my limitations.
- ❑ I can say no easily.
- ❑ I am compulsively self-disciplined.
- ❑ I am comfortable speaking with people in all disciplines and at all levels of an organization.

Although the specific number of checks on the page is not significant, your willingness to face the reality of what it takes to be a consultant is *very* significant. Each time you are unable or unwilling to check a box, you increase the gap between you and success.

Here's an explanation of each statement in the quick quiz:

• *Are you willing to work sixty to eighty hours each week to achieve success?* You are about to enter the world of the entrepreneur. Perhaps you will be able to decrease the number of hours after your business is up and running, but until then the hours will be demanding. Most successful entrepreneurs require less than eight hours of sleep a night. Time is always a critical element to entrepreneurs. In his book *Entrepreneurs Are Made, Not Born,* Lloyd E. Shefsky (1994) teaches readers how to learn to get by with less sleep! You will eventually become more disciplined about your use of time, learn to juggle many things at once, and identify priorities.

• *Do you love risk and thrive on it?* As a consultant you will live with constant uncertainty. The biggest risk relates to finding enough steady work to pay the mortgage. Even if you land a yearlong project with an organization, the person who brought you in may not be there as long as you are. The possibility of a change in management through a promotion, transfer, or layoff could put the project, and thus your contract, in jeopardy.

• *Do you have a thick skin? Does being called a pest, beltway bandit, or con man bother you?* Consultants are not always respected. How will you react the first time your profession or your personality is criticized?

• *Are you good at understanding and interpreting the big picture?* Clients will often hire you because they believe that you will have a unique advantage and be able to see the organization from a different perspective. You will constantly need to think outside the parameters that your client explains. You will often need to be a quick study in how the organization works, and you will need to be adept at asking the critical questions that will result in the insight your client needs.

---

*Be a quick study in how
an organization works.*

• *Do you pay attention to details?* Although you must see the big picture for your client, you will also be running a business that will require you to focus on the details of accounting, proofreading, and scheduling, among others.

• *Are you an excellent communicator?* This is critical. I cannot think of a single consultant who does not need to be a superior communicator. If you did not check this box, I would seriously recommend that you obtain additional training and development in communication before you attempt a consulting profession. It is basic, and it's required. You must be able to communicate clearly and completely. You must be a good listener.

• *Are you a good writer?* Written communication is almost as important as verbal communication. You will write reports, marketing materials, letters, proposals, and client materials. In many cases your work will go before top management. If your writing is not as good as it should be, you may want to hire someone to proofread your work or even complete the writing for you.

• *Do you like to sell yourself?* Knowing how to impress a client with your skills and abilities without bragging is an art form. It is often a matter of your attitude. You must believe in yourself and be able to convince a client that you can achieve what your client wants you to achieve.

• *Can you balance logic with intuition, the big picture with details?* A consultant must be able to put on whatever hat is required to do the job. You may be buried in the details and logic of your cash-flow projections when a client calls and asks you to brainstorm the needs of the community in 2020. Your marketing plan will be a balance of logic and intuition. You must be flexible. You must be able to tap into all your skills and attributes.

• *Do you know your limitations?* Only you know what they are. Are they physical? Social? Financial? Might they prevent you from doing what needs to be done? We all have limitations. It's how we manage them that counts. One of my limitations is an inability to make small talk. I overcome that by planning ahead for situations in which I will be expected to make small talk. If you don't know what your limitations are, ask someone who knows you well.

• *Can you say no easily?* You will need to say no to some projects because they aren't right for you. (More about that in Chapter Five.) You must also stay focused on your strategy. It may be tempting to accept a project that's not right for you—especially if you don't have anything on the horizon. You also must be realistic about the amount of work you can take on. Initially it will be better to overestimate the time a project will take than to have quality suffer because you spread yourself too thin.

• *Are you compulsively self-disciplined?* You must be a self-starter. You must be compulsive about your financial records. You must be compulsive about planning and developing materials for your clients. You must be compulsive about billing your clients.

• *Are you comfortable speaking with people in all disciplines and at all levels of an organization?* Depending on the project you have accepted, you may find yourself talking to crane operators, secretaries, supervisors, janitors, teachers, presidents, welders, scientists, or cooks. You must feel comfortable with them so that they feel comfortable with you.

Be compulsive about
billing your clients.

How are you doing? Ready to learn more about the skills of a consultant?

Talents and Tolerance

Whether you believe you can or you can't,
you will prove yourself correct.

Henry Ford

The most important reason to become a consultant is because you want to. Whereas Chapter One focused on what it takes to *become* a consultant, this chapter focuses on the skills and the personal stamina you will need to *remain* a consultant. It forces you to explore the upside and the downside of working out of your home and the potential barriers to your success.

The most important reason to become
a consultant is because you want to.

You may be surprised to think of yourself as an entrepreneur, but you must examine this aspect of becoming a consultant. Your professional skills, abilities, knowledge, and experience provide the content. Your entrepreneurial abilities will determine how well you run your business. Both are required to be a successful consultant.

SKILLS FOR SUCCESS

As a consultant, you will possess skills that are valued and needed by clients who are willing to pay you for them. Naturally, many of the skills required will be dependent on the niche you will carve out for yourself. Whether you work in the manufacturing or insurance industry, whether you focus on training or organization development, you will want to acquire the skills necessary to put you at the high end of the knowledge curve.

As a training consultant, for example, you may become certified by one of the larger training supplier companies, such as the Ken Blanchard Companies, DDI, or the Forum Corporation. In this case you will need strong delivery skills. A training consultant who also designs training must have design skills. If you expect to broaden your consulting to working with clients on performance issues, you will need to add analytical, measurement, and process improvement skills to your list.

If you decide to be a consultant who coaches, you will need to be familiar with a variety of assessment tools and certified to use them; you will also need to be an excellent communicator and to know how to help another individual establish goals, among other skills and competencies.

In addition to these specific skills, there are general consulting skills which show that you are a professional. Exhibit 2.1 provides a self-evaluation to determine whether your skills and characteristics are a match for the profession. Complete it by jotting comments in either the Strength or the Needs Improvement column and the Natural or Needs Attention column. Then read the following sections to determine which of the listed skills are important for you.

Prospecting and Marketing. Prospecting, or looking for clients, will require much of your time when you first start. Having clients is the only thing that will keep you in business. Prospecting and marketing will ensure that the phone keeps ringing.

---

*Having clients is the only thing
that will keep you in business.*

Promoting and Selling Yourself. You can market your services, but people will be hiring you. You must feel comfortable discussing your successes.

Exhibit 2.1. Consultant Skills and Characteristics.

Rate your strengths

Skills	Strength	Needs Improvement
Prospecting and marketing		
Promoting and selling myself		
Diagnosing client needs		
Identifying mutual expectations		
Pricing projects		
Dealing with paperwork		
Understanding business data		
Designing materials		
Conducting training		
Facilitating meetings		
Depth of experience		
Breadth of experience		

Characteristics	Natural	Needs Attention
Leader		
Decision maker		
People turn to me for decisions		
Enjoy competition		
Self-confident		
Enjoy working long, hard hours		
Always plan ahead		
Self-disciplined		
Sell myself with confidence		
Financial acumen		
Reasonable risk taking		
Family support		

Which skills and characteristics need the most improvement and attention?

How will you gain necessary skills or experience?

How will you adapt to necessary characteristics that are not naturally "you"?

Diagnosing Client Needs. In some cases you will meet with your clients and they will tell you exactly what they want you to do. Sometimes they will ask you what needs to be done. And sometimes what they say they want is not what they need! Your diagnostic skills will tell you what to do in all cases.

Identifying Mutual Expectations. The ability to lead a candid discussion with your client to reach agreement on what each of you needs, wants, and expects as a result of working together will ensure that your projects start on the right foot.

Pricing Projects. How long a project will take, how many on-site days are needed, how long it will take to design and develop the materials, and how many trips you will make to the client's location will all affect the price tag you place on a project.

Dealing with Paperwork. Developing processes to track clients, money, and work and organizing your office so that you will be able to locate everything that you file will be critical to your success.

Understanding Business Data. This book offers numerous methods for tracking your data, such as expense records, profit-and-loss statements, and revenue projection forms. Your ability to read them, analyze them, and know what they are telling you is important for your financial health.

Designing Materials. Even if you don't design your own materials, you must be able to spot quality in materials for purchase and compare the pros and cons of different models. You must be able to look at an activity and tell how much time it might take or whether it is appropriate for your client.

Conducting Training. You may not bill yourself as a trainer, but you will train in many ways. You may coach a CEO, mentor a manager, or do some one-on-one training with superintendents on the floor. Internalizing adult learning theory will ensure that you are always ready for those teaching moments.

Facilitating Meetings. You very likely will be called on to facilitate meetings for your client. Brush up on meeting-management skills as well as facilitation skills. You will be seen as a model in many situations. These skills will help you hold your own.

Depth of Experience. How deep is your experience? If you are specializing in an area, you should know all you can about it. Read your professional journals and keep up with the latest books in your area. As a specialist, you have expertise in a particular field, industry, or focus area.

Breadth of Experience. How wide is your experience? You must be enough of a generalist to know what else applies in the situation you are dealing with. You should know where you can go for help when you need it. As a generalist, you will be expected to have a heavy dose of common sense to provide an outside perspective and to cut through internal politics. You will have a wide range of experience.

A balance of breadth and depth is a critical advantage your client will look for. It is also important to decide whether to present yourself as a specialist or a generalist. The more specialized you are, the more difficult it will be to obtain a wide variety of business; the more generalized you are, the less credible you may be in a potential client's eyes.

> *The more specialized you are, the more difficult*
> *it will be to obtain a wide variety of business;*
> *the more generalized you are, the less credible*
> *you may be in a potential client's eyes.*

PERSONAL CHARACTERISTICS OF SUCCESSFUL CONSULTANTS

Consulting is a profession of contrasts and high expectations. You will need to be not only multiskilled, sensibly focused, knowledgeable, and widely experienced but also capable of maintaining a delicate balance of personal characteristics. Your clients expect you to be confident, but not arrogant; assertive, but not pushy; intelligent, but not a nerd; personable, but not overly friendly; candid, but not critical; understanding, but not too sensitive. They will also want you to be creative and visionary, but at the same time logical and practical. You will need to see the big picture, but also watch out for the details that might trip you up.

This affords you quite a challenge! Clients will be just as interested in your personal characteristics as in your skills. Although clients will ask you to discuss your skills, they will evaluate your characteristics. As unfair as it may seem, many contracts are awarded on personality. Clients may consciously (or unconsciously) understand that they will need to work with the consultant they are considering. I recently had a discussion with a vice president of a Fortune 300 company who emphatically told me that he simply did not trust the last consultant he interviewed, but could not say specifically why. (I got the job.)

Although clients will ask you to discuss your skills,
they will evaluate your characteristics.

ROLES YOU MAY PLAY

Although there are hundreds of roles you may play as a consultant, the following examples will give you an idea of what a client may expect of you. As a consultant, you may come in at any point in a situation facing a client. Although the examples here are somewhat oversimplified, they may help you identify the role that you can fill most effectively.

Identify the Problem. You may enter when a client knows something is wrong in general, but just cannot identify what: morale is down, communication is poor, turnover is high, and profits are questionable. In this case, you may be asked to identify the problem. You will probably be required to gather data, interview people, study the bigger picture, recognize interfaces, and benchmark other organizations. The roles you will play include interviewer, analyzer, synthesizer, categorizer, and researcher.

Identify the Cause. You may enter when a client knows there is a problem: sales are down, time from concept to market is too long, or defects are high. The client knows there is a problem, but does not know what the cause is. In this case, you may be asked to identify the root cause of the problem. You will need to understand the basics of problem solving, how to uncover the root cause, how to communicate with process owners, and how to challenge the status quo. You may need to have a heavy dose of expertise in the specific area. The roles you will play include expert resource, auditor, devil's advocate, mediator, and problem solver.

Identify the Solution. You may enter when a client knows there is a problem and has identified the cause: sales are down because the competition has introduced a new product, time from concept to market is too long because the staff doesn't work well together, or defects are high because the supplier is unreliable. In this case, you may be asked to identify a solution or solutions. You will probably need to research outside initiatives in the same or other industries. You may need to locate other resources or to coordinate and facilitate open discussion. You will need to help others identify potential ideas. The roles you will play include processor, idea generator, facilitator, and adapter.

Implement the Solution. You may enter when a client knows there is a problem, has identified the root cause, and has determined the solution: attract a new customer base, work better as a team, or improve supplier communication. In this case, you may be asked to implement the solution or change. You will be expected to make things happen. If you must install the new, you may also be required to get rid of the old. You will need to deliver information and assist others to communicate effectively. You may need to supervise installations and reconfigure the workforce. The roles you will play include catalyst, implementer, change agent, mentor, communicator, and coordinator.

Each of these situations requires you to play different roles. Obviously there is a lot of crossover, but think about your talents and which roles you could fill best. What are your strengths? What do you most enjoy doing?

The Independent Consultant Association recently conducted a study of its members, who were asked to consider a consultant's role and describe the "ideal" consultant. The following are the top ten responses:

1. Knows how to methodically diagnose any problem, structure, or organization.
2. Is constantly learning and growing.
3. Never misses a deadline.
4. Can prepare a compelling report with clear, helpful graphics.
5. Knows how to tap the right and left sides of the brain.
6. Loves the client and becomes a true friend.
7. Understands how to use leverage for clients as well as in the consultant's practice.
8. Is technologically competent.
9. Knows how to run or participate in a meeting with equal effectiveness.
10. Knows what's going on in the world and is generally well-read.

e-Idea

Check the consulting section of the Careers in Business website. It provides a variety of information, including skills and talent required, recommended books on jobs in consulting, facts and trends in consulting, and information about practice areas in consulting. Check it out at www.careers-in-business.com/consulting/mcsal.htm.

Now that we've examined the skills you may require and the roles you may play, let's look for signs that you may not be cut out to be a consultant.

SIGNS OF A MEDIOCRE CONSULTANT

In almost thirty years of consulting, I've observed hundreds of consultants. Many were very good, and some were mediocre. You aren't starting your business to be mediocre, so now's the time to acknowledge some of the practices and characteristics that lead to mediocrity:

- A belief that being a consultant means that you can be just who you are without concern for what your clients expect and refusing to be flexible to fit their environment when necessary.

- An inability to identify practical marketing tactics or finding excuses to avoid implementing them.

- An inability to recognize an opportunity when it is slapping you in the face—for example, clients or potential clients saying, "Do you know anything about . . ." or "Something that is really bugging me is . . ." or "I'd like some help with. . . ." These are all cries for help. Listen! Listen! Listen! Your next project may be speaking to you!

- An insistence on using a model or solution that you are familiar with rather than creating or finding a new one that would be more appropriate.

- An insistence on doing the same things over and over, not creating new materials or trying new options.

- Limited desire to continue to grow and learn.

- No recognition that your consulting practice is a business.

Average is just average. Is that what you want to be?

YOUR PERSONAL SITUATION

Before you quit your job and buy your business license, take time to identify any personal situations that may make the profession difficult for you. I've listed five that people frequently identify. You may have others. The best way to discover these may be to discuss your own situation with a friend, your spouse, or a significant other.

Financing the Business

Even if you leave your present job with the promise of six months of consulting work, there is no guarantee that you will have your next projects lined up when that income stream ends.

You may become so tied up in the project that you don't take the time to prospect for new projects. Or you may decide that you deserve some time off before you plunge into your business. In either case, you may not have a steady income following your initial project.

What can you do? Do you have savings or other cash that you can draw from during your initial start-up or later if you have no income? Can you cut back on personal or business spending? Can you obtain a line of credit from your bank? Consulting has its ups and downs. Be sure to set some money aside in a liquid investment for times when things are not going as well as you would like. It may be difficult to adjust to the fact that consulting does not produce a regular paycheck.

Consulting does not produce a regular paycheck.

Working Alone

Leaving the hustle and bustle of an office sounds great initially, but once you spend several days in the same room without seeing anyone except the mail carrier, you may begin to go stir crazy. You may miss the opportunity to work as a team. You may miss the synergy that groups can create, and you may miss the social interactions.

What can you do? You can at least arrange to have lunch with someone once each week. You can plan to meet other consultants regularly. Even though discussion is likely to turn to work, you will still appreciate the camaraderie.

Working from Your Home

At first working from your home sounds like an ideal situation. Get up when you want to. No traffic to face. No time clock to punch. Work in your shorts and

T-shirt. Listen to your favorite radio station. Brew fresh gourmet coffee in the morning. Eat a bagel while you're proofing a proposal. Walk outdoors at any time during the day. Flick the television on to hear the latest news. Pick up the kids from school. Read at your desk after everyone has gone to bed. Perfect day—right?

How about the day things don't go as well? The dog barks just as you are about to close an important sale. Your daughter spills milk on the proposal that's on its way to the post office. Your home-based office has spread to the living room. You need to leave for an important meeting, and your son hasn't returned with the car. Your spouse is upset because you spend every waking hour in your office.

Both kinds of day are equally possible. You will need to face the reality of both. Think about how you can balance working at home and living at home.

Being a One-Person Company

Think about how you will feel when a client asks you how many people are in your company. Will you feel proud of being on your own, or will you feel somehow inferior? How will you feel about doing your own typing, copying, errands, dusting, vacuuming?

An important factor to consider is backup support. What will you do when one of your clients is counting on you to facilitate a critical meeting and you are at home ill? Identify someone who could fill in for you. You could make a reciprocal agreement with several other consultants in your area.

Needing Family Support

Family support is critical. Starting your business will be difficult enough. You don't need your family saying, "We told you so!" when something goes wrong. Obtain 100 percent support from all immediate family members before you hang out your shingle.

The five personal situations I've described here are the ones consultants mention most frequently as interfering with their ability to function. Each has its own solution. You must recognize the possibility of any of these problems coming up and plan your own solutions.

You've examined your skills, looked at your characteristics, explored the roles you may play, faced your personal situations, and evaluated your talents, and you have determined that you are a match for the profession. The rest of this book assumes that you have decided to open your own consulting practice.

CAUTION: BUSINESS OWNER AHEAD

So far in this chapter we have focused on what it takes to be a successful consultant. You are headed for the entrepreneurial ranks. You are about to become a business owner.

Estimates generally are that 80 percent of all start-up businesses fail within five years. Responsibility for success or failure rests almost entirely with the person who started the business. What are some of the reasons for this high failure rate?

- Mistaking a business for a hobby.
- Asking friends and relatives for advice.
- Borrowing money from friends and relatives.
- Mismanaged money.
- Lack of business plan.
- Poor marketing.
- Lack of pricing knowledge.
- Inability to manage growth.
- Lack of commitment.
- Failure to set and revise goals.
- Inability to develop, monitor, and understand financial statements.
- Inability to balance business and family.
- Underestimation of time requirements.

Although there is no way I can prepare you psychologically for the long hours, the endless frustrations, the demands for patience and persistence, the multitude of ups and downs, and the desperate need for planning when there is no time for planning, I can tell you what characteristics are likely to pave your way to success.

ENTREPRENEURIAL CHARACTERISTICS

Although all the experts do not agree about what makes a successful start-up business owner, the following seem to be mentioned most often.

First, you have to want to do it! Let's face it. You're tired of working for someone else, and the idea of doing your own thing appeals to you—really appeals to you. You have already taken the first step. You've decided that you want to start a business, and, yes, you want to ensure that it is still around five years from now. What's next?

Self-confidence is on almost all lists. Be honest with yourself. If you don't believe in you, who will? Most consultants have a good dose of self-assurance—believing that they can do whatever they set their minds to. Before starting my business, I can remember thinking, "This is such a sure bet; I can't *not* succeed!"

Most entrepreneurs have a sense of urgency. They have places to go, things to do, people to see, and successes to pull off. They seem to have more energy than most people and a need to do things *now*. Interestingly enough, most require fewer than the usual eight hours of sleep each night.

e-Idea

Entrepreneur magazine has a great website with all sorts of informative downloadable articles. Check it out at www.entrepreneur.com.

Entrepreneurs are willing to work hard—to do what it takes to achieve success. Long hours don't scare them. They also play hard—and competitively!

Entrepreneurs have a need to control and direct. They want the responsibility and authority that comes with owning a business. They like making decisions; they do not like being told what to do.

They have the flexibility to think differently as the need arises. They can be either creative or analytical; they can be big-picture thinkers or detail-oriented.

Maintaining a positive attitude gets entrepreneurs through the ups and downs. They truly do look at problems as challenges. They are certain a solution exists and welcome the learning that accompanies identifying the problem and solving it.

They are good decision makers. They usually rate neither high nor low in risk taking, but are good at weighing potential outcomes. They are decisive, and they move forward. They don't hesitate or procrastinate. They are also willing to change a course of action if the expectations for success are less than they had hoped for.

Entrepreneurs are creative problem solvers. They are conceptual thinkers and see relationships that others may not. They excel at creating order out of chaos.

They may be obsessed with quality—quality of service, quality of product, quality of a project. They are naturally committed to excellence and do not need the quality gurus to inspire them!

Good health is almost imperative, given the preceding list! I believe that health has a lot to do with positive thinking and the fact that entrepreneurs just don't have time to get sick.

Do you have what it takes to be a business owner? Can you cut it as an entrepreneur? Find out with the evaluation in Exhibit 2.2.

Exhibit 2.2. Entrepreneurs: Do You Have What It Takes?

Rate yourself on the following qualities. They represent the thinking of several authors about the requirements of a successful business owner. Spend ample time pondering these questions and answer honestly. Although this survey can only give a general picture of what it takes to be a successful entrepreneur, only you can decide if the move is right for you. Rate yourself on the following 1–4 scale:

1 = strongly disagree   **3** = agree
2 = disagree   **4** = strongly agree

Circle your answer

1.	I usually try to take charge when I'm with others.	1	2	3	4
2.	I can do anything I set my mind to.	1	2	3	4
3.	I have a high tolerance level.	1	2	3	4
4.	I believe I can always influence results.	1	2	3	4
5.	I am complimented on my ability to quickly analyze complex situations.	1	2	3	4
6.	I prefer working with a difficult but highly competent person rather than a friendly, less competent one.	1	2	3	4
7.	I can fire employees who are not producing.	1	2	3	4
8.	I am willing to leave a high-paying, secure job to start my own business.	1	2	3	4
9.	I push myself to complete tasks.	1	2	3	4
10.	I can work long, hard hours when necessary.	1	2	3	4
11.	I need to be the best at whatever I do.	1	2	3	4
12.	I do not become frustrated easily.	1	2	3	4
13.	I thrive on challenges.	1	2	3	4

The Business of Consulting, Second Edition. Copyright © 2007 by John Wiley & Sons, Inc. Reproduced by permission of Pfeiffer, an Imprint of Wiley. www.pfeiffer.com

Exhibit 2.2. Entrepreneurs: Do You Have What It Takes?, Cont'd.

14.	I become bored easily with routine tasks.	1	2	3	4
15.	I dislike being told what to do.	1	2	3	4
16.	I have a higher energy level than most people.	1	2	3	4
17.	I have held numerous leadership positions.	1	2	3	4
18.	I enjoy accomplishing a complex task by myself and have the ability to do so.	1	2	3	4
19.	I can change my course of action if something is not working.	1	2	3	4
20.	I am seen as a creative problem solver.	1	2	3	4
21.	I can balance the big picture and details of a business at the same time.	1	2	3	4
22.	I can predict how my actions today will affect business tomorrow and in the future.	1	2	3	4

23. I need at least _____ hours of sleep to function effectively.
   1 = 8 hrs   2 = 7 hrs
   3 = 6 hrs   4 = 5 or fewer hrs

24. I have at least _____ years of experience in the business I will start.
   1 = 1 yr   2 = 2 yrs
   3 = 3 yrs   4 = 4 yrs

25. Over the past three years, I have missed a total of _____ days of work due to illness.
   1 = over 15 days   2 = 11–15 days
   3 = 6–10 days   4 = 0–5 days

Scoring: Total the numbers you circled

90–100	Go for it!
82–89	Good chance of success
74–81	Pretty risky
73 and below	Better continue to collect a paycheck

This chapter focused on the required talents and characteristics of consultants. You can begin to appreciate the multitalented person a client will expect. You now probably have a better picture of the drawbacks as well as the rewards of consulting. If you are excited by the opportunity and challenged by the adventure, you are ready to begin thinking about what you need to do to start.

Dollars and Sense

The harder I work the luckier I get!

Samuel Goldwyn

Determining what to charge clients is usually the most difficult decision for a first-time consultant. Yet it is a decision that you must make before you can begin to solicit business. Your client will most likely want to know, "How much will this project cost?"

There are really two issues: (1) how much money you need and (2) how much a client is willing to pay you. Although they are closely related, it is important to keep them separate in your mind. On the one hand, if the two amounts are relatively close or if clients are willing to pay you more than you require (what an exciting problem to have!), you'll find it easy to balance your budget. On the other hand, if you suspect that you require more than clients are willing to pay for your services, you may want to reconsider opening a consulting practice.

Let's examine each of these issues: How much money do you require? and How much should you charge for your services?

HOW MUCH MONEY DO YOU REQUIRE?

Determine how much income you will require as a consultant in one of two ways. The first way is to calculate in detail your salary, taxes, benefits, and business expenses for one year. A second way, the "3× Rule" (pronounced "three times rule"), will provide a quick estimate of your requirements.

Calculation Method

Your perceived value is one way to start. What do you believe you should make in a year? Starting here makes sense because an annual salary is the way most of us think of our value. Don't forget benefits, including insurance, retirement contributions, self-employment taxes, and vacation time. You may identify each benefit individually or simply add on 25 to 33 percent as an estimate. After that, develop a budget for running your business. Exhibit 3.1 will help you remember most of your expenses. In addition to annual expenses, you will have some one-time start-up costs. Chapter Four provides more details about these. Use Exhibit 3.1 to estimate the amounts you will need to cover your salary, benefits, taxes, and business expenses. Total these to determine how much money you will require annually.

The 3x Rule

If you don't want to take time now to identify your business expenses, the 3× Rule will give you a close estimate. The 3× Rule is used by many consulting firms to determine how much to bill clients (and in some cases how much business to generate as well) in order to pay salaries to themselves, cover overhead, and contribute to profit for the company. For example, consultants with a salary of $50,000 are expected to bill at least $150,000 each year. Does this seem excessive? Do you wonder what happens to all that money? You already know that $50,000 is earmarked for your salary. The other two-thirds pays for fringe benefits, such as insurance, FICA, unemployment taxes, worker's compensation, and vacation time; overhead, such as marketing, advertising, electricity, professional development, telephone, supplies, clerical support, and management; downtime, those days when consultants are traveling, off for a holiday, or in training; and for development and preparation time. The additional money also covers days that cannot be billed due to an inability to match available consultants to client dates.

If you plan to work out of a home office and do not plan to hire support staff the first year, you might be able to whittle your requirements down to a "2× Rule," but your budget will be tight, and you may experience cash-flow problems. (More about cash flow in Chapter Six.) Be cautious about playing a tight numbers game.

Exhibit 3.1. Calculating What You Require.

Your Salary for One Year _____

Your Benefits
    Health insurance _____
    Life insurance _____
    Disability insurance _____
    Retirement _____
                     Total Benefits _____

Taxes
    Self-employment _____
    Social Security and Medicare _____
    State income tax _____
    City tax _____
    Personal property tax _____
                     Total Taxes _____

Business Expenses
    Accounting, banking, and legal fees _____
    Advertising and marketing _____
    Automobile expenses _____
    Books and resources _____
    Clerical support _____
    Copying _____
    Donations _____
    Dues and subscriptions _____
    Entertainment _____
    Equipment leases _____
    Interest and loan repayments _____
    Liability insurance _____
    Licenses _____
    Lodging (nonbillable) _____
    Materials (nonbillable) _____
    Meals _____
    Office supplies _____
    Postage _____
    Professional development _____
    Rent _____
    Repairs and maintenance _____
    Telephone _____
    Travel (nonbillable) _____
    Utilities _____
                     Total Business Expenses _____
                     Total Required _____

The Business of Consulting, Second Edition. Copyright © 2007 by John Wiley & Sons, Inc. Reproduced by permission of Pfeiffer, an Imprint of Wiley. www.pfeiffer.com

Your Circumstances

As you begin to put numbers on paper, you must also consider your personal circumstances. Are you the primary breadwinner in your family? Can someone else pick up some of the slack as you are starting your business? What can you contribute from your savings as you start your own consulting practice? (*Note:* Many experienced consultants recommend that you have a six- to twelve-month cushion.) What work can you count on immediately? How long will it take to generate additional work?

As many companies downsize, they offer employees "consulting contracts" as part of a severance package. This may be an ideal scenario for you. It usually means that you are responsible for specific projects identified by your former employer for which you receive an amount that is somewhat less than your former salary. The projects may require less than half of your time, and you can use the rest to generate and conduct other business. Generally these agreements extend for less than one year and are nonrenewable. Many budding consultants find this an ideal way to start.

HOW MUCH SHOULD YOU CHARGE?

Deciding how much to charge is difficult because you naturally feel modest and do not want to charge too much, but also cannot afford to charge too little. Here is how to decide how much to charge for your services.

Determine Typical Charges

Charges are determined by many factors. The greatest determining factor is the client: the business or industry, the size and location, the demand, and the history of consultant use. The next determining factor is the consultant: the level of expertise, the amount of experience, and the person's stature. This unique supply-and-demand situation creates a wide price range. I've worked with consultants who have charged as little as $200 per day and as much as $55,000 for a one-hour speech! So what's realistic?

Training magazine published its 2006 Annual Salary Survey in the November 2006 issue. The overall average for consulting was just over $100,000 per year. The Northeast region had the highest average at almost $136,000, and the Mountain region had the lowest at $64,000. This is a 29 percent increase over 2005 and is attributed to consultants being used more.

The type of client determines acceptable fee ranges. Generally, for-profit companies have more in their budgets for your services than do nonprofit organizations. Usually, the larger the company, the larger the discretionary funds available. My limited research on the Web and with colleagues finds that daily rates for consultants working in the corporate arena are $600 to $5,000; those in government, $400 to $4,500; those in nonprofit fields, $0 to $3,500; and those in church-related work, $0 to $2,500. As you can see, these figures show a wide range both within and among the categories of clients.

The larger the company, the larger the discretionary funds available.

Also check your market area for services similar to yours but priced much lower. For example, a local mental health clinic may offer a stress-management class for $10. A community college may offer a time-management course for $35. If either of these areas is your specialty, you may have a difficult time convincing companies to pay $1,000 per day—even if you do customize the materials for them.

Location of both the client and the consultant will also affect the fee charged. Ranges are different in different areas. It is natural to expect that consultants in large cities, such as New York, Boston, or Los Angeles, will charge more than consultants in smaller towns.

Finally, the consultant determines the fee. What expertise do you have? Is it unique or commonplace? How much experience do you have? With what kind of clients? Do you work internationally? Nationally? Statewide? Locally? How well known are you? What perceived value do you add due to your stature in the business, the books you've written, or your university affiliations? The answers to each of these will help you determine your rate.

Determine Your Fee

Although it may be interesting to know that some consultants charge more for one day than you may presently make in a month, the real question is how to determine what you should charge.

You can determine a fee in one of two ways. You can start with the requirements you compiled and plan toward that end, or you can approach the problem from the standpoint of what the market will bear.

Plan with the End in Mind. To use this method, return to your calculations to obtain the amount that you need for living and business expenses for one year. Think in terms of how much billable time is actually available. There are fifty-two weeks in a year, and you will probably take off at least two of them. In addition you must account for New Year's Day, Memorial Day, July Fourth, Labor Day, Thanksgiving, Christmas, and other holidays. This leaves about forty-nine weeks or 245 days, assuming a five-day week. Generally, you will average between two and three billable days per week or a maximum of 120 days per year, for two reasons. The first is that you will need time to run your business. You will need to market, network, write proposals, travel, bill clients, and complete many other administrative details required to manage a business. In addition, you will need to develop your skills, learn new techniques, and keep up with the changes in your field as well as the industries in which you work. As a consultant you must maintain your professional edge.

The second reason it is highly unlikely that you will bill more than 120 days in one year is the difficulty of matching your clients' needs with your available days. You may find that all your clients need you the same week in September. You may need to turn down some of those billable days. Then again, you may find yourself with a week or two in December with no billable days. Exhibit 3.2 will help you determine your actual billable days.

Let's work through an example. You have determined that you require $50,000 to live for a year. You added $20,000 for taxes, $7,500 for retirement, and $6,000 for various kinds of insurance. This brings what you need to bill to $83,500.

Let's suppose that you will begin by working out of your home and that you expect overhead to be small for your first year, about $2,100 per month, or $25,200 per year. Now the total amount that you must bill is $108,700. Because this is your first year in business, you know it will take some time to build a client base. You decide to play it safe and plan on eighty days of consulting.

Next you will divide the total dollar amount, $108,700, by eighty. That gives you a daily rate of $1,358.75. Most consultants would round that figure to $1,300 or $1,400 for each billable day.

You should consider one last thing. A successful business makes a profit each year. Don't confuse your salary with your business profit. A profit is your reward for owning the business and incurring the risks that ownership entails. A 10 percent profit is very respectable for a first year in business, so you may want to add $10,000 for a profit margin. This increases what you will need to bill for your first

Exhibit 3.2. Actual Billable Days.

Days in a Year	365
Weekend Days	− 104
	= 261
Time Off	
Vacation, personal (5–15 days per year)	− _____
Holidays (6–12 days per year)	− _____
	= _____
Marketing (1–2 days per week)	− _____
Administrative (2–4 days per month)	− _____
	= _____
Down time (15–30 percent)	− _____
Days you expect to work	[ ]

year to $118,700. Using the original eighty billable days, that amounts to almost $1,500 per day.

Does $1,500 per day sound high for your first year in the field? It may be. You may need to return to your original budget. Can you cut expenses? Could you do all your own typing instead of using a temporary service? Can you decrease the amount you require to live? For example, could you not take an expensive vacation, or could you use some of your savings for living expenses? Can you increase the number of billable days? Perhaps your present employer will retain you to complete existing projects, or you could work weekends to add more days. Any of these will change the equation to lower your billable rate. Use Exhibit 3.3 to calculate your consulting fee.

The Business of Consulting, Second Edition. Copyright © 2007 by John Wiley & Sons, Inc. Reproduced by permission of Pfeiffer, an Imprint of Wiley. www.pfeiffer.com

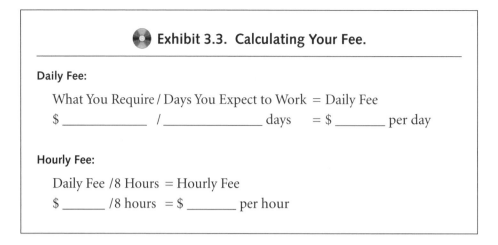

Exhibit 3.3. Calculating Your Fee.

Daily Fee:

What You Require / Days You Expect to Work = Daily Fee

$ _____ / _____ days = $ _____ per day

Hourly Fee:

Daily Fee /8 Hours = Hourly Fee

$ _____ /8 hours = $ _____ per hour

Although this exercise is an excellent way to determine your billable rate, you must also consider what a client will be willing to pay for your services. You certainly do not want to price yourself out of the market your first year!

Determine What the Market Will Bear. Place a price on your head by determining what you believe the market will bear—that is, how much you believe your targeted clients will pay for your services. Realize that you are not charging what you are "worth" but what clients are willing to pay. In his book *The Consultant's Calling*, Geoff Bellman (2002) says, "We are not talking about what you and I are worth; we are talking about what you and I can get. . . .Your ultimate value as a consultant or as a human being is not being put on the line in this negotiation." This is an important distinction. Geoff goes on to say, "You can't put a financial value on who you are, so don't mix up your struggles about personal worth with your efforts to sell your services."

If you use this method, remember to look at your competition. As a new consultant, you may want to collect as much information as you can about what clients are paying for services and what consultants are charging for services. Don't be surprised if this information is difficult to obtain. I have found most consultants to be quite closed about what they charge. Of course you need to pay attention to the Sherman Anti-Trust Act to ensure that you will not be accused of price fixing!

e-Idea

You may feel better about your value if you find out what you are worth at www.payscale.com. You can input information about yourself—for example, where you live, where you graduated, your certification and degrees, and number of years of experience—to calculate a current compensation analysis. You will get the basic information for free or a more detailed salary report for a six-month membership at a minimum fee. You can find another salary comparison at www.salaryexpert.com. At www.careerjournal.com, you can create and print out salary tables for various consulting positions. Use these only as additional data points.

If you decide to follow what the market will bear, you will want to explore some other issues to help you determine your fee. Ask yourself these questions: What's your specialty? How common is your expertise? What is unique about your experience? What industry are you targeting? What constitutes a typical consulting fee for companies in this industry? Where is your market? What is the range of fees organizations pay in this market? Who else offers similar services? What do they charge? Use Exhibit 3.4 to help you sort through the factors that will determine your rate. The more Xs in the left column, the higher the rate you will be able to charge.

Pricing Strategy

Whether you decide to plan with the end in mind, go with what the market will bear, or use a combination of the two methods, you must still select a pricing strategy. Your figures will result in a range, so you will have to determine whether to charge at the high end or the low end of the range. Experience shows that most new consultants select the lower price. They feel that if they price low, they will find more contracts to "get started."

However, pricing services too low is the biggest mistake that new consultants make. Choose the high end of the range—for several reasons. First, the higher price means that you will need to accept fewer contracts. This allows you to manage your time better, giving you the flexibility to deal with all those unforeseeable things that crop up when starting a business. It also allows you to spend more time with your clients; you can give them better service rather than worry about your next contract. Charge a price that allows you to do the job with superior quality.

Exhibit 3.4. How Much Will Clients Pay?

Place an X in either the left or right column next to the item that most accurately describes you and your potential clients.

My Consulting

___ Expertise in high demand	___ Minimal demand for expertise
___ More than 20 years in the the industry	___ Less than 10 years in industry
___ High name recognition	___ Little name recognition
___ Rare area of specialty	___ Specialty readily available
___ Published work is well known	___ No published work

My Clients

___ High-paying industry	___ Low-paying industry
___ For-profit organizations	___ Nonprofit or government
___ Large organizations	___ Small organizations
___ Large city	___ Small city
___ Coast locations	___ Midwest
___ High use of consultants	___ Minimal use of consultants

Total _____   _____

---

*Charge a price that allows you
to do the job with superior quality.*

Second, your consulting rate sends a message. True or not, a higher price often is equated with higher quality. A low price may send a message that you are not worthy of important projects. A low bid may help you acquire some early projects, but may also be a reason that clients are uncomfortable hiring you again—especially if the project was not large enough for you and the client to develop a solid relationship. Achieving the reputation of being the cheapest consultant in town means only that you are "the cheapest consultant in town"!

Third, if you offer what clients need, they will most likely pay the price you request without questioning it. It will be much easier to start high than to increase your rates at a later time.

SELECTING A PRICING STRUCTURE

The discussion so far has focused primarily on a daily fee. There are other possible pricing structures. Often the industry you serve or the kind of consulting you do will determine the pricing structure you choose.

Daily Rate

Training, organization development, or management development consultants typically charge by the day. That day may be six to twelve hours long depending on the task at hand. If you are conducting training that begins at 8 A.M., you will probably need to arrive before 7 A.M. to set up the room—or even set it up the night before the session. The session may last until 4:30 P.M., but participants may stay around to discuss the day with you. After they leave, you may still want to organize the room and your materials for the next day, study your notes, or examine work that was generated by the participants during the day. It may be 6 P.M. before you leave for the day. An eleven-hour day may be the norm, and you do not charge overtime for the additional hours.

Billing by the day may make you seize as many days of work as possible—even when they don't fit into your schedule well. When a day has passed without a billable client, you have lost that income potential forever. Billing by the day limits your earning power to the number of days in a year. This puts strong emphasis on days worked as opposed to results achieved. Remember that a billable day is a billable day; once it's gone, it is lost forever.

A billable day is a billable day;
once it's gone, it is lost forever.

Hourly Rate

Consulting fees charged by the hour are standard in some industries, such as computer programming, executive coaching, and engineering. In this case, you will provide a range of hours (minimum and maximum) you expect the job to require. Travel time is not generally billed in any of the other pricing structures; it is charged in the hourly rate structure.

Both a daily rate and an hourly rate require the client to assume the risk for the total cost of the project. Thus these pricing structures are more typically used for training or tasks that have clearly defined time parameters and outcomes. In less defined situations, a daily or hourly rate penalizes the clients if the consultant is slow, and penalizes consultants if they are efficient!

Fixed-Price Projects

Establishing a firm-fixed price for a complete project is how I prefer to bill. The client and the consultant identify and agree on specific results that mark the completion of a project. Although some consultants resist this method of pricing, due to the risk involved if the price is too low, my experience shows that this is the trend. Tom Peters (1997) says, "It's a project-based world. If you're not spending at least 70 percent of your time on projects, you're living in the past." In his book *Million Dollar Consulting,* Alan Weiss (2002) advocates this approach and states, "If you want to make a million dollars or more in this profession, charging by time units isn't the route to get there."

You may have to bid on a fixed-price basis if you work for government agencies. Responding to a Request for Proposal (RFP) from any organization may also require you to determine a fixed price for an entire project. An RFP is often used when several consultants are competing for a job.

I prefer this pricing structure for several reasons. First and most important, the client's employees can call at any time for assistance and, unlike my attorney, I won't start the timer. Second, the method is performance- and results-oriented. We are paid for what we accomplish. Third, this method is the best match for a custom design. Fourth, this method is better for larger contracts. Several large contracts are easier to manage than dozens of little ones.

How can you determine a price? First, estimate how much time you expect the project to require. If this is your first time using this method, you may still want to use a daily rate to find a ballpark price. With this method, you assume the risk of the total cost of the project. Ethically, you cannot charge more than the original quoted price—even if you lose money. We have lost money on a couple of projects due to poor estimating. In these situations, we have always continued to provide the highest-quality work and have not disclosed our predicament to the client. This would be unprofessional. It certainly taught us good estimating skills quickly!

Per Person

Charging by the number of participants who attend a session is another way to look at pricing. It is typically used by trainers offering public seminars. Government agencies may want you to use this type of fee structure because it more closely matches their budgeting structure. If you do choose this method, consider an up-front agreement that you will be paid for a minimum number of participants. In other words, if you require payment for a minimum of eighteen and only sixteen people attend, you will still be paid for eighteen.

Retainers

Retainers were very popular in the 1960s and 1970s and are making a comeback today. A retainer establishes a set fee that the consultant receives on a regular basis, generally monthly. A retainer typically covers a span of twelve months. The client is assured that the consultant is available on an as-needed basis. The client and consultant determine an approximate amount of time that will be required monthly. The advantage to the consultant is a regular income; the drawback is that the consultant must plan around the needs of the client.

Conditional Fee

Some organizations pay a fixed price to a consultant on the completion of a clearly defined task. This method may be used by search firms in executive recruiting, where the conditional fee is paid only after the recruiting consultant provides the organization with four qualified candidates for a specific position.

Percentage Fee

Percentage fees are used when the financial outcome of the project is easily and clearly measurable. The consultant agrees to a percentage of the financial success of the project. This method works well for sales or marketing consultants. The client and the consultant agree that a percentage of the financial gain or savings will be paid to the consultant. A consultant can do very well with this arrangement, and the client is assured that the consultant will focus on the bottom line. A drawback for the consultant is that the results may not be measurable until some time after the project has been completed.

No matter which pricing structure you choose, you still must determine how much you require as well as how much you believe the market will bear.

OTHER PRICING DECISIONS

Pricing involves many other decisions. You must clarify what you think about the following before you can discuss costs with a client.

Definition of a Day

If you have decided to charge by the day, you must determine what constitutes a day. If you attend meetings at your client's business from 10 A.M. until 3 P.M., is that one day? If you work on a project in your office from 7 A.M. until 7 P.M., is that one day? Do you count hours? Do you count calendar days? How will you define one day? Although we typically charge by the project, when we use daily rates we charge for one calendar day, no matter how many hours we work. Regardless of how you determine the length of a day, be sure to decide prior to working with clients.

Half-Day Events

What if a client needs you on-site for four hours and you are basing your charges on full-day rates? Should you charge half your regular rate? We recommend that you charge more than half. Why? First, you will spend the same amount of time going to and from the site. Second, you will probably spend the same amount of time in preparation. And third, this billable day is spent! You have little chance of using the rest of the day in billable work. So what can you do? You may wish to bill for something more than half a day's rate, but less than a full-day rate. Or you may wish to do as I do, which is to charge a full-day rate, even for a half-day event.

Perceived Value

Your price may send a message to potential clients about your expertise. I notice consistently that new consultants tend to establish fees that are lower than the market would bear. If your price is too low, you may be inadvertently telling clients that you are not as good as other consultants. You want your client focused on the value of the services that you will provide. An astute client will question whether you can successfully complete the project at the rate you have quoted.

Proposals or Sales Meetings

We do not charge for writing proposals. We see it as a cost of doing business. If we initiate a sales call, we do not charge for the time or expenses. Nor do we charge if the client requests a visit and it is local (within a two-hour drive). However, if the client initiates a sales call that will require an overnight stay or airfare, we do request payment of out-of-pocket expenses. To open this discussion in a professional manner, I usually say, "Would you like us to make travel arrangements and bill you at cost? Or would you like to make the travel arrangements and let me know what they are?"

Pro Bono

Work that you complete for free is good for your business, good for the community, and good for your soul. I set aside at least fifteen days each year to do pro bono work for professional organizations, such as ASTD; volunteer groups, such as the American Red Cross; or schools or government agencies that cannot afford to pay. In these cases I do not charge a reduced fee. I tell them that I have only two fees: my client fee and free. The more you give, the more you get. Try it.

OTHER CHARGES

Besides your billing rate, you will incur extra charges that will be reimbursed by the client.

Travel Expenses

Travel, lodging, and meals are generally an additional charge to the client. Bill the client for the same amount you paid. It may be a common practice in other professions to tack on a "handling fee" for expenses, but it is not accepted in consulting. You will be expected to provide receipts for your expenses. If you work for government agencies, you will hear the term *per diem,* which refers to a preestablished daily rate that has been determined for the city in which you are working. This fee, allowed by the Joint Travel Regulations, is expected to cover your lodging, meals, tips, and sometimes local travel. If you are traveling on a per diem basis, find out what the rate is prior to making your travel arrangements so that you can stay within the maximum amount allowed.

Materials

There are three possible ways to handle charges for materials that will be used during the consulting project: (1) materials can be included in your daily fee; (2) materials can be an additional charge to the client and can appear as an additional line item on the invoice; or (3) materials can be provided or produced by the client. When a contract includes many repeat sessions, you can save clients money by providing them with masters for the materials and allowing them to make their own copies. This saves you time and eliminates your need to transport materials for each session.

Overhead

Most consultants' fees include the cost of overhead. However, some larger firms itemize the charges for typing, data entry, editing, data analysis, and other off-site activities. Some firms also track and charge for telephone calls and other correspondence. Although it is unlikely that as a start-up consultant you will do that, you should be aware of this practice. If you ever find yourself competing on a daily or hourly rate basis with one of the large consulting firms, and you wonder how it can charge less per day or hour than you do, dig deeper. You will find that the firm's total sum will most likely be greater than yours due to all the additional charges.

Travel Time

Will you charge for travel time? A very small portion of consultants itemize travel time as billable to the client at a reduced rate. Most simply consider it a cost of doing business.

e-Idea

If you are a member of the American Society for Training and Development (ASTD), you have access to the Ask a Consulting Expert website column (www.astd.org/astd/resources/consulting_community). Many of the questions submitted address money issues.

FEE INCREASES

If you think setting your initial fees is difficult, wait until you are faced with increasing your fees. You will have many questions on your mind: "Will they pay more?" "Will I lose some of my clients?" "How do I tell them?" I remember sitting next to the Elizabeth River with a friend trying to decide whether I should increase my fees from $750 to $800 or $900. In the end my friend convinced me to go for it!

Although I've never experienced a negative reaction to fee increases, I know that some consultants have. An increase in your fees may result in a loss of clients. However, if you give your clients enough time to adjust their budgets and you're not increasing your rate by some astronomical figure, your clients will most likely understand. A six-month notice is generally considered fair, ethical, and appropriate. We tell our clients about an increase verbally, then follow up with a written note. In addition, we include a reminder with the first invoice at the new rate. This is one time that you cannot overcommunicate.

How do you know that it's time to increase your fees? You'll know when you are so busy you don't have time to increase your fees! It's a simple matter of supply and demand—or so I once thought. At one point in my career I had about twice the work I could handle, so I increased my fees. In fact, I doubled them, thinking that my projects would be cut in half and that I would break even financially with less work. That didn't happen. Instead, when I raised my fees it created a perception that I was more valuable! Raising my fees actually *increased* business.

Sometimes when you increase your rates, your proposals are bumped into a new category, requiring approval by a higher level of management. This is good because higher levels in any organization generally have larger budgets and more discretionary funds. A difference of $13,000 one way or another is not as critical to a vice president as it is to a line manager. Lesson learned? Don't underestimate yourself. If you add value, the work will be there.

If you add value,
the work will be there.

For another perspective, be sure to read Geoff Bellman's book *The Consultant's Calling.* I'd like to be able to tell you to read just one chapter, but I can't do that. The book represents a philosophy, and to appreciate its holistic nature, you need to read the entire book.

ETHICS OF PRICING

Although Chapter Nine is dedicated to the ethics of consulting, three issues about pricing ethics deserve to be mentioned here.

Determine a Consistent Pricing Structure

The highest compliment that I can receive from a client is to hear that we are ethical. The fastest way to undermine that trust is to price inconsistently for different clients. To ensure that this does not happen, identify a clear and consistent pricing structure for all your clients. Charging one client $1,000 for one day of training and another on the other side of town $1,300 for the same type of training will cause problems. Clients get together at their industry professional meetings and share what they are doing. You do not want them to discover a difference in your pricing.

Some situations do exist in which you might not charge the same for all clients or for all work, but be certain that these occasions are clearly spelled out in your pricing strategy. Be certain that you adhere to your own strategy. Three situations in which you might charge different prices follow:

1. *The work is different.* You might use a different pricing strategy for different kinds of work—one price for work done on-site and another for work done at your office. You might have a consulting fee and a training fee and perhaps a design fee that is less than either of them. You may charge a different fee for speaking engagements than for training. And, of course, if you are subcontracting with other consultants, you will always charge less, as they acquired the contract with their marketing investment and bear the burden of risk.

2. *The organizations are different.* You may choose to give a discount to non-profit organizations, associations, government agencies, church or school groups, or even your favorite charity. But always identify a measurable reduction and be consistent. Why would you give one nonprofit group a 10 percent discount and another 50 percent? You may have a good reason, but it won't necessarily make sense to others. Being clear about your pricing strategy will help you maintain an ethical image. Remember that your discount strategy is something that you have determined ahead of time. It is not something you negotiate with a client.

3. *The time period is different.* You may be in a situation where the client asks you to do the work in a shorter than normal time period. To accomplish this you might need to work weekends, bring in additional people to help with the project, or both. In this case you would be justified in raising your typical rates, and I am guessing that the client will be happy to pay a premium to get the task completed. The time period might also be different because it is a long-term contract—say over a year. In this case you might be justified in providing a discounted rate for repeat business because you will not need to spend time constantly getting up to speed as you would if you were starting with a new client each month.

The point in each of these three examples is that there is something different—unique—that justifies a different pricing strategy. The key word here is "strategy." Know your strategy and stick with it.

Save Bargains for Department Stores

Although we all love a sale, consulting is not a postseasonal business. It is unethical for you to lower your rates simply because clients do not have adequate funds in their budgets to cover the amount you first quoted. How could this happen? You determine that your rates for the project will be $15,500. The client responds that there is only $10,500 in the budget for the project. It is very tempting (especially if you don't have any work lined up for the next few weeks) to say, "Okay, I'll do it for $10,500." This is one of the ways that consultants gain a bad reputation. If you can do it for $10,500, why did you ask for $15,500? Does that mean that you had $5,000 worth of fat in the proposal? It will make a client question your ethics and the ethics of all consultants.

The only way that you can lower the price of an original quote is to eliminate some of the services, so that there is a true trade-off for the services you offer. For example, you might say, "We could do it at the lower price if you copy the training materials there, compile the evaluations yourself, and provide all the equipment." Or you might eliminate a more valuable service, saying, "We could do it at the lower price, but it would mean that I would not spend a day at your company interviewing people in order to customize the participant materials." When I take this approach, two things usually happen. First, I feel good about myself when I do not succumb to the monetary temptation. Second, the client usually does not want to give up the service and most often says that the money will be found someplace.

If neither of these types of suggestions work, be prepared to walk away from the project. I have walked on at least a dozen occasions. Every time, the client called back to say he or she could "scrape up the money" somehow. I'd like to believe that something greater occurred. I believe that I was educating the client about appropriate consulting ethics.

Don't sell yourself short. If you find that new clients often ask you to reduce your rates, you may want to research the marketplace in which you are working. Have you priced yourself above what the market will bear? If yes, you have at least two choices. First, you may want to lower your prices. To do this you may need to decrease the services you presently provide to clients or decrease your cost of doing business. Second, you may want to locate another market in which your fees are more competitive.

Charge Higher Rates for a Specific Project

The ethics of increasing your rates are even fuzzier than those for reducing your rates. If you are up-front and candid with your client, it's probably okay. Why would you raise your rates? I can think of at least two reasons: the client wants the task completed in a ridiculously short amount of time, or the client insists on using you for a project that you dislike. In either case, you are most likely justified in quoting an increased fee—especially if you are candid in your explanation to your client.

MONEY DISCUSSIONS

During discussions with your clients, you may want to take the responsibility for bringing up the topic of cost. Talking about money is difficult for some people. Take the lead by saying, "You probably want to know how much this will cost." When I open the discussion, I often see relief on clients' faces—they're grateful that I brought up the subject.

Sometimes during that first discussion, you may see potential complications with the project, perhaps an unusual timeline or something unique that you haven't done before. This may make it difficult to price the project on the spot. In this case, you can say, "I'm not sure of the price at this time. Let me go back to my office and put a proposal together that will outline a work plan and the cost. I will have the proposal on your desk tomorrow." This buys you time to plan the project and to price it appropriately. Don't allow yourself to be forced into providing a "rough estimate." An exact figure the next day is better for both you and the client. Naturally, you must live up to your promise to deliver the proposal and price quote when you say you will.

VALUE OF A GUARANTEE

If you are just starting your consulting practice, you might consider offering a 100 percent satisfaction guarantee. If the client is not satisfied with your work, you will return the full amount. Sound risky? It shouldn't. If you don't believe in yourself, who will? If you don't believe in your ability to meet and exceed clients' needs, perhaps you are considering the wrong profession. You should not be practicing on clients. You should know your abilities and be able to guarantee the job.

---

*If you don't
believe in yourself,
who will?*

I've offered a 100 percent money-back guarantee from my first day in the profession. Many of my first clients gave me a chance because the guarantee provided reassurance that I was confident in my ability to complete the project successfully. If I wasn't successful, they wouldn't have to pay. Since that time, many have said the guarantee made the choice easy. As one of my clients from NASA said, "It was a win no matter how we looked at it!"

A guarantee does two things for you and your business. First, it makes it easier for the clients to say yes to you. They have nothing to lose. Either you accomplish the task that needs to be done or it doesn't cost them a thing. Second, it tells the client that you are confident and competent at what you do. What better way to begin a consulting relationship?

Establishing your fee and pricing structure may be the most difficult decisions you must make in "the business of consulting," but it's not impossible. Don't let it prevent you from moving forward.

---

*A guarantee tells the client
that you are confident and competent
at what you do.*

Starting . . .

chapter
FOUR

If you put everything off till you're sure of it, you'll get nothing done.

Norman Vincent Peale

Are you chomping at the bit to get started? That's a good sign. You are excited about tackling all the things necessary to begin your business. One of your biggest questions will be, "How much will it cost to start my consulting business?" The answer is that it will be surprisingly less than you imagine.

But there is much more to consider than start-up costs when you begin a business. You must select a name, choose an accountant, determine a business structure, develop your business plan, and define your niche in the field.

From the moment you begin your business, image plays a key part in how successful you will be. This chapter provides tips on how you can look like a million from day one—on a shoestring budget!

This chapter also explores the age-old question, "I need project experience to be hired; how do I find a project to get that experience?" I'll give you numerous ideas about how to land that first client.

Let's begin your start-up tasks by talking about what's important in a name.

WHAT'S IN A NAME?

When selecting a name, consider two important aspects: it should project the image you desire, and it should be easy to remember. Your business name is not something you will want to change. It will identify you for many years, and changing it is an expensive proposition. So choose carefully.

The name of your company should tell a prospective client something about what you do. One of my favorites in this category is Toys " Я " Us. If your name does not explicitly state what you do, like ebb associates inc, you may want to add a "tag line." A tag line is three or four words that explain what you do. My tagline is "consulting, training, design" to better define the work we do.

The name you select will have implications for how your clients view you and your business. For example, you might choose to use your name. The advantage of "Pam Schmidt Consulting" is that it tells potential clients who you are and the nature of your business. The drawback is that it limits your clients' perspective of your business to one person. Pam may have ten people working for her, but the name will prevent that information from surfacing.

What's your vision for the future of your consulting business? Will you have employees? Associates? Partners? Your name should allow for your future growth or challenge. Many consultants use "Pam Schmidt and Associates" or "The Schmidt Group" even though Pam may be starting out on her own. The name conjures up a team of people working together. Doing this allows the company to grow into the name.

The drawback of using your name is that it may be a problem for those who may join the firm in the future. Your clients will want the best. They will want you. In this case they will assume that Pam is the best of the team and without knowing her capabilities may think that they haven't gotten the best if they do not get Pam. Of course if you have strong name recognition, such as "The Tom Peters Group," you may want to take advantage of it.

"PJS Consulting" has less emphasis on Pam. Another consideration is that this name tells the client what the company does. "Team Consulting" is even more specific. The drawback, however, is that it may be too restrictive and may not allow for expansion when the company wants to branch out to "Strategic Planning" or "Talent Management," for example.

Some company names are related to the location. Again, just be sure you do not limit yourself. "Midwest Marketing" may have a certain ring to it in Madison, Wisconsin, but when you gain a reputation, will the name project the image that will encourage a store on Madison Avenue to hire you?

e-Idea

Are you stuck trying to come up with a name? Go to www.naming toolbox.com or www.entrepreneurs.about.com. The first is software for generating names; the second is a website that specifies a naming process and offers other services for entrepreneurs. When you get to the second website, click on "Starting a Business."

Your name will be a marketing tool, and even though you want something that is easy to remember, you do not want to be too cute, as it may not project the business image you desire. This includes names that have double meanings. There are certainly exceptions to every rule. One successful consulting firm is called "Team Up," and they are very clear that building teams is all they will ever specialize in.

Think about all the ways that your business name will be used: website, email address, stationery, business cards, pens, T-shirts, even coffee mugs! Consider the length of the name. Long names will not fit on computer-generated labels. If you are thinking about working internationally, research the translation of your name into other languages. Also be aware that if your company name begins with "The," such as "The Schmidt Group," it will be alphabetized under "The" in the telephone directory unless you specify differently. Who would think to look under "The"? Just for fun, check your local telephone business directory under the word "the."

By the way, if your business name is anything besides your own, you may be required to register your business name with the secretary of state's office in the state in which you intend to do business. Also, if you use any name in addition to the one you've chosen, you must file a Certificate of Trade Name or a "Doing Business As" (DBA) certificate. For example, your corporation may be Greene Ventures, Inc., and you may name your consulting practice Corporate Computer Consulting. This approach allows you to do business in states where someone else is already known as Greene Ventures, Inc. Further, this approach allows you to incorporate once and maintain flexibility for various new start-ups. Contact your local city or state officials for more information. Finally, if you want to trademark your company's name, you will need your attorney's assistance.

e-Idea

Use your favorite search engine to conduct a quick-and-dirty check to locate how the name you have selected is being used. Of course this is not all-inclusive. You may also access information about business names and their protection on www.nolo.com.

CHOOSING AN ACCOUNTANT

Your next task is to select an accountant. You're thinking, "Hey! Why do I need an accountant? I haven't made any money yet!" That may be true, but you have many decisions to make that will be dependent on good advice.

How do you find a good accountant? I do not recommend that you use your second cousin Joey. You are making life-changing decisions and need someone who is knowledgeable (Joey probably is), experienced (Joey may be), impartial (Joey will have difficulty), and not personally involved with you (not Joey!).

You will find a good accountant the same way you have probably found the best employees, restaurants, and barbers—by networking and asking others. Start by asking successful people, preferably other consultants, who they use for accounting. Try to identify the qualities you are looking for so that you can describe your "ideal" accountant. First, you want someone who understands what you want—even if *you're* not sure yet. Ideally you will find someone who has experience with small consulting start-ups. Interview a few accountants before you select one with whom you will work. This relationship is one of the most important to your business. It is worth the time to look for someone with whom you can partner on your most intimate business matters—money.

It is worth the time to look for someone with whom you can partner on your most intimate business matters—money.

I tried several accountants before I found one who met my needs. I wanted someone who would challenge me, keep me abreast of new tax and investment laws, and take risks with me. I finally found the right person because I was able to describe what I was looking for in one phrase. I wanted a "creative accountant." That may seem like an oxymoron, but when I used this phrase while interviewing accountants, I could tell by their immediate response whether they understood what I was looking for. Stephanie did. She keeps me informed, suggests options, challenges my reasoning, looks for creative alternatives, and allows me to take risks within legal boundaries. Stephanie practices in Virginia Beach, but that did not stop me from working with her for the ten years that I lived in Wisconsin. The relationship works—even from a distance. It continues to be a successful partnership.

The first decision your accountant can help you with is to determine the business structure that will be best for you. Many of your other decisions will be based on your business structure.

BUSINESS STRUCTURE

Selecting a business structure is one of the first and most fundamental decisions you must make. This is more critical than you might initially think, as it influences nearly every aspect of operations, such as how much you pay in taxes, the extent of your personal liability if anything goes wrong, and your ability to raise money for business expansion. There are four basic types of business structures: sole proprietorships, partnerships, corporations, and limited liability companies.

Note that some of the following information may be valid only in the United States. Check into your country's business structures and tax laws.

e-Idea

The IRS can provide you with tax information online. Go to the IRS website at www.IRS.gov and click on "Business" under "Contents." You will be able to access information on tax considerations related to the legal structure you choose, download tax worksheets and forms, and participate in online small business workshops.

Sole Proprietorship

A sole proprietorship is the simplest form and creates no separate legal entity. Usually your Social Security number will serve as your company's federal taxpayer ID number. Federal tax reporting for sole proprietorships is the easiest of the four structures, requiring only the addition of a Schedule C on which you list business income and take deductions for expenses. The structure incurs no additional tax liabilities beyond yours. Although the fact that no separate legal entity is created is usually considered an advantage, it also poses a concern. It means that any legal or tax liabilities that transpire become your personal liabilities. For example, if a client sues you for business reasons, you are personally liable, and your personal assets are at risk.

Partnership

Like sole proprietorships, a partnership is not a separate legal entity. The difference is that you will need to obtain a separate federal employer ID number, known as your FEIN. Your partnership will file a partnership return, even though it pays no separate federal tax. The business losses and income are reported on the partners' personal tax returns. The division of profits will be governed by a partnership agreement. The decision to share equally or on a percentage basis is usually dependent on contributions of cash, experience, property, labor, and perhaps even reputation or earning power of each partner. Legally you and your partners are all personally responsible for liabilities incurred by any of the other partners or the partnership as a whole. Because so many terms must be spelled out in the partnership agreement—for example, the rights and obligations of each partner or what happens if one partner dies—a partnership can be more complicated than it may initially appear.

Corporation

Corporations differ from the first two structures in that they are separate legal and tax entities. Your personal liability is limited if the corporation is sued. Corporations are formed when individuals invest assets to create equity. To incorporate you must file articles of incorporation, create corporate bylaws, and fulfill other state requirements. Stock must be issued, even if you are the sole shareholder. The corporate structure that you are most familiar with is the "C" corporation, which is required to pay income taxes separate from you and the other shareholders.

A subchapter-S corporation (commonly called an S corp) is an option for smaller groups. This special structure is available to U.S. organizations of thirty-five or fewer shareholders. There are other guidelines, which your accountant will share with you. One of the advantages of the S corp is that you will avoid double taxation on income to the corporation and dividends to you. The income is passed through to the shareholder (you), which you report on your personal return. By the way, both corporate structures require you to submit annual paperwork.

I usually recommend the S corp for a start-up consulting business. It has all the legal protection without much added expense. If you later decide to bring others into your business, the documentation is in place.

Limited Liability Company

A relatively new business structure, the limited liability company (LLC) has the limited liability of a corporation, but the flexibility and tax status of a partnership. An LLC must file articles of organization and an operating agreement with state authorities. Tax reporting is similar to a partnership, but liability is limited to the assets of the LLC.

Because choosing the right business structure is essential for maximizing your success, it is a choice you will want to make with expert advice. Call your accountant.

e-Idea

The Small Business Administration's website at www.sba.gov is an excellent source of business information. Once you access the site, click on "Starting a Business" on the home page. You will find a Start-Up Kit, "Your First Steps," and many other topics that will provide information about starting your business. You can also access special interest groups and electronic mail forums.

BUSINESS PLANS

You will need to prepare a business plan. Unless you will try to woo investors, it can be quite simple. Your business plan allows you to put everything that is in your head on paper in an organized way. This will help you stay focused on what is important to you. View your business plan as a working document that you refer to regularly. Make it work for you. Later, as you make new business decisions, you can return to your plan to identify what you might change, how to go about changing, and how that change might affect the rest of your business.

> *View your business plan as a working*
> *document that you refer to regularly.*

The business plan format shown in Exhibit 4.1 can be downloaded from the enclosed CD, and you can simply answer the questions. It has everything you need to create your business plan. However, you can purchase software to simplify the process even more.

e-Idea

If you would like to see another option for writing a business plan, check out the software at www.business-plan.com. Automate Your Business Plan for Windows is the companion software to the book *Anatomy of a Business Plan.* One advantage of this program is that all the spreadsheets are linked. Numbers that you input or change will automatically be reflected on all related spreadsheets.

Business PlanMaker Professional (version 4) is another software program you may consider. It will help you with everything from designing a business card to producing financial projections. You can import data from QuickBooks and peruse links to websites that have information to start or grow your business.

Exhibit 4.1. Business Plan Format.

A Business Plan

for

[company name and logo]

ebb associates inc

Date

Owner
Address
Telephone
Email
Website

Exhibit 4.1. Business Plan Format, Cont'd.

Table of Contents

The table of contents provides another opportunity for you to impress your business plan reader by showing your organizational skills. This table of contents lists the suggested sections.

Table of Contents

Business Description

Market Analysis

Competitive Analysis

Marketing Plan

Management Plan

Financial Plan

Appendixes

> **Financial Statements**
> [list each]
>
> **Supporting Documents**
> [list each]

Business Description

Begin the actual narrative with an introduction that states the purpose of the business plan. Follow this with a description of your consulting business. Use the following questions to guide you. You may divide the description into sections covering your plans for the business, the work you will conduct, and the business's demographics. This will most likely be the longest and most important section of your business plan.

- Introduction that states the purpose of the business plan

- Your plans for the business
  - What is the mission, vision, and purpose of your consulting business?
  - What are your goals for the business? (Your goals should be specific, measurable, and time-bound.)

- The Work
  - What specific activities does the business do to raise revenue?
  - What services or products will it provide? What is the mission of your business?
  - Why do you believe your business will succeed?
  - What relevant experience do you bring to the business of consulting?

- Demographics
  - What's the name of the business? The address? What are the telephone and fax numbers? What's the email address? What is the Web address?
  - Who is(are) the owner(s)?
  - What's the business structure? If the business is incorporated, where?
  - What information is important about the start of this business? For example, is it a new business or an expansion of an existing business? What was the start-up date?

Exhibit 4.1. Business Plan Format, Cont'd.

Market Analysis

Your market analysis will be most beneficial if you can quote statistics about consulting, your consulting specialty, or the industry you have chosen. You may find some of this data in industry journals or on the Internet. *Training* magazine and the American Society for Training and Development conduct research each year that might provide data for some of you. Kennedy Publishing is another good source.

- What industry or industries are you targeting?
- Are you in a stable, growing, or declining industry?
- What is occurring now or is expected to occur in the future that will affect your business either negatively or positively?
- Who are your current customers?
- Who are your potential customers?
- What are the demographics of your current and potential client base?
- What is the size of your potential market? What percentage do you expect to penetrate?
- What's the estimated total market value available to you in dollars?

Competitive Analysis

You should spend some time examining the competition you expect to face.

- Who is your competition?
- How would you describe your competition in the geographical and specialty areas you have targeted?
- How do your consulting products or services differ from your those of your competitors?

Exhibit 4.1. Business Plan Format, Cont'd.

- How do your competitors' pricing structures compare to yours?
- What experience do your competitors have?
- How strong is your competitors' name recognition?
- What share of the market do these targeted competitors have?
- Is your competitors' business increasing, decreasing, or remaining steady?
- Why would someone buy from them instead of you?
- How do your competitors market themselves?
- What are your comparative strengths and weaknesses in sales or marketing?
- What differentiates you from your competitors?

Marketing Plan

You can use the following questions to develop a simple marketing plan. Remember, however, that you will develop a more in-depth plan in Chapter Five.

- Describe your market niche in detail:
  - What size company will you serve?
  - What specific geographical area will you serve?
  - What kind of organizations will you serve?
  - Will you serve special situations, such as start-ups or mergers?
- What is your pricing strategy and structure? How does your pricing strategy and structure differ from that of your competitors?
- What marketing tactics will you pursue? What advertising? What promotion?
- How will you implement these tactics throughout the year?
- What expertise will you use to develop your marketing plan?

Exhibit 4.1. Business Plan Format, Cont'd.

Management Plan

Answer these questions about how you intend to manage your consulting business.

- Who are the key players in your business? What are their duties, compensations, and benefits?

- If you are the sole employee, how will you manage all that needs to be completed? What is your starting salary?

- What resources are available if you need assistance?

- When do you expect to hire additional personnel—if ever?

- What experience do you bring to the business in marketing, sales, managing a business, and other supporting roles?

- What is your education level?

- What professional support will you use, such as an attorney, accountant, or banker?

- What banking services will you use, and where? What process will you use to establish credit?

Financial Plan

Use these questions to write a narrative. Support your narrative with financial statements in an appendix to your plan.

- What assumptions are you making as a basis of the plan, such as market health, start-up date, gross profit margin, required overhead, payroll, and other expenses?

- What expenditures will you require for start-up?

Exhibit 4.1. Business Plan Format, Cont'd.

- What are your cash-flow projections for each month of your first year? What are your three-year per exhibit projections?

- Do you have a line of credit? How much?

- What is your personal net worth as displayed in a financial statement?

- Where do you expect to find financing, and under what terms? How will the money be used—for example, overhead, supplies, marketing?

Where Will the Money Come From?

- You could take money from your savings account.
- You could borrow against your retirement account.
- You could obtain a loan on the equity in your house.
- You could borrow against your life insurance policy.
- If you have stocks, you could go on margin against them.
- You could obtain a line of credit from your bank.
- Your spouse could increase his or her living expense contribution.
- You could sell something—for example, a motor home or sailboat.
- You could cut back on some of your spending—for example, cancel your vacation trip.
- You could obtain a business bank loan.
- You could get a loan from the Small Business Administration (SBA).
- You could ask a friend or colleague to sponsor you.
- You could borrow against your credit card. (Don't do this unless you have an immediate and very good opportunity in hand.)

Create Financial Documents

Exhibits 4.2 through 4.6 provide the answers and supporting documentation for completing the financial section in your business plan. You will include them in the Financial Statements appendix. (Please note that before you consider Exhibit 4.2 "final," you will be using it as a working document, possibly playing with the numbers a bit. See the next main section, "Start-Up Costs.")

Exhibit 4.2. Start-Up Expenses.

	Estimated Cost
Furniture	
Desk and chair	$_____
Filing cabinet	$_____
Bookcases	$_____
Table	$_____
_____	$_____
_____	$_____
Equipment	
Computer	$_____
Software: _____	
_____	
_____	$_____
Printer/scanner	$_____
Copier	$_____
Fax machine	$_____
Adding machine	$_____
Calculator	$_____
Telephone system	$_____
Answering machine	$_____
Cell phone	$_____
Postage scale	$_____
Postage meter	$_____
_____	$_____
_____	$_____
Office Supplies	
Stationery	$_____
Paper: Fax	$_____
Printer	$_____
Special	$_____
Three-hole punch	$_____
Daytimer or PDA	$_____
Pens, pencils	$_____
Tape, glue, other adhesives	$_____
Scissors, rulers, miscellaneous	$_____

⊙ Exhibit 4.2. Start-Up Expenses, Cont'd.

	Estimated Cost
Seminar Supplies	
Pocket folders	$_____
Three-ring binders	$_____
_____	$_____
_____	$_____
Marketing Supplies	
Website	$_____
Business cards	$_____
Brochures	$_____
Pocket folders	$_____
_____	$_____
_____	$_____
Corporate Set-Up Fees	
Professional fees	$_____
Legal fees (incorporation)	$_____
Business name search	$_____
Accounting fees	$_____
Banking start-up	$_____
Insurance	$_____
Licenses and permits	$_____
_____	$_____
_____	$_____
Personal Living Expenses	
Remodeling: accommodate office	$_____
Moving van	$_____
_____	$_____
_____	$_____
Unanticipated Expenses	
_____	$_____
_____	$_____
_____	$_____

Exhibit 4.3. Budget Format.

Net Salary for One Year _____

Benefits
Health insurance	_____	
Life insurance	_____	
Disability insurance	_____	
Retirement	_____	
	Total Benefits	_____

Taxes
Self-employment	_____	
Social Security and Medicare	_____	
State income tax	_____	
City tax	_____	
Personal property tax	_____	
	Total Taxes	_____

Business Expenses
Accounting, banking, legal fees	_____
Advertising and marketing	_____
Automobile expenses	_____
Books and resources	_____
Clerical support	_____
Copying	_____
Donations	_____
Dues and subscriptions	_____
Entertainment	_____
Equipment leases	_____
Insurance and loan repayments	_____
Liability insurance	_____
Licenses	_____
Meals	_____
Office supplies	_____
Postage	_____
Professional development	_____
Professional fees	_____
Rent	_____
Repairs and maintenance	_____
Salaries (employees)	_____
Seminar expenses	_____
Telephone	_____
Travel	_____
Utilities	_____

Total Business Expenses _____
Total Required for One Year _____

● **Exhibit 4.4. First-Year Cash-Flow Projection.**

	Jan	Feb	March	April	May	June	July	Aug	Sept	Oct	Nov	Dec
Revenue												
Total Revenues												
Expenses												
Accounting/banking/legal												
Advertising/marketing												
Automobile												
Benefits												
Books/resources												
Clerical support												
Copying												
Donations												
Dues/subscriptions												
Entertainment												
Equipment leases												
Interest												
Insurance												
Licenses												
Lodging												
Materials												
Meals												
Office supplies												
Postage												
Professional dev.												
Rent												
Salaries												
Taxes												
Telephone												
Travel												
Utilities												
Total Expenses												
Monthly Cash Flow												
Cumulative Cash Flow												

The Business of Consulting, Second Edition. Copyright © 2007 by John Wiley & Sons, Inc. Reproduced by permission of Pfeiffer, an Imprint of Wiley. www.pfeiffer.com

	Year 1	Year 2	Year 3
Total Revenue	_____	_____	_____
Expenses:			
Salaries	_____	_____	_____
Benefits	_____	_____	_____
Taxes	_____	_____	_____
Marketing	_____	_____	_____
Administrative	_____	_____	_____
Total Expenses	_____	_____	_____
×5 % Inflation*	no	_____	_____
Expenses and Inflation*	no	_____	_____
Projection (Revenue–Adjusted Expenses) After Inflation	_____	_____	_____

*Note: No inflation is added the first year.

Print Your Business Plan

Once you've completed your plan, have it edited and proofed. You may wish to give it to several people: some who know the consulting business well, and others who can edit for typos, spelling, and grammar errors. Make the corrections and print out a clean copy of your business plan on high-quality paper. You may wish to put it in a document binder with a clear front. If you have pocket folders that you are using for your business, you may wish to tuck the plan inside as a finished product. Whatever you do with the plan, do not put it on a shelf.

Exhibit 4.6. Personal Financial Statement.

Assets

Cash _____

Savings accounts _____

Stocks, bonds, and other securities _____

Accounts, notes _____

Life insurance (cash value) _____

Rebates, refunds _____

Autos, other vehicles _____

Real estate _____

Vested pension plan or
retirement accounts _____

Other assets _____

Total Assets _____

Liabilities

Accounts payable _____

Real estate loans _____

Other liabilities _____

Total Liabilities _____

Total Assets Less Total Liabilities = Net Worth _____

Plan to Use Your Business Plan

Keep your business plan handy and use it to help you make decisions. Check your business progress against the plan at least quarterly to keep yourself focused. Of course, if something is not working, you will change your direction. Staying "focused" does not mean staying the course even when something is not working. You will modify your strategies if they are not as effective as you originally envisioned.

Keep your long-term vision in mind and continue to move in that direction. Consider the following to ensure that your business plan serves its purpose:

- Check the data from which you are operating to ensure they are still current.
- Read the *Wall Street Journal* daily to be knowledgeable about the industries in which you work.
- Subscribe to *Harvard Business Review* and *Fortune Magazine* (at least) to stay on top of business and management trends.
- Read biographies of the leaders you respect to inspire new ideas for your consulting business.
- Attend conferences that focus on improving your skills and knowledge in the areas you have designated as needing improvement.
- Learn as much as you can from customers about their present needs, but also become adept at predicting their needs.
- Never hesitate to pick up the phone and call someone in your networking sphere to discuss something in your plan that doesn't seem to be working.
- Use all of the information from the previous seven suggestions to update your business plan and ensure that you are focused on an appropriate vision.

Schedule a Review with Yourself

After you complete your business plan, and before you leave this chapter, schedule a date with yourself to review your business plan. This date should be in six to twelve weeks, depending on where you are in the process of establishing your consulting business. If you're just starting out, "meet" in six weeks; if you have been consulting for some time, you could wait as long as twelve weeks. You decide. What seems appropriate to you?

e-Idea

During your planning you will most likely want access to as many resources as possible. Two websites that you will want to check out are maintained by *Entrepreneur* magazine (www.entrepreneur.com) and the Wall Street Journal Center for Entrepreneurs (www.startupjournal.com). Both provide ideas that may be useful to you. Note: during your research, it is a good idea to bookmark sites that you find particularly helpful.

START-UP COSTS

Now you will need to determine whether you have the money to start or to expand what you are already doing.

Start-Up May Cost Less Than You Think

Consulting start-ups usually fit into the low-cost category because starting a consulting practice can be surprisingly inexpensive. Exhibit 4.2 lists everything you need to start. As you review the list you might be thinking, "I already have a computer. I could use the fax services at the copy center down the street. It can't be that expensive to have stationery and business cards printed. And I could work out of my home office initially." As you total the expenses on Exhibit 4.2, you may find that you could start with as little as $3,000. (As noted earlier, once you have created a final version of this form, you will include it as part of the appendixes to your business plan.) Should you need a start-up loan, you will at the very least need to create a personal financial statement. A simplified version is displayed in Exhibit 4.6; you may have already completed this as part of creating your business plan.

Home Office Advantage

Because few clients will visit you at your office, working out of your home is a wonderful option. Just remember that it will take discipline to stay focused on writing your marketing letters instead of watching television, to continue to pay the bills rather than visit the refrigerator. A home office offers financial advantages because you will be able to deduct a proportionate amount of your home's utility costs, taxes, or rent. Keep in mind that the IRS may require proof that your home office is used exclusively for business. Also, a home office is sometimes a red flag that alerts the IRS to an audit, with potential tax implications.

e-Idea

Download IRS Publication 587, which provides comprehensive information about working from your home. It addresses depreciating your home, business furniture, and equipment; qualifying for a deduction; calculating expenses; and, of course, record keeping. It supplies you with worksheets and instructions so that you can calculate your own deductions.

Given all the ways that you can reduce start-up expenses, the cost of starting a consulting business should not deter you. My only caution is this: do not cut corners. Your professional image is at stake right from the start.

YOUR NICHE

The opportunities available to you as a consultant are so broad that you must narrow the choices. Doing so will help you be more efficient and will ensure that you can achieve depth in an area. Some of this will come naturally due to your skills and the experiences you have had. Other decisions may be dependent on the kind of lifestyle you have chosen—for example, whether you wish to travel.

As you narrow your choices, you will define your niche or what service you will offer and to whom. There are many ways to define your niche. Consider three things: (1) the work you will do, (2) the type of client you will serve, and (3) the location where you will work.

The Work You Will Do

You probably already know what work you will do, but be aware of other opportunities for future growth. You may define your work by the *role that you play*—for example, trainer, facilitator, coach, technical adviser, process consultant, content expert, or resource.

You may define your work by the *level of the organization* with which you will work—that is, frontline employees, first-level supervisors, managers, or executives.

You may define your work by your *topic expertise*—for example, team building, time management, leadership, computer programming, mergers, investing, or regulatory laws.

You may also define your work by the *structure of the groups* with whom you work—for example, teams, intact work groups, or individuals.

What work will define your niche?

The Type of Client You Will Serve

Determine the type of clients you will serve by considering the general category, the industry, special situations, and the size of the organization.

Decide whether you want to work in the for-profit or nonprofit organizational category. Within the for-profit sector you can consider manufacturing, service, and so on. Within the nonprofit sector you can consider associations; educational institutions; local, state, or federal government agencies; or others in the public sector.

You can further narrow your niche by focusing on a specific industry. If you have decided to work in the for-profit service sector, you may narrow that down even more by selecting health care, hospitality, or finance. Focusing on a small number of industries can build your credibility in each.

You may choose to work with organizations that have special situations. These could include small family-owned businesses, start-up businesses, merged organizations, or high-growth businesses.

The size of organization on which you focus gives you credibility with other organizations of like size. You may decide to work only with Fortune 500 firms. You may decide to work only with small organizations. I consider a small organization as one with fewer than one hundred employees, a medium organization as one with one hundred to two thousand employees, and a large organization as one with over two thousand employees. You may also consider the organization's revenue. In some cases, the unit of measurement is industry specific. Hospitals, for example, measure their size by number of beds.

What type of client will you serve that will define your niche?

The Location Where You Will Work

Although this may be the easiest consideration to understand, it is not always the easiest to define. It may be difficult because your industry is broad based, such as the hospitality industry, which can be found almost everywhere. Location refers more to your preference than to anything else and could be defined as local, statewide, regional, national, or international. What location will define your niche?

However you define your niche, ensure that it is broad enough that you have an adequate pool of clients, yet narrow enough to provide focus for you.

YOUR IMAGE

Your image is the most important marketing asset you have. In fact, as you start, your image is a critical attribute of your business as a whole. You do not have products to display; you do not have clients to brag about you; you do not have experiences to discuss. All that you have is *you* and the image you present. Therefore, it is imperative that you invest in making your image all that it can be. Your name, your logo, your visual look, the public's recognition and affection are all vital to your success. Your corporate identity is your most valuable possession.

Here's some good news: you can look like a million on a shoestring budget right from day one! The secret? Ensure that everything you do reeks of quality. Nothing should leave your office unless it looks impeccable, sounds professional, and feels flawless. Quality should touch all the senses.

You can look like a million
on a shoestring budget
right from day one!

If you send a letter, it should exude quality in how it looks, sounds, and feels:

- *Looks.* It should be aligned on the paper correctly. The type should be dark black, printed with a new ink cartridge. The stamp and envelope label should be affixed straight.

- *Sounds.* The letter should be error-free. It should be written using correct grammar. The tone should send the message you desire. It should be written for the interest of the reader. If possible, the letter should begin with the word "you."

- *Feels.* The letter should be printed on the highest-grade paper money can buy. The reader should feel the quality in the paper. If you need to save money, do it somewhere else; the pennies you will save by buying second-grade paper will not be worth the harm it may do to your image.

Create an image for your business. Invest in a logo. A logo is an important image builder, but it is also an important marketing tool, as it provides a recognizable identity for your consulting business. Keep these points in mind when designing a logo:

- It should have immediate impact. Instead of receiving a passing glance, will it attract and hold attention?

- The logo should accurately represent what you do. Is the logo specific enough to tell an uninformed person what you do, yet broad enough so that it will grow with you?

- As the cornerstone of your brand, a logo should represent your image positively. Do you want to project a serious and professional image, an optimistic and whimsical image, or something else?

- The best logos are memorable. Is the logo pleasing to look at and unique enough that someone will remember it?

- A good logo is also practical. Will it copy well? Does it lend itself to use on stationery, business cards, brochures, websites, and promotional materials? It should be as effective on a business card as it is on a billboard.

e-Idea

A traditional design firm will charge $2,000 to $10,000 for a corporate logo. Instead, you can use one of the online firms. Check the websites of these three firms online: www.LogoDesignPros.com, www.Logojeez.com, or www.LogoWorks.com. I like all three because they have samples you can view, guarantee your satisfaction, provide fast turnaround (three to four days), and, most important, offer reasonable pricing (packages from $199 to $599). The third company, Logo Works, was recognized as one of America's fastest-growing companies by being listed on *Entrepreneur* magazine and PricewaterhouseCoopers's Hot 100 list for 2006.

Printed materials that represent your business should also be created with quality in mind. If you own a copier, buy the best that you can afford. When you make copies, be certain that they don't pick up the dirt specks from your copier's glass. What's the secret? Clean your copier glass often with a copier glass cleaner. If you use the services of a local copy shop, build a relationship with the manager and employees. Let them know how important it is that your copies be clean, straight, and on high-quality paper.

What else can you do to look like a million? The following quick ideas will help. Keep your eyes open for other ideas and add them to your list:

- Design stationery and business cards. The investment may seem high at this time, but it will pay off very quickly. Your paper products speak first for you. A professional design says, "I'm serious about my profession!" The logo companies listed earlier also design these products at a reasonable price.

- Design a professional-looking fax cover page. You can use Exhibit 4.7 as a model.

- Use overnight express carriers to send all proposals and important communication to clients.

- Clip documents with gold paper clips.

- If you are working from your home, be sure to have a second telephone line installed immediately. It may be cute if your three-year-old answers the phone when Aunt Sadie calls, but it's not cute when the vice president of human resources calls to ask a question about your proposal.

- Ensure that your invoices are complete, correct, and businesslike. Help your business appear bigger by using a numbering system that begins with a number greater than one. You could simply start with 301. Or you could present a series of numbers such as 13-076-11. The middle number is the sequential number of the invoices; the last number is the year; and the first number is just for luck!

- Use your answering machine like voice mail. First, invest in a high-quality machine that is dependable, allows you to obtain messages from remote locations, and does not play a charming chime while the client awaits the tone. Change your message daily to encourage callers to leave a message. Smile when recording your message; the feeling comes through. Say something like, "Hello! You've reached the voice mail of Annie Trainer. Today is Thursday, October 30, and I will be away from the office. I will check for messages today, so please leave your name and telephone number. I look forward to speaking with you and hope yours is a great day!"

In addition to the ideas mentioned here, you will want to think about the image you project in general. When I first went into business, I wanted to project a subtle professional image. I wanted to speak quietly, but professionally. To express this image, I chose to use all lowercase letters in the corporate name. I carried out the

⊙ Exhibit 4.7. Fax Form.

ebb associates inc
box 8249
norfolk, va 23503
757-588-3939
757-480-1311/Fax

Fax To: _____   Location: _____

From: _____

Date: _____   Total Pages: _____
                                                      (Including Cover)

---

theme further by printing gray on gray. Since that time my business has changed, as has my outlook on the world. I decided to shout a little. The corporate name, ebb associates inc, is still in all lowercase, and we shout with happiness using red, white, and metallic gold—again on high-quality paper.

What image do you want to project? The name of your company, the graphics you choose, the tone of your website, your title, the color and style of paper, the color of the ink, the style of brochure you distribute, the content of your marketing pieces, and the tone of your correspondence—all these things complement each other and together create your image. Every interaction you have with your clients will express your image. Make sure it's the one you want.

e-Idea

Unify your Web address and email address—for example, Elaine@ebb web.com. It becomes a marketing tool and is easier for your clients to remember. It adds to your professional image as well.

EXPERIENCE

Remember when you were looking for your first job? It seemed that every job required experience, but how could you get experience without a job? It was a crazy circle. Well, you may feel as if you are in that same place as you look for your first consulting project, and may be asking yourself, "I need experience to get a project, but how do I get a project to get experience?" Landing your first client can be easier than you think if you plan ahead, expand your networking, and identify creative options.

Plan Ahead

It usually takes one to six months from the day you first speak with an organization until the day you begin the project. This means that you must decide either to maintain an income while you are establishing yourself or to live off money you have saved for the start-up period of your business.

Your planning should include your present employer. A common way to transfer from your present job to consulting is to have your current employer become your client. You must plan this carefully. Identify which projects you could complete, list the benefits for your employer of utilizing your services, and allow enough time for your employer to accept this idea. Of course, the risk you run is that your employer may not agree with your plan. This may put you in a difficult situation until your final employment date.

Another way your present employer could assist with your transition is to allow you to work part-time while you use the rest of your time for business start-up. If your employer is gracious enough to allow this to happen, make certain that you give your part-time work your full attention. It may be very difficult to focus on the same old job when you are starting an exciting new adventure. Nevertheless, remember that your employer is doing you a favor; you owe the company 110 percent in return.

Expand Your Networking

Before you leap into a start-up, examine your network. Have you maintained an active network of professional contacts? If not, give yourself at least six months to build this network before starting your consulting practice.

Join professional associations and attend their meetings to identify organizations that might use your services. A word of caution, however. There is no greater turnoff to a corporate manager than to be accosted by a wannabe consultant at a professional meeting. Do not ask for work or make appointments at the meeting. So what's the point of my even suggesting that you attend these events?

Attend meetings with plans to meet people who may use your services. Most people are attending for business-related reasons, so it will be appropriate for you to initiate conversations about the projects in which they are involved. Find topics about which you both enjoy talking. The next day, follow up with a note expressing a common interest, your pleasure at meeting him or her, or some other theme that was a result of your discussion. *Be sincere.* If you cannot be sincere, forget it. You will appear pushy and hungry. A test of your sincerity is whether you want to follow up even when you sense that there is no potential project at the present time. The key phrase here is "at the present time." True networking is an investment in the future. Follow your note with a phone call to set a date for lunch or a meeting to explore opportunities or simply to learn more about the organization.

Identify other networking opportunities that can move you toward your goal, including the following:

- Make a list of everyone you know who could lead to business opportunities. Then follow up with a telephone call or a note.
- Volunteer to make presentations at local, state, and national conferences and meetings.
- Identify organizations that might use your services. Request fact-finding meetings with some of the decision makers.
- Take other consultants to lunch to gather ideas for identifying business contacts.
- Search your local newspapers for people you would like to meet.

Chapter Five covers the topic of marketing once you are in business; however, many of the ideas in the chapter can be used as you network prior to starting your business. But be sure to expand your networking list before you begin to count on a full-time salary from consulting.

Identify Creative Options

The most creative tactic I used to break into the consulting business was to work part-time for a small consulting company for three months without pay. I agreed not to contact their clients and to work as an employee under their corporate name. It was a true win-win for both of us. I was able to observe the business generation (finding clients) and billable (serving clients) processes in action and to gain experience with actual clients that I could use as references. They acquired a skilled trainer who added value to their business, worked without pay, and would not pirate their clients. Because I worked part-time, I could implement what I learned to build my own business during my off hours.

If you don't want a long-term arrangement like mine, you can provide pro bono work for community, government, or nonprofit organizations. These organizations usually have limited funds and appreciate the services that you can provide. This can be the beginning of your list of clients served.

You could also subcontract full- or part-time with a large training firm that certifies trainers, or you could subcontract with other consulting firms. The first could be an easy route, especially if you have been certified to conduct training programs for the organization while employed at your present company. The drawback, however, will be conducting repetitive training material. The second approach may provide more options in terms of projects or actual consulting. The drawback here is that you must suppress your ego to represent the prime firm's name. Drawbacks for both are that you will bill about one-third to two-thirds of your typical billable rate. The advantages are that you will have an income and will be able to build your own business while working part-time in the field.

If you're looking for something more full-time, you could join an existing firm to gain experience. The obvious drawback is that it continues to put off even longer the opportunity to begin your own consulting business.

Although any of these ideas can serve as quick starts to becoming a consultant, some may also slow the process of starting your own business. Only you can weigh the pros and cons of each start-up tactic. Only you can weigh the advantages of finding work versus finding the work you want. Only you can make the final decisions. Exhibit 4.8 will help you think of everything you need to make decisions for a successful start-up.

e-Idea

Be sure to reserve a website domain name. This is a simple process, but finding a good one that works for you and has not already been taken can be challenging and frustrating. Over thirty million domain names have been registered, so it may require some creativity to find a domain name that will meet your needs. Just because a domain name is available does not mean that you can use it without incurring liability for trademark infringement. The least expensive way to obtain a domain name is to be the first one to register by contacting one of the authorized issuers of domain names, known as a "registrar." To obtain a new domain name:

- Go to the website of an authorized registrar. I like www.000Domains .com because it's only $13.50 per year for each domain name, and they have good tools for bulk administration of domain names. The most popular registrars are Network Solutions and Register.com.

- Use the registrar's online search function to see if your desired domain name is taken.

- If your domain name is available, follow the registrar's instructions to complete the registration form and pay by credit card.

Exhibit 4.8. Start-Up Checklist.

- ❑ Describe your business, its services, and its products.
- ❑ Identify your market.
- ❑ Analyze your competition.
- ❑ Assess your skills.
- ❑ Name your business.
- ❑ Determine your financial requirements (budget) and your pricing structure.
- ❑ Identify start-up costs.
- ❑ Select an accountant.
- ❑ Determine your business structure.
- ❑ Check on zoning laws, licenses, and taxes.
- ❑ Select your location.
- ❑ Apply for a fictitious name (called a DBA for "doing business as").
- ❑ Develop a business plan that includes:
    - ❑ Business description
    - ❑ Marketing plan
    - ❑ Management plan
    - ❑ Financial plan
- ❑ Obtain a tax ID number from the IRS.
- ❑ Apply for a city business license or home occupation permit if necessary.
- ❑ Select a banker, attorney, and insurance agent.
- ❑ Open a business banking account.
- ❑ Arrange for financing (or set aside capital for a worst-case scenario).
- ❑ Obtain business insurance.
- ❑ File legal documents to register your business.
- ❑ Set up your financial records.
- ❑ Select a logo; order business cards and stationery.

- You obtain a domain name for a period of one to ten years. If as the domain name owner (the "registrant") you fail to renew the domain name at the end of its term, its registration will be revoked, and another party may acquire it.

If you really want to start your own consulting firm, do it now. If you don't, a year from now you will wish you had started today.

A year from now you will
wish you had started today.

. . . And Staying in Business

None of the secrets of success will work unless you do.

A fortune cookie

Starting your business is the first difficult step. The second is staying in business. Staying in business as a consultant means that you have a continuous flow of clients. In his book *The Secrets of Consulting*, Gerald M. Weinberg (1985) states, "The best way to get clients is to have clients." That is a very true statement. Unfortunately, it is not of much value to you if you have just started your business!

So how do you "get" clients so that you "have" clients? Obviously, you cannot just sit back with your stack of business cards on your desk and wait for the phone to ring! You may be the best consultant in the world, produce the best materials, know the most innovative solutions, provide the best service, and be the most knowledgeable in your field. However, if no one knows about you, what are your chances of finding clients? Slim to none! So you must let people know that you are available for consulting. You must market your products and services. You must promote yourself. As the fortune cookie says, you must work at it.

A successful business can be measured by an adequate supply of clients, a professional image, and an ethical reputation. Each requires your attention and energy.

All three will happen at the same time, and they will all happen all the time. Everything you do will affect your business success, as measured by your clients, your image, and your reputation.

Chapter Four addressed your image. Chapter Nine addresses building an ethical reputation. This chapter addresses how marketing will ensure that you have an adequate flow of clients to stay in business.

You must promote yourself.

Consultants must be marketing-oriented. In the beginning you may need to market yourself tirelessly, using every tactic at your disposal. If the term "marketing" scares you, think in terms of simply putting the word out that you are in business. You must get the word out. You *must* promote yourself.

This chapter helps you prepare a simplified marketing plan and explores marketing with little or no money. As you explore your own ideas to keep yourself in front of your clients, stimulate your creativity with the 113 marketing tactics we've listed. The chapter will help you plan the most efficient and effective networking activities and show you how the dreaded "cold call" can be fun when you warm it up and refocus your attitude.

This chapter gives you advice and suggestions for staying in business once you've started.

A MARKETING PLAN

More volumes must have been written about marketing your professional services than about any other topic. The topic of marketing can be pretty complicated. You may find yourself reading about marketing goals, objectives, strategies, tactics, promotions, and practices. You may read about the marketing mix. Some marketing experts discuss the "four P's" of the marketing mix: product, price, place, and promotion. Other experts discuss the "eight P's and an S": product, price, place, promotion, positioning, people, profits, politics, and service. You will read about advertising, public relations, and media. Then there are discussions about personal versus impersonal promotion or direct versus indirect marketing. You can read about personal selling, client-centered marketing, leveraging your clients—well, you get the idea.

Right now you do not need a degree in marketing. You must find out how to put the word out that you have consulting services to offer. Although this may seem like an overwhelming task, and one you would rather skip, don't be tempted. Developing a marketing plan is critical if you are to stay in business.

You may say, "What? Another plan?" The answer is yes. Your marketing plan will convert your ideas and intentions into commitment and action. Your marketing plan will guide you through the year so that you never push the important task of marketing to the back burner.

You must put your plan in writing. A written plan puts discipline into your ideas, enables you to measure success, and provides data for future use.

We touched on a marketing plan in Chapter Four when you prepared a business plan. You have two choices: (1) if you went through that exercise and have the information, you can now use it as input to this more specific marketing plan, or (2) if you did not spend time yet, you can use this process to develop a more specific marketing plan and slip it into your business plan.

Format for a Marketing Plan

A marketing plan can become quite complex. The format presented here is a simplified version that will be especially helpful if you have never written one before. Exhibit 5.1 will take you through eight easy steps. You will find that marketing is a combination of intuition and logic. The eight-step format will move you through the process comfortably. It will ensure that your resulting marketing plan does what it is supposed to do—put your name out there!

Marketing is a combination of intuition and logic.

---

1. Analyze the Present. If you're just starting, there will not be much to analyze. However, a year from now or if you've been in business for awhile, you will want to ask these questions:

- How am I perceived in the marketplace?
- How do I compare to my competition?
- What's happening to revenue and profits?
- How satisfied are my customers?
- How do customers, colleagues, and competitors describe me, my performance, and my results?

◉ Exhibit 5.1. Marketing Plan.

1. Analyze the present.

2. Clarify your strategy.

3. Set measurable six- to twelve-month goals.

4. Select marketing tactics to accomplish your goals.

5. Identify resources.

6. Develop an annual marketing plan.

7. Implement your plan.

8. Monitor your results and adjust as needed.

Responses to these questions will guide you as you focus on whether you project the image you desire, whether you have the competitive edge you desire, whether you are as financially successful as you desire, whether you meet your clients' expectations, and whether you have the reputation you desire.

If you have been in business for more than a year, complete this subjective analysis. If you are just starting, imagine your future. Alan Kay often says in his speeches, "The best way to predict the future is to invent it." Next year, you will have something to analyze. Today, each of your answers may still be described as your preferred future—the one you are inventing!

2. **Clarify Your Strategy.** Where is your business heading? You have already completed some analysis in the first chapters. Chapter Eleven will take you through a visioning exercise that may also help clarify this question. The following are some questions you might ask now:

- What size company do I want to serve?
- What geographical area will I serve?
- Will I work for government, nonprofit, or for-profit organizations?
- In what industry will I specialize?
- Will I serve groups or individuals?
- Will I serve special situations, such as start-ups or mergers?
- What projects do I want to conduct?

Your answers will reflect the kind of business you wish to develop. These questions will help you generate a list of potential customers with whom you want to do business.

Your strategy might be to focus on medium to large financial institutions located along the East Coast that are facing mergers and need assistance working toward efficient, shared visions of the future.

3. **Set Measurable Six- to Twelve-Month Goals.** You know how important goal setting is. Be specific. Make sure you can measure yours and add time limits to them. Here are some examples:

- Generate $100,000 in repeat business from July 1 to January 31.
- Generate $140,000 in new business from July 1 to January 31.

- Acquire three new clients by February 28.
- Acquire one new client in the banking industry by February 28.
- Present at one new conference in the next calendar year.

4. Select Marketing Tactics to Accomplish Your Goals. Generally, advertising and direct mail do not work very well for promoting consulting, but there are hundreds of other things you can do.

This is where the fun begins. We have listed 113 self-promotional tactics in this chapter. Use some of them or, if you prefer, use the list to spark your own tactics. Tactics are actions, including anything from cold calls to hot presentations, that put your name in front of potential clients. Examples include actions such as these:

- Make twenty-five contacts in the banking industry.
- Submit proposals to at least three new conferences.
- Submit an article to the *Pfeiffer Consulting Annual.*

5. Identify Resources. There is a cost to marketing. Whether you speak at conferences, write letters to the local newspaper, make calls to potential customers, purchase magazine advertising, publish a newsletter, or rent a booth at a trade show, there is a cost. You must weigh the cost and the benefits to determine if a particular marketing strategy makes sense for you.

But resources mean more than money. Resources can also mean people who are able to provide you with information or assistance. For example, you may have targeted a certain industry on which you would like to concentrate. You could publish an ad in one of the industry's trade journals, or you could go to lunch with someone you know in the industry to brainstorm ideas for approaching organizations within the industry.

6. Develop an Annual Marketing Plan. Your marketing activities will be more appealing if you break them down into small steps. For example, if you have chosen ten potential clients with whom you have a speaking relationship, and you have decided you would like to focus on them in an attempt to turn them into clients within the year, part of your plan might look like this:

- Ask Wisconsin staff to help identify ten clients by July 5.
- Research the clients by July 15.
- Brainstorm potential mailing content with Edie.
- First mailing out August 5.
- Second mailing with article September 5.
- Follow-up phone call September 20.
- Autumn greetings October 8.

Exhibit 5.2 is a marketing calendar. Notice that you can track the dates and the expected cost of each month. You can tell at a glance what you intend to do each month, where your focus is, and which months are heavy or light in activities.

7. Implement Your Plan. There is not much to say here. You've planned the work; now work the plan. Don't fall behind. Marketing results may not show up for six months. You cannot go back to fix anything that was not implemented six months ago.

8. Monitor Your Results and Adjust as Needed. Although a plan provides you with your best guess at the moment, you may need to adjust at times. For example, you may have focused your business on small companies. After you start, you may find that the demand is there, but the revenue is not sufficient. Perhaps you will need to refocus your client mix. You may add some medium-size companies to boost revenue. This will be a portion of your analysis before you develop your next marketing plan.

Develop a Marketing Plan for Free

Most business schools require their marketing majors to develop full marketing plans. Students usually write plans for the school itself or for nonprofit agencies connected to it. Most would rather write a marketing plan for a real business. Why not yours?

Two things will make this a successful experience for you. First, allow enough time. Writing the plan will probably be a long process occurring over a full semester. You will want to speak with the professor the semester before. Second, stay involved. Your input will be critical. You will need to provide the correct data so that the plan will

💿 **Exhibit 5.2. Annual Marketing Planning Calendar.**

Marketing Activity for 20XX		Jan	Feb	Mar	April	May	June	July	Aug	Sept	Oct	Nov	Dec
	Dates												
	Cost												
Total Budgeted Costs													

The Business of Consulting, Second Edition. Copyright © 2007 by John Wiley & Sons, Inc. Reproduced by permission of Pfeiffer, an Imprint of Wiley. www.pfeiffer.com

be based on accurate assumptions. In addition, your involvement will increase the enthusiasm of the students and the professor. Even if the plan is less than perfect due to the students' inexperience, you may receive good advice from the professor.

DO I NEED A WEBSITE?

Do you need a website? One word: yes. When I first entered the profession, every potential client asked for my brochure. Today every potential client asks for my website. Your website is today's brochure. (This does not mean that you do not also need a brochure—you do for your client's convenience and for kinesthetic folks who like print material.) The business world assumes that if you are in business you have a website. You need one. It is a self-serve marketing tool that is open 24/7. I am always surprised when I meet a potential client for the first time, and they tell me they have already been on my website. Websites are good for generating more leads as well as qualifying those leads.

In Chapter Four I tell you how to get started with a domain name. You can either design your website yourself or hire someone to design it for you. You can have lots of bells and whistles for $7,000 or more, or you can hire someone in a cottage industry to design a very simple website for you for under $900. Heck, if you have children in junior high or high school, they probably have a pal who would design it for you for less. Keep in mind that you still need to know what you want and need on your site. Be sure you are very clear about its purpose.

Once it is up, keep your website up-to-date and refresh it with something new at least monthly. How do you bring traffic to your website? The primary way to promote your website is to create valuable content. Search Engine Optimization (SEO) is the process of modifying web page content to improve the search engine ranking of the page. According to Pew Internet Research, over 70 percent of people who are looking for products and services on the Internet use search engines. Therefore, SEO will increase the number of visitors. Be sure that the signature on all your emails has the powerful tagline that invites the recipient to click on the link and visit your site. Be sure that your Web address is on all your documents, brochures, newsletters, business cards, and promotional materials. You may also wish to write Web articles and submit them to article directories. Finally, if you want to bring more traffic and keep people returning, give something of value away—for example, free e-books, articles, games, self-assessments, or podcasts.

e-Idea

Consider adding a chat room to your website. You can communicate with your visitors, learn about them by reading their conversations, answer their questions, or even teach a free online class using your chat room.

SURPRISING BUT PRACTICAL THOUGHTS ON MARKETING

You may not feel comfortable about marketing, but the following thoughts will put you at ease and help you think of more ideas on your own.

Market All the Time

The drawback with a calendar of marketing activities is that it suggests that there are certain days of the month that you will be marketing and certain days that you won't. The truth is that you are marketing all the time. Every experience with every client, every conversation with a colleague, every visit to a professional meeting, every comment to a friend is a marketing event. You are selling yourself. As a consultant, you represent your product or service. People around you are making decisions (subconsciously at least) about whether they can or will use your services.

The time to market is all the time.

Marketing all the time also means that you must religiously complete the marketing activities on your calendar. You may find yourself too busy with a current project to complete the marketing event that you had planned (for example, contacting two organizations in the next city or going to lunch with a colleague). Yes, you must complete the project, but if you tell yourself that you are too busy to complete the marketing also, you will come to the end of the busy project and not have another project to be busy on! Yes, the time to market is all the time. And the most important time to market is when you are too busy to market!

The most important time to market
is when you are too busy to market!

Keep Yourself in Front of Your Clients

You can do this in three ways. First, you can physically be in their presence. When working on-site, I frequently pop in on the CEO, president, HR director, or the person who hired me, even if we were not scheduled to meet. I'm sure some of you are shuddering at my lack of formality, but it represents who I am. I can get away with this. You may need to schedule meetings. The point is, make time for them.

Second, you can keep yourself in front of your clients with permanent, practical year-end gifts. We always look for something unique, something special. We have gained a reputation for creative gifts. For example, one year we sent miniature mugs filled with gold paper clips. They were high quality and useful, and they put our logo on everyone's desk every day.

Third, you can keep yourself in front of your clients by ensuring that things periodically go across their desks—for example, articles, notes of interest, books, announcements, cards, seasonal greetings, or even cartoons! Find a reason. When someone joins our firm, we send a special announcement. For example, when Garland joined our firm, we sent a miniature chalkboard and chalk with the message, "Chalk another one up for ebb associates."

e-Idea

Email a URL that leads your client directly to an article of interest or a resource that you recommend.

Have a Strategy

Well, that certainly isn't rocket science! True! You must determine the kind of client on whom you will focus. This second step of your marketing plan is critical. Do not skip it!

You must have a strategy for several reasons. The most important is that you need to know where to focus your energy. If you have decided to focus on large businesses as your niche and you continue to do work with the federal government, you may work the same number of days, but you may not reach the financial goals you set. You will learn from that experience.

Even with a strategy, many consultants stray from it and get their business into trouble. So it is not enough to have a strategy—you must also implement it. Besides, if you do not have a strategy, how will you know when you stray from it?

Go for the Big Fish; You'll Spend the Same Time Baiting the Hook

When I started my business, I decided to focus on medium- to large-size businesses. This strategy is one of the best decisions I ever made. Many new consultants focus on small businesses as their first targets, perhaps because large organizations are more intimidating. In general, small businesses have smaller training and consulting budgets. Because the decision to hire a consultant may be a small business's one and only budgeted consulting expense for the year, the company may take longer to make the decision.

In contrast, large businesses make numerous training and consulting purchases in a year. They may feel more comfortable taking a risk on a new consultant. Because this is not their one and only decision for the year, they can make hiring decisions faster. In addition, if you did a great job, you will have a better chance at repeat business with a larger organization. Small organizations may want to have you return, but may not have the budget.

Go for the big fish;
you'll spend the same
time baiting the hook.

Don't let the size of the organization scare you. The people who manage organizations need good consulting, no matter what the size. You will invest the same amount of time marketing your services to a large organization as to a small one. Your payoff, however, may be much greater.

Keep an Eye on Your Competition

One of the difficulties of being a consultant is being alone and outside the employment loop. Although keeping up with what is going on in your field is psychologically difficult, not keeping up can be financially devastating. What your competition does will affect your marketing plans.

Although you may have a specialty, be aware of the trends around you. How will a surge in downsizing affect what you provide? How will the latest management fad affect your philosophy? How will the changes in technology affect your service delivery?

Keep an eye on your competition. Read your professional journals: Who's advertising? What are they selling? Who's writing articles? Attend conferences: Who's presenting? What are they expounding? What's the buzz in the hallways? Visit bookstores: Who's writing? What topics are being published?

If you are not going to lead the profession, you must at the very least stay in touch. Your clients expect that of you.

Wallow in Your Junk Mail

Junk mail is a marketing research gift. Read it! You can spend thousands to find out what your competition is doing, or you can acknowledge the free research delivered to your door every day. I often hear consultants complain about the piles of advertising they receive, especially in conjunction with conferences for which they have registered. Instead, welcome your junk mail as the gift it is.

What can you gain from your junk mail? You can develop a sense of the trends in the field. Trends are always changing. Is stress management "in" this year or "out"? Use junk mail to spark ideas for your own marketing. Notice that I said spark ideas—not steal them. Junk mail can keep you informed of new people who have entered the field.

Don't bemoan your junk mail delivery. Instead, be grateful for all the competitive information that has just been dumped in your lap. Don't throw it away! Read it. Study it. Wallow in your junk mail!

Wallow in your junk mail!

Mail a Lumpy Envelope

The idea is to capture the recipient's attention so that the envelope is opened. You certainly don't want to think that your envelopes could be placed in someone's junk mail stack!

Over the years, we have mailed dozens of lumpy envelopes. We've mailed typical things such as staple removers and holiday ornaments, but we've mailed the unusual, too, such as:

- Tree-shaped pasta in January to send greetings for a "tree-mendous" new year with many "pasta-bilities."

- Light-up yo-yos at the end of 2001 stating that "it's been a year of ups and downs."
- Tape measures asking the recipients how they measure up.
- Crayons to complete an interactive creativity brochure.
- Pewter sea shells that spoke of uniqueness and beauty.
- Light-up stemmed glasses to send special congratulations.

When there is nothing to make a large lump, we may add confetti to celebrate a business success or tiny stars to say congratulations. We have acquired a reputation for our lumpy envelopes. Some clients will only open our envelopes over a wastebasket. This marketing tactic has gained us a reputation for being creative and fun. In fact, deciding what the next lump could be is one of the most delightful things I do.

Mail a lumpy envelope.

Personalize Your Marketing

One of the rules of consulting states that a consultant should not be too close to the client because it prevents objectivity. I intentionally and completely ignore that rule. I want to get to know our clients as people and in doing so celebrate their humanness as well as their professionalism.

I do not do this as a marketing tactic. In fact, when I first started the business, most of my exchanges with clients were very informal and personal. I claimed that we did no marketing, until Ian, one of my clients, asked what I thought I was doing when I sent him a handmade thank-you card. Whether it's marketing or not, I do believe that the personal touch builds a strong relationship with my clients and potential clients.

How do we personalize marketing? We send cards filled with confetti to congratulate clients on job promotions. We send birthday cards. We send custom-designed cards to celebrate graduations, births, engagements, weddings, anniversaries, new cars, trips, a new life focus, a new house, a move. Most recently we have discovered singing cards—a bargain at less than $5. We send lots of cards—always with a handwritten message.

We send articles of interest about a favorite subject, hobby, child's college, vacation site, competitor, or mutual friend. We may send items that have a special meaning, such as Georgia O'Keefe stamps, job ads, special coffee, music CDs, books (lots of books), pens, photos, good-luck tokens, or stones.

We send many notes to follow up on conversations. Sometimes we add items. I once had a conversation with a vice president of a large bank about the best training activity he ever saw: analysis of the task of eating a piece of pie. Following that conversation, I sent him a piece of pie to tell him how much I enjoyed our conversation. Another time I had a discussion with a publisher in which we both marveled at the magic of television. I followed up by sending her a children's book, *How Things Work,* that talked about the magic of television.

Remember that I do these things because I like people and I enjoy doing them! Although my approach may be seen as a marketing tool, I see it as a people tool. It may not work for everyone. I do it because it's who I am and I enjoy it. If it's not sincere, this kind of contact will backfire. If you are doing it "just to market your services," do not do it.

Know How to Acquire a New Client

Acquiring a new client requires ten times as much effort as acquiring repeat business. I quoted Weinberg (1985), "The best way to get clients is to have clients," at the beginning of this chapter. This is true for two main reasons: first, if you are producing results, your clients will recommend you to other clients; second, if you are producing results, your clients will invite you back for additional projects.

----

*Acquiring a new client
requires ten times as much effort
as acquiring repeat business.*

Many books written by successful consultants state that you will spend 25 to 40 percent of your time in marketing activities. I probably spent 80 percent of my time during the first months of start-up, but since then I have spent no more than 10 percent of my time marketing, and most of that is of a very personal nature.

Use Your Clients to Market Your Services

The ideal situation for any consultant is to find that your clients speak highly of you and recommend you to other clients. Nothing, absolutely *nothing* is more valuable to you than a client's recommendation. You earn that by exceeding your customers' expectations, adding value at every point, producing the highest-quality results, building trusting relationships, and modeling the highest ethics. In other words, doing a good job. Do good consulting!

Our vision statement says, "Our clients are so satisfied that they will market for us." Although it has taken a long time to achieve that vision, we have. We can trace more than 80 percent of our business back to three of our original clients.

113 TACTICS FOR LOW-BUDGET MARKETING

You need business. You need marketing tactics. You want to make a name for yourself, promote yourself, enhance your image, and build your reputation. But you have little money! What can you do? The following ideas will help you start. All will give you visibility and ensure that you stay in business. Some of these are common sense, and you may already have thought of them. Others may be too unusual for you. All of them should spark your creative thought process. All of them are tactics we have used.

1. Attend professional conferences to network.
2. Attend conferences for the industries that you serve.
3. Submit press releases to the media regarding your major consulting engagements, awards, published articles or books, or appointments.
4. Invite potential clients to a minipresentation to give them an idea of your expertise and services. Sometimes called showcases, these are often held in local hotels where food and beverages are served to encourage a more social atmosphere.
5. Find a reason to call special clients.
6. To build credibility, become certified in your professional field; for example, earn a CMC (Certified Management Consultant) from the Institute of Management Consultants, or the CPLP (Certified Professional in Learning and Performance) from ASTD. Then announce it to your clients.

7. Join local civic organizations.

8. Join organizations that represent the industries you serve.

9. Join your professional organizations.

10. Attend local chapter meetings for the professional, civic, and social organizations to which you belong. Network! The greater the number of follow-up notes you write, the greater your success!

11. Plan to meet three new people in every networking situation.

12. Every time you meet a potential client, even a remotely potential client, follow up with a personal note.

13. Scan your newspaper for awards local businesspeople have received and send a note congratulating them. I like to include the article as well.

14. Speak at meetings and conferences of civic and professional organizations.

15. Identify and meet with people who can advance your career.

16. Take a client to lunch.

17. Meet with other consultants. If they are offered a project outside their scope of work, they may pass it on to you.

18. Bring the doughnuts if it's not in the client's budget.

19. When you are not given a project, send a thank-you note saying you appreciated being considered. Compliment them on their choice—your competition.

20. Talk to a client about a new idea.

21. Send articles that will interest your present and potential clients.

22. Send a card for atypical holidays: Thanksgiving, Valentine's Day, St. Patrick's Day, Ground Hog Day, Independence Day.

23. Tie a client message to a holiday—for example, "We're thankful to have you as a client," "We're lucky to have you as a client," or "We have a reason to celebrate."

24. Send a lumpy envelope for a holiday: a gourd for Thanksgiving, candy hearts for Valentine's Day, a four-leaf clover for St. Patrick's Day, a sparkler for July Fourth.

25. Send birthday cards for both people and companies.

26. Send "congratulations" cards for promotions.

27. Send personal, handwritten thank-you notes.

28. Listen to everything your clients are telling you. Find their needs.

29. Pass your extra work on to a trusted colleague. It will come back to you.

30. Help your client locate other consultants who can do work you are not qualified to do.

31. Share your expertise freely with clients and other consultants: advice, ideas, materials, instruments. It will come back to you.

32. If you send brochures, announcements, or other information in the mail, package them in a unique way, such as an oddly shaped envelope, a tube, or a colored envelope.

33. Send postcards when you're on vacation.

34. Page through a corporate specialty catalogue to locate something around which you could build a theme. You will be surprised at some of the creative items you can purchase for under $2.00.

e-Idea

Visit one of the following specialty shops to receive their catalogues or just peruse their products online: 4imprint, at www.4imprint.com; Crestline Company, at www.crestline.com; Oriental Trading Company, at www.orientaltrading.com.

35. Visit a toy store looking for something around which you could build a marketing theme.

36. Send pictures of your support staff to your clients as a way to introduce the people who assist them by phone.

37. Support your local charity in the name of your clients. Send an announcement to your clients stating the details.

38. Sponsor a community event, such as a 10K run.

39. Buy T-shirts for your employees, colleagues, or even clients.

40. Sponsor an offbeat memorable event. Perhaps you could rent your local theater for an afternoon and invite clients' children for a free showing.

41. Spread good rumors about your business, such as "We deliver high quality at a reasonable rate."

42. Invite an executive to breakfast.

43. Write letters to the editor of your newspaper or your professional journal.

44. Write newsworthy articles to publish in newspapers—for example, information about people in the industry, recent changes in an industry, or the "story behind the story" that made the headlines.

45. Write a column for your local newspaper. After the column is established, you can sell it to other newspapers.

46. Publish your own newsletter.

e-Idea

Publish an electronic newsletter, but heed the cautions of experts. Your newsletter should be filled with useful information, resources, and helpful ideas. It should not be filled with advertisements or rewritten old press releases. It should be written professionally, be grammatically correct, and address controversial issues of interest to your subscribers.

47. Write articles for your professional journal. Contact the editor to obtain a calendar of topics for the year.

48. Purchase professional-looking reprints of your article and send them to present and potential clients.

49. Write a book.

50. Send a copy of your book to present and potential clients.

51. Send any book your client would appreciate.

52. Invest in the best stationery and business cards you can afford.

53. If you are not ready to develop a brochure, create a fact sheet that concisely explains the benefits of your services.

54. Create a list of satisfied clients that you can share with potential clients.

55. Develop an autobiographical sketch that focuses on your strengths, lists some of your clients or the industries in which you work, and identifies your accomplishments.

56. Post your business card or literature on public bulletin boards.

57. Ask your clients for referrals.

58. Give an award to one of your suppliers. This becomes a marketing tool for both of you.

59. Create a list of ten tips representing your specialty, such as "Ten tips for more efficient meetings," "Ten ways to reduce stress," or "Ten do's for financial planning." Print them on high-quality paper with your name and telephone number. Mail them to clients or give them away at professional events.

60. Enter your projects in industry award competitions.

61. Collect testimonials from customers, experts, or celebrities and use them to spice up your marketing materials.

62. Serve on a board for your community college, a local company, an association, or a charity.

63. Thank your clients—often.

64. Give something away free.

e-Idea

If you have promised to send a white paper you have written, an instrument you have developed, a strategic plan you have compiled, or the summary of a planning meeting you have conducted for your client, save it to a memory stick and send it to your client. Your delivery will be classy, and your deliverable will be with your client on the memory stick!

65. Refer new customers to your clients.

66. Provide new information to your clients on a regular basis.

67. Create your own mailing list. It should include everyone you meet in the line of business every day. We have a primary mailing list and a secondary mailing list. The primary list receives everything we send. The secondary list exists primarily for new product sales brochures. Your mailing list is a valuable marketing tool.

68. Offer a full money-back guarantee.

69. Trade show booths are generally very expensive, but you may be able to share one with another organization, or you could trade the cost of the booth for services to the association. Creativity, bed sheets, and lots of action can make up for the lack of glitz and glamour of the more typical booths.

70. Start all letters with "you" followed by a compliment.

71. Purchase space in a directory or consultant database. Be sure to check on the rules. They may want a percentage of each project you obtain from the listing.

72. Keep your key contacts alive. Plan how you will stay in touch with them, how often, and in what way.

73. When asked what you do, be prepared to further describe your consulting practice. Identify two or three quick examples to add more detail.

74. Love what you do. It will show.

75. Visit an industry trade show to compile a list of potential clients in an industry. You can visit their booths, speak with their employees, and pick up their literature.

76. Keep a supply of business cards with you. Hand them out freely everywhere you go.

77. Open a conversation with the person sitting next to you on the plane—especially if you are in first class.

78. Offer a finder's fee to colleagues who generate a project for you.

79. Prepare marketing around a theme; for example, send a ruler or tape measure asking potential clients how they measure up.

80. Find something that gives your correspondence a special touch. I've used round gold paper clips and small cards that have a special message sealed under a perforated flap.

81. Do things that make people feel special, such as using their names in the middle of the notes you write to them, sending pictures that you took at their team-building session, tracking down a special request they mentioned, or attributing an idea to them.

82. Respond to Request for Proposals (RFPs) from government agencies.

e-Idea

Log on to www.FedBizOpps.gov to watch for opportunities to submit a proposal to the federal government for work in your area of expertise. Some states have similar sites.

83. Read *How to Become a Rainmaker,* by Jeffrey J. Fox.

84. Following a presentation, have everyone toss a business card in a hat for a drawing. After drawing for the prizes, send a personal note to all who submitted a business card thanking the individuals for their attendance.

85. Contact your college roommate and ask for an introduction to an organization.

86. Donate a service or product to charity.

87. Stage a publicity stunt.

88. Agree to be interviewed on radio.

89. Conduct a survey. Publish the results. Share the results with clients.

90. Send samples of your materials or products to potential clients. For example, a computer software consultant could send a demo CD; a management consultant could send a self-evaluation.

91. Keep your website up-to-date. A rule of thumb: update your website with a new article or tool at least once each month. Link to other websites that may interest potential and current clients.

e-Idea

Your website is important, but remember that people spend more time off the Internet than they do on it. Find non-Internet ways to build online traffic. Given that many people do not open direct mail, find ways to get them to open your mail. For example, send a lumpy envelope (idea 24) or send something that does not need to be opened, such as a coconut or a glossy postcard with an intriguing message.

92. Teach a class at a college or university.

93. Sponsor a round-table breakfast for members of a specific industry in one locale.

94. Volunteer your services to the media as a source of information about a specific industry. You will most likely be called for a quote.

95. Create a list of success stories you have had with past clients, such as an effort that resulted in a savings of $3 million each year and shortened the time from concept to catalogue by eleven months.

96. Keep your travel expenses to a minimum. Your present clients will notice and appreciate it.

97. Call a former client if you plan to be visiting the city where the client is located.

98. Practice a perfect handshake—not too firm, not too weak.

99. Create a key contact list. Update it and use it regularly.

100. Call future clients to request their quarterly reports. Use them to learn about the companies before visiting.

101. Purchase a focused mailing list from your professional association. Follow up the mailing with phone calls.

102. Purchase tapes of the speeches you give at conferences and send them to potential clients.

103. Write a letter to a television programming manager describing your idea for an appearance on television. Identify the connection to the show and the benefits to the viewers.

104. Start your own cable show.

105. Ask your neighbor for an introduction to an organization or individual.

106. Send geographic mailings before you visit a city. Send a note to several people letting them know you will be in their city. Follow up with a phone call to set a meeting time.

107. Make friends with secretaries and receptionists. All of them!

108. Host a summer picnic.

109. If you are a trainer, offer to conduct a pilot training program for a potential client for free.

110. Create a list of "client questions," questions you have used when meeting clients that have proven to be successful in getting to the heart of their problems.

111. Place ten cold calls.

112. Write a warm letter.

113. Most important, always give your client at least 113 percent of what they expected.

These 113 marketing tactics are just a start. You can think of others. The key is to find ways to promote who you are and what you do—and in the process to have fun! Looking for more in-depth marketing information? *Marketing Your Consulting Services* (Biech, 2003) is another resource that will answer all your questions.

CONTACTS WITH POTENTIAL CLIENTS

Many people assume that contacting potential clients will be difficult and should therefore be avoided. It is easier than you might think.

Cold Calls

What is a person's greatest fear about making cold calls? Rejection. What can positively be guaranteed about making cold calls? Rejection. So create a positive cold-call attitude. I have a friend in sales who lives by cold calls. The numbers he works with are daunting. He says he must make one hundred cold calls to find ten people who will talk to him. Of those ten people, two will agree to meet with him, and one will purchase his product.

So what if someone says no, hangs up, or is rude? Don't let it bother you. You must refocus your attitude. You were not rejected; your services were rejected. The person did not need your services at this time. When you run into someone who frankly cannot use your services and he or she cuts the phone call short, you should *silently thank the person for not wasting your valuable time.* Rather than feeling rejected, you can feel thankful. Say "Thank you for your candor and have a great day!" Create your own cold-call attitude.

Cold Call Warm-Ups

Quite honestly, I have made only a few cold calls in my life. I prefer to make warm calls. Although this takes more time, I believe I have better results, and I enjoy the process more. To start, I warm up the client with a letter—not just any old letter, but one that I have written specifically for the client. This will require research.

e-Idea

Begin your research on the Web. Identify a list of twenty to thirty potential clients with whom you would like to do business. Use your favorite search engine to gather as much data as you can about each.

I visit the local library to continue the research. I use the library's resources, including local business magazines, journals and periodicals, local business newsletters, the newspaper, the city directory, manufacturer and business directories, and any other resources available. Each of these has an index that makes it easy to research the list of clients. I use Exhibit 5.3, the company profile, to synthesize the information I find.

Exhibit 5.3. Company Profile.

Company Name _____

Address _____

_____

Telephone _____   Website _____

Employees _____

Management Positions

_____   _____

_____   _____

_____   _____

Products and Services _____

_____

History _____

_____

_____

Financial Information _____

_____

Organizational Philosophy _____

_____

_____

Relationship to My Consulting Services _____

_____

Additional Relevant Information _____

_____

Resources Used _____

_____

Enlist your librarian to help in your search. Librarians hold a wealth of knowledge. If possible, I also copy articles that I find. I gather information for two key purposes: first, to learn as much as I can about the organization and, second, to have enough information to compose a unique letter that will grab the reader's attention. Examples of several of these letters are displayed in Exhibit 5.4.

Begin by making sure you are sending the letter to the right person. Double-check the spelling of the person's name and the person's title. Focus on the recipient in the first paragraph. Demonstrate that you know what is important to him or her. The second and third paragraphs should connect the recipient to the need for consulting services in some way and establish your qualifications. Both of these paragraphs must be customized. For example, when referring to past clients, select only those who are related to the recipient by industry, location, or size. If that is not possible, select only a couple of your most impressive clients. In the last paragraph, tell the recipient what to expect next. I developed this format over twenty years ago and continue to obtain remarkable results.

I usually find information for 30 to 50 percent of clients on the initial list. After I return from the library, I compose the marketing letters and mail them. I follow the letter with a telephone call on the date that is stated in the letter.

Of the people I contact in this way, 95 percent are interested in speaking with me, and more than half of them agree to a meeting within a month. Of those, about half become clients in less than one year. The rest become contacts, resources, or clients in the future. These odds are much better than for cold calls, and the process is more fun. I enjoy the challenge of the research and the creativity of composing the letters. I particularly like beginning a relationship in this positive way.

_Librarians hold a wealth
of knowledge._

Exhibit 5.4a. Sample Introductory Marketing Letter.

July 12, 20XX

Robert R. Birkhauser, President
Auto Glass Specialists, Inc.
2810 Syene Road
Madison, WI 53713

Dear Mr. Birkhauser:

Auto Glass Specialists is one of Madison's phenomenons. In just over twenty years you have transformed an innovative idea into a successful business spanning five states. Your expertise for repairing windows in cars, trucks, and heavy equipment is now available in twenty-three locations, with sales pushing $15 million. Strong management and hard-working employees achieved these results.

At ebb associates we recognize the important role the employee plays in the successful growth of any company. Further, we have found that improving employees' communication skills results in improved productivity and increased profit. Do you realize that just one one-hundred-dollar listening mistake by each of Auto Glass Specialists' two hundred employees can result in a loss of $20,000 each year? Improved communication skills can decrease mistakes, increase your profits, and improve customer relations.

ebb associates specializes in communication training. We present workshops and seminars focusing on improved communication and will custom-design a program to meet your needs at Auto Glass Specialists. Our clients, including Tenneco Automotive and Cardinal Glass, recognize our commitment to meeting their needs, providing excellent follow-up, and obtaining results. We'd like to help you, too, so that you can improve the quality and increase the quantity of work by maximizing the potential of your human resources.

I would like to call you within the week to schedule an appointment to discuss how we can assist you to meet your goals at Auto Glass Specialists. I am enclosing a list of the course titles that we can customize to meet your specific needs. I look forward to meeting and working with you.

Sincerely,

Elaine Biech
ebb associates

Exhibit 5.4b. Sample Introductory Marketing Letter.

July 12, 20XX

Roger Brown, President
Rocky Rococo Corporation
First Gilman Corporation
333 West Mifflin Street
Madison, WI 53703

Dear Mr. Brown:

From Brown's Diner to fifteen units and franchising plans is a success story that could only be written by the best Chicago pan-style pizza. This exceptional product is a result of your high standards for consistency and quality. In addition, we know that Rocky Rococo values people highly. You do not want customers to wait too long; yet you want them to experience the best pan-style pizza in the nation. You offer variety yet consistency—thus your unique system of selling pizza by the slice. You want families to feel at home—thus your new Hostess Program.

We at ebb associates value people, too. In fact, staying in touch with the needs of a company and its employees is our specialty. We work with companies that are interested in improving their productivity through improved communication. Managers and supervisors who participate in our training programs have found that, as their communication and management skills improve, so do the quality and quantity of work. ebb associates presents workshops and seminars on supervisory training, management development, sales training, and customer relations. Our clients, including Land O' Lakes, Dorman-Roth Foods, Hershey Chocolate, and many others, recognize our commitment to meeting their needs, providing exceptional training, and obtaining results.

Opening eight new stores in the next year in such places as Oshkosh, La Crosse, and Milwaukee will not be an easy task. We at ebb associates would like to show you how improved communication can result in a smoother expansion plan, reduce mistakes, and continue to improve customer relations.

I will call you within the week to schedule an appointment to discuss how we can assist you to meet your goals at Rocky Rococo. I am enclosing a list of the course titles that we will customize for your specific needs.

Sincerely,

Elaine Biech
ebb associates

Exhibit 5.4c. Sample Introductory Marketing Letter.

July 12, 20XX

Terry Voice, President
Pizza Pit Ltd.
2154 Atwood Avenue
Madison, WI 53704

Dear Mr. Voice:

Free, fast, hot delivery has placed Pizza Pit a step ahead of the rest. In fourteen years you have turned this unique idea into a successful business with over $6 million in sales. Pizza Pit has grown from one location to a chain of nine Dane County stores with franchising plans on the board. Two hundred franchised units in five years is an ambitious goal—one we're sure you will achieve!

At ebb associates we recognize the important role employees play in the successful growth of any company. Further, we have found that improving employees' communication skills results in improved productivity and increased profit. Your anticipated rate of growth will require you to be on top of the communication needs of your staff for a smoother expansion.

ebb associates presents workshops and seminars that focus on communication for supervisory training, management development, sales training, and customer relations. Our clients, including Land O' Lakes, McDonald's Corporation, and many others, recognize us for our commitment to excellence in training, customizing to fit individual company needs, and obtaining results.

Enclosed is a list of the course titles that we will customize to meet your needs. I will call you within the week to schedule an appointment to discuss how we can assist you to meet your expansion goals at Pizza Pit. I promise a free, fast, hot delivery!

Sincerely,

Elaine Biech
ebb associates

Exhibit 5.4d. Sample Introductory Marketing Letter.

July 12, 20XX

Albert H. Felly, President
Felly's Flowers
205 E. Broadway Street
Madison, WI 53716

Dear Mr. Felly:

We know that you at Felly's Flowers take pride in the individual care you give each of the plants you grow. You water almost all of the six hundred species of plants by hand to insure that they grow and flourish. You have an automatic fertilizing system, but again, acids and fertilizers are provided only if needed. We recognize that Felly's reputation for high-quality plants and flowers can be attributed to the individual attention you provide for each.

Just as you are an expert at growing flowers, we at ebb associates specialize in communication training. We recognize that individual care must be given to employees if a company is to grow and flourish. Did you know that 50 percent of all mistakes in the business world are made due to misunderstanding, not lack of skills or job knowledge? Therefore, improving employees' communication skills is vital to the success of any business.

ebb associates presents workshops and seminars that focus on improved communication. We work with companies, such as Famous Fixtures, General Casualty Company, James River Corporation, and many others, that are interested in improving their productivity through improved communication. These companies recognize our ability to meet their needs, provide excellent follow-up, and obtain measurable results. We'd like to provide training for the Felly's staff so that you, too, can decrease mistakes, increase profits, and improve customer relations.

Improving employees' communication skills is one of the ways to fertilize the desired growth of a company. I would like to call you within the week to schedule an appointment to discuss how we can assist you to meet your goals at Felly's Flowers. I am enclosing a list of the course titles that we can customize for your specific needs and look forward to meeting and working with you.

Sincerely,

Elaine Biech
ebb associates

Exhibit 5.5 provides a list of questions to ask potential clients. You can use these to guide your discussions on the telephone or in person.

 Exhibit 5.5. Questions to Ask Potential Clients.

1. What does your company (division, department) value most?
2. What are your company's (division's, department's) vision and mission?
3. What is your strategy to achieve your vision and mission?
4. What are your company's (division's, department's, leadership team's) strengths?
5. What's going well for your company (division, department, team)?
6. What are the greatest challenges you will face over the next two years?
7. What prevents you from achieving your goals (objectives, mission)?
8. What do you see as the greatest need for improvement?
9. What prevents you from making that improvement?
10. Describe the communication process in your company (division, department). How well does it work?
11. If you had one message to give your company president (CEO, board of directors, manager), what would it be?
12. What should I have asked, but did not?

Ways to Track Client Contacts

After you begin to contact clients, you will want to track whom you called when, what they said, what you sent them, and when they have asked you to call again. Exhibit 5.6 will help you keep this information organized. Date the follow-up column to confirm when you completed actions you agreed to take.

Exhibit 5.6. Client Contact Log.

Organization/ Phone Number	Contact Person	Date	First Contact	FUP*	Date	Second Contact	FUP	Date	Third Contact	FUP

*FUP = Follow-Up

The Business of Consulting, Second Edition. Copyright © 2007 by John Wiley & Sons, Inc. Reproduced by permission of Pfeiffer, an Imprint of Wiley. www.pfeiffer.com

Questions Clients Will Ask

Clients who have used consultants in the past will ask many of the same questions. Most will want to know what you do. Know how to tell your story in a sixty-second sound bite. I experience the following variations repeatedly:

- What are the deliverables? What will the final product look like?
- What are the critical milestones? At what point will progress, quality, quantity be checked? How?
- How much will this cost me? (Answer this one using the word "investment"—for example, "Your investment for completing this project will be $13,900.")
- What are your billing practices? How often will you invoice me?
- How can you help me with the kickoff of this project?
- Whom do I contact if there are problems or concerns?
- How can we stay in contact?
- How can you help me communicate with my boss?
- What is our responsibility at each phase? How will you involve our employees?
- How will you evaluate the success of this project?

---

*Know how to tell your story
in a sixty-second sound bite.*

If Your Clients Don't Ask

What if the client does not ask questions? Perhaps your client has little experience working with consultants. You will still want to ensure that your discussion covers certain basics. If your client does not ask, introduce the topic by saying, "You probably want to know. . . ." This puts the topic on the table in an efficient way. The list of questions in Exhibit 5.5 can be adapted for this purpose.

If you have read Peter Block's *Flawless Consulting* (and you should have if you are considering a consulting career), you undoubtedly recognize that you are moving into the contracting phase of the consulting process. Contracting is ensuring that both you and your client are as explicit as possible about your needs, wants, and expectations of one another. Contracting is covered more completely in Chapter Seven. The contracting discussion is an important link to writing a good proposal.

PROPOSALS AND CONTRACTS

Proposals and contracts are two written documents that you will probably use at some point in your career. Each serves a purpose for staying in business.

Proposals

I use proposals frequently and like them. Often I am asked to submit a proposal as a step in competing for a project. At other times I am asked to submit a proposal to clarify a previous discussion. The proposal will identify *who* will do *what* by *when* and for *how much*. I actually like to write proposals. It clarifies the project in my mind, and I find myself developing creative possibilities during the process.

A proposal typically includes a purpose statement, a description of the situation as it now exists, a proposed approach that the consultant will take (this may include data gathering, design of materials, content relationships, delivery of services, and implementation), a timeline, the consultant's qualifications, and the investment required to complete the plan.

I guarantee that you will write the best proposal if you listen to what your client says and take good notes. Do not take this statement lightly. In fact, reread it. Take it in. After reading our proposals, clients often say complimentary things about them, such as, "This is exactly what we need! How did you know?" We knew because we listened, and we fed back their exact words. Consultants make a big mistake by putting things in their own words. If the client has requested an attitude survey, identify it that way in your proposal. An "employee satisfaction survey" may be more meaningful to you, and the resulting survey may have the identical words on paper. Unfortunately, your client will not know that.

*You will write the best proposal
if you listen to what your client says
and take good notes.*

Exhibit 5.7. Sample Proposal.

Progressive Discipline:
Consistency Is the Key

Purpose

This proposal is submitted at the request of Jack Smith, vice president of human resources, National Underwriters. It includes the situation, a suggested approach, timeline, and expected investment for the effort.

The Situation

The goal of National Underwriters' progressive discipline training is to ensure that progressive discipline is handled consistently across the company. To ensure that this occurs, supervisors must be able to:

- Identify employee behaviors that must be changed, based on National Underwriters' performance and policy standards.
- Define and implement the progressive discipline process consistently.
- Document in detail the steps to be taken.

This session will ensure that supervisors leave with a clear understanding of how to ensure consistency.

In addition to ensuring consistency, supervisors will also be able to:

- Understand the cost to the company of inconsistency.
- Define the progressive discipline regulations for the state in which each supervisor works.
- Identify the legal ramifications of inconsistent actions.
- Review the policy statement and locate it within the employee handbook.
- Clarify the concept of "fair dealing."
- Identify skills necessary to decrease the number and intensity of difficult disciplinary situations.

- Make consistent decisions when presented with an unclear situation.

- Discuss the importance of consistent progressive discipline in relation to the statements "The Client Comes First" and "People Make the Difference."

Supervisors will become experts to ensure consistent treatment of every employee in the organization. To ensure this, we will custom design a session using your examples, your language, your progressive disciplinary process, and your standards of conduct. Your unique needs will be addressed.

Proposed Approach

Information and Data Gathering. To design a relevant training session for you, data gathering is required. To accomplish this we will do the following:

- Interview Jack Smith, vice president, and Donna Dopp, corporate attorney, to determine their desired objectives for this session.

- Interview National Underwriters' attorneys for examples of past lessons learned.

- Interview HR and line managers who have experienced the progressive discipline process.

- Review job descriptions, training curriculum, employee-orientation materials, and other documentation that defines expected supervisory performance.

- Request a list of supervisors and their experience, including tenure, training, and previous relevant work experience.

- Review your vision and strategy statements for the next five years, historical information, names and positions of key people in the organization, a listing of jargon and acronyms we may need to know, and other documentation you deem appropriate.

Exhibit 5.7. Sample Proposal, Cont'd.

Custom Design. Your materials will be custom designed for the organization, making it much easier for supervisors to accept, learn, and implement.

Our data gathering will provide examples that we will build into the training design, corporate jargon we will learn and use, strategies to ensure that the training "sticks," and actual situations that we will develop into role plays, case studies, and other hands-on activities.

In addition, the design will ensure that critical factors of adult learning theory are built into the session. The training will do the following:

- Build on the knowledge and concepts the participants already possess.
- Use actual corporate examples.
- Relate the learning to the needs of each participant.
- Allow opportunity for interaction and questions.
- Provide hands-on skill practice.
- Build in mechanisms for participant feedback.
- Present a plan for immediate action and feedback.
- Provide a job aid for supervisors to ensure consistency of the process.

Content. Final content will be determined as a result of the data-gathering process. The session will ensure that participants achieve all objectives identified in the first section of this proposal. Final content will be determined at a meeting scheduled for March 14, 20XX. All of the content will be directly related to National Underwriters. Examples will be based on four areas within the company:

- Software development.
- Data centers—account processing.
- Item or check processing.
- Small manufacturing/software companies.

Materials. National Underwriters will be given an exclusive copyright for all participant materials designed for this project.

Conducting the Course. We believe this course will require one day's training, allowing supervisors to return to their offices at the end of the day. We recommend that a maximum of eighteen participants attend. If that number increases, it will be necessary to increase the session time.

Implementation. At your request, a pilot session will be held on May 16, 20XX, in Troy, Michigan. Your staff will conduct the session, and six to eighteen of your first-line supervisors/managers will participate to ensure that we have perfected the materials before they are presented to the rest of the organization. The pilot is also important to ensure that the timing is adequate for your employees.

We will observe this session to provide feedback to your trainers, to ensure that the materials meet your unique needs, to answer any implementation questions, and to determine whether changes need to be made. In addition, we will facilitate an evaluation following the pilot session in which participants will be asked to provide answers to the following questions:

- What should be emphasized more? Less?
- Do we need to increase the time spent in any area? Decrease time spent in any area?
- Is there too much material for the time available? If so, what should be cut? Should additional training hours be added? How else can this information be learned?
- Have we missed anything? What should be added?
- What errors must be corrected?

Exhibit 5.7. Sample Proposal, Cont'd.

This evaluation process serves to guarantee our work. Any changes or corrections will be provided without additional charge.

Follow-Up. A critical but often overlooked step in the training process is the follow-up to reinforce the skills. We will provide ideas that will be initiated by your training staff and the supervisors. These could include such suggestions as:

- A "rap" session open to anyone in supervisory positions to ensure continued growth, to answer concerns or questions, and to enhance teamwork among supervisors.
- Peer mentoring.
- A reading list.
- A "lessons learned" board.
- A refresher session.

Timeline

March 14, 20XX	Decision on final course objectives
March 22, 20XX	Interviews and data gathering begin
April 4, 20XX	Design begins
April 18, 20XX	First draft available for National Underwriters
May 9, 20XX	Final approval by National Underwriters
May 16, 20XX	Pilot

We can begin the data-gathering stage by mid-March and have the design completed by mid-May. Other dates can be finalized on acceptance of this proposal.

Exhibit 5.7. Sample Proposal, Cont'd.

Investment and Responsibilities

We would like to have one contact person within the company who is knowledgeable about the project and who understands the goals. This individual will assist us with scheduling interviews, distributing information, and answering our questions.

The investment includes the design and delivery of all aspects of the effort outlined in this proposal, including, but not limited to:

- All planning and coordination.
- All data and information gathering and compilation.
- All interview preparation, coordination, and facilitation.
- A one-day session titled "Progressive Discipline: Consistency Is the Key."
- A pilot session on May 16, 20XX.
- A training guide for HR trainers.
- Participant materials for the pilot session.
- Audiovisual materials for the pilot session.
- A master of "Progressive Discipline: Consistency Is the Key" participant materials.
- A master CD of the PowerPoint presentation.
- An exclusive copyright for all participant materials designed for this project.

Your investment for course design, pilot observation, and exclusive copyright is $42,900. In addition, travel will be billed at cost.

The terms of this proposal are effective through June 30, 20XX.

Executive-level and/or expert trainer references are available.

Specify an effective date—for example, "The terms of this proposal are effective through April 30, 20XX." You do not want to get caught by a client who has a proposal that is two years old and for which the budget was just approved. Why is this a problem? First, the fee you quoted may be lower than what you presently charge. Second, you most likely have grown and have improved your skills, so the process you proposed may be outdated. Finally, an effective date reduces the amount of time a client will keep you dangling.

We like to use the word "investment" (as opposed to cost or price) when we write proposals. It echoes our philosophy: what we do adds value and does not just cost money.

Proposals are often written in competition with other consultants. They may range in length from one to fifty pages. A one-page proposal may be considered a letter of agreement. An informed client will be as interested in the content of the proposal as in the price. Exhibit 5.7 provides an example of a proposal.

e-Idea

Don't just send your proposal as an attachment to an email. That's so ho-hum! Send a CD that incorporates a video clip. Perhaps it is of you in action leading a team-building session. It could be you delivering a message about how you work with the client. It could be endorsement statements from some of your clients.

Contracts

Contracts are legal documents that bind both parties to the content stated. I personally do not like them because I believe they start the relationship on a basis of implied mistrust. On the other hand, many consultants feel that a contract simply clarifies responsibility. Whether you are a fan of contracts or not, they usually involve an organization's legal department, which often holds up the project for a time. Except for our government work, most of our work is conducted on the basis of a clarifying proposal or a handshake.

What should contracts look like? What should they say? No matter how complete we have been or what we have written in contracts, legal departments

Exhibit 5.8. Sample Contract.

Agreement

Agreement made and entered into this 3rd day of January 20XX, by and between _____[client]_____ of _____[address]_____ (hereinafter "Purchaser") and _____[consultant]_____ of _____[address]_____ (hereinafter "Consultant").

In consideration of the mutual covenants and promises contained herein, and for good and valuable consideration, the parties hereby agree as follows:

I. Project Responsibilities and Obligations

Consultant will develop and implement a Member Service Staff Training and Intervention plan as further detailed in Exhibit A to this contract, which is hereby incorporated by reference. Implementation of said plan will be based on input and guidelines provided by Purchaser. Implementation of said plan will include, but will not necessarily be limited to, the following components:

A. Gathering Information and Data;
B. Designing Three Training Courses;
C. Conducting Training Courses;
D. Designing Training Materials; and
E. Providing Consultation Services.

These are detailed further in Exhibit A herein. Delivery of services shall reasonably conform to the timeline set forth in Exhibit B.

Responsibilities for each party shall be as follows:

Purchaser
1. Provide one contact person who is knowledgeable about the project and who understands the goals of this effort. This individual will assist with establishing meetings, scheduling interviews, copying and distributing information, and completing other coordination tasks.

Exhibit 5.8. Sample Contract, Cont'd.

2. Provide copies of the participant materials for the last four sessions of Member Services Staff Training.

3. Provide training space and all audiovisual equipment for the training sessions, including an LCD projector and screen and two flip charts for each session. Recording and playback equipment will also be required for the two-day Train-the-Trainer session.

Consultant

1. Complete all aspects required to implement the plan outlined above, including, but not limited to:

   - All planning and coordination
   - All data and information gathering and compilation
   - All interview preparation, coordination, and facilitation
   - Design of a one-day session titled Member Services Staff Training
   - Design of a two-day Train-the-Trainer session for six to ten individuals
   - Design of a one-day Coaching session for supervisors
   - Training materials for Member Services and Coaching sessions
   - A training guide and outline for the Train-the-Trainer session
   - Participant materials for the pilot of the Member Services session, the Train-the-Trainer session, and the Coaching session
   - All audiovisual materials

2. Provide materials ensuring the Purchaser's self-sufficiency following the implementation, including but not limited to:

   - Master of Member Services Staff Training participant materials
   - Master of Member Services Staff Training PowerPoint

Exhibit 5.8. Sample Contract, Cont'd.

3. Provide an agreement following the final follow-up on-site visit that outlines arrangements for shared copyright for all participant materials designed for this project. The agreement will state that the materials shall be used by the Purchaser for internal use only. The materials may not be sold. The materials may be used externally with written permission from Consultant.

4. Invoice monthly for work completed plus travel expenses.

II. Consideration

In exchange for Consultant's services, as set forth in Section I above, Purchaser will pay Consultant monthly, total compensation not to exceed ninety thousand three hundred dollars ($90,300). Consultant will be paid as services are rendered in any given month as set forth above, excluding 5 percent ($4,515), which will be held until completion of the full engagement. Final payment will be made within thirty days of receipt of a bill itemizing charges incurred to complete all services.

III. Travel Expenses

In addition to the consideration set forth in Section II above, Purchaser will pay to Consultant reasonable and necessary expenses as specifically set forth herein. Reimbursement of expense shall include charges incurred for travel (airfare, mileage, car rental, and/or train fare), lodging, and meals during trips to the Purchaser's site. All travel expenses shall be procured at the lowest cost available. Travel dates are outlined in Exhibit B.

Reimbursement for travel expenses shall be paid within thirty days from invoice date by Purchaser on submission of receipts, evidencing out-of-pocket expenses incurred by Consultant.

IV. Term

This agreement will take effect as of the date indicated in the introductory paragraph above and shall extend until Consultant's completion of all services

Exhibit 5.8. Sample Contract, Cont'd.

set forth in Section I unless earlier termination by the Purchaser on the giving of written notice. On any such notice of termination, services by Consultant shall be discontinued and compensation will cease to accrue.

V. Confidential Information

A. On being notified that a party to this Agreement considers information confidential, each party hereto agrees not to disclose the confidential information of the other party, directly or indirectly, under any circumstances or by any means, to any third person, without express, written consent obtained in advance. Each party hereto agrees that it will not copy, transmit, reproduce, summarize, quote, or make any commercial or other use whatsoever of the other party's confidential information, except as provided herein. Each party agrees to exercise the highest degree of care in safeguarding the confidential information of the other party against loss, theft, or inadvertent disclosure and agrees generally to take all steps necessary to ensure the maintenance of confidentiality.

B. On termination of this agreement or as otherwise requested, each party agrees to deliver promptly to the other party all confidential information of that party, in whatever form, that may be in its possession or under its control.

VI. No Transfer

This Agreement shall not be assigned or transferred by either party without the express written consent of the other party, obtained in advance.

VII. Taxes

Both parties shall promptly pay all applicable taxes of every kind, nature, and description arising out of the establishment, nature, and operation of its business in connection with the event described in this Agreement.

Exhibit 5.8. Sample Contract, Cont'd.

VIII. Notices

All notices to be given and communications in connection with this Agreement shall be in writing and addressed to the parties at the following addresses:

Consultant	Purchaser
[Consultant]	[Client]
[address]	[address]
[address]	[address]

IX. Effect of Partial Invalidity

The invalidity of any portion of this Agreement will not and shall not be deemed to affect the validity of any other provision. In the event that any provision of this Agreement is held to be invalid, the parties agree that the remaining provisions shall be deemed to be in full force and effect as if they had been executed by both parties subsequent to the expurgation of the invalid provision.

X. Modification of Agreement

Any modification of this Agreement or additional obligations assumed by either party in connection with this Agreement shall be binding only if placed in writing and signed by each party or an authorized representative of each party.

By the Parties:

_____   _____
Name, Title   Name, Title
[Client]   [Consultant]

_____   _____
Date   Date

have always slashed them apart. I recommend that you have the client's legal department initiate the contract. It will save you a great deal of time and frustration. If you believe a contract will provide you with security or clarity, use it. Quite honestly, I believe a well-written proposal meets our needs better. We use contracts when it makes the client feel more comfortable with the new relationship.

Contracts frequently include terms (effective dates), project scope, deliverables, confidentiality, communication, staffing, supervision of the consultant, scheduling, payment schedule, incentives and penalties, termination terms, the cancellation policy, arbitration arrangements, transfer of responsibilities, taxes, and modifications to the contract. Exhibit 5.8 provides a simple version of a contract drawn up by a client.

HOW TO REFUSE AN ASSIGNMENT

There will be times when it is better to walk away from an assignment than to accept it. I was once called to conduct a team building for a manager for whom I had completed some previous work. During our second planning discussion, he began to make some unusual requests—all directed toward one employee. It turned out that he was not really looking for a team-building session, but for evidence and documentation that could be used to fire someone on his staff! Needless to say, I turned the job down.

In another situation, our firm was selected based on our proposal and interviews to coordinate a major change effort that would occur over an eighteen-month time frame. One of our contingencies was a satisfactory meeting with the CEO. When I met with him, I found that he supported the change for all the wrong reasons and that it was unlikely that his support would continue when the going got tough. I ended our conversation with, "It doesn't seem that you are ready for this change. We will be unable to accept this challenge until you can guarantee your full support." There was a lot of sputtering and disbelief. He had never heard of a consultant turning down work. I left saying that if he wanted me to help him prepare for what was ahead, I would do so, but otherwise we would not accept the project. He called that same afternoon, and I spent several sessions with him explaining exactly what he was getting himself into.

Yes, there are times when you will refuse an assignment, including some of the following:

- The client asks you to do something unethical or clandestine, or you just feel uncomfortable about the project.
- The project lacks support from the right levels of management.
- The project is doomed for failure. It is unethical to take the client's money in that situation.
- The scope is too large for the money available.
- The project requires a steep learning curve for you, but the time is not available for the learning to occur.
- You do not have the time to do the project with your usual high quality.
- The chemistry is missing between you and the client.

WAYS TO STAY IN BUSINESS

Many things can happen to ensure that you stay in business. Only one thing will ensure that you go out of business—lack of work. Staying in business is dependent on a steady flow of clients. Put your marketing plan together and then use it! You will starve waiting for the phone to ring.

*You will starve waiting
for the phone to ring.*

The Cost of Doing Business

Error is only the opportunity to begin again, more intelligently.

Henry Ford

Even if your business is up and running quickly, you land a couple of big contracts, and you have satisfied customers, you must study the numbers to know whether you are financially successful. Study your numbers? Here's what you are looking for:

- *Cash flow.* Will you have enough money to pay your bills this month?
- *Expenses.* Where is all the money going? Which expenses are constant (those that do not change when business increases or decreases, such as rent, salaries, and insurance)? Which expenses vary depending on the level of business, such as travel, printing, and professional fees?
- *Overhead.* What does it take to keep your business open?
- *Profitability.* Which contracts are the most lucrative?
- *Capital.* What business expenses are good investments?
- *Invoices.* How readily are they being paid?

This chapter helps you examine various aspects of recording, tracking, and reading your numbers. It also offers suggestions to improve your financial picture and provides forms that will save you weeks of work. The advice in this chapter can prevent dozens of mistakes.

PLAN FOR THE WORST

To keep myself out of financial trouble, I follow this advice: plan for the worst-case scenario, but act as if you're living the best case. There are two messages inherent in this statement. First, *don't spend your money until it's in your hands.* One of your clients may not pay you on time; the loan you were counting on may not be approved; an unexpected expense may occur, such as replacing your computer.

---

*Plan for the worst-case scenario,
but act as if you're living the best case.*

The first message is practical, but the second message is philosophical. "Act as if you're living the best case" refers to the message you are sending to yourself and others. As a strong believer in positive thinking, I am convinced that much of my company's success is due to the fact that I expect it. I believe I will succeed. You must also *live the best case for your clients.* Never hint to a client that business is less than great. Suggesting that your business is having financial difficulty will make clients nervous about your stability and even wary about your ability to perform the job. I've noticed that even the smallest complaint, such as "Our paper wasn't delivered on time," can cause concern. So do not mention your problems to your clients. You want confidence, not sympathy.

---

*Do not mention your
problems to your clients.*

Whenever you play with your numbers, remind yourself to "Plan for the worst-case scenario, but act as if you're living the best case." Most consultants do exactly the opposite.

Plan for problems. Portray prosperity.

WATCH YOUR CASH FLOW

You can be very profitable and still go out of business. A surprising statement? Yes, but true. Your books can display a 20 percent profit on every project, but if cash flowing into your business does not meet cash flowing out, you will find yourself in a very difficult situation. Cash-flow problems are the number one reason that small businesses fail. You can control cash flow. Try some or all of these suggestions to prevent cash-flow problems.

You can be very profitable and still go out of business.

Bill Immediately

Make billing for work you have completed your number two priority. (Meeting customers' needs should always be your first priority.) Complete and mail your clients' invoices as soon as you finish the work. The same day is not too soon. Many organizations, including federal government agencies, have a thirty-day time frame from the date they receive the invoice to the day they cut the check. If you wait a week or two to send the bill, it could be a full sixty days before you receive cash for the work you completed. Remember, they cannot pay you if you don't bill them!

They cannot pay you if you don't bill them!

Billing immediately is important for reasons beyond preventing cash-flow problems. The sooner you bill, the more pleased the client will be about paying immediately. Unfortunately, the value of your services diminishes with time. A client may begin to think that what you accomplished was actually a very small aspect of the total success of the project or even that the solution was his or her own, not yours! The lesson? Bill while the client is most satisfied with your work.

Use a Reliable Delivery System to Send Invoices

Ensure that your client receives your invoice. Send your invoices in a priority mail packet. The cost will be a little over $4.00, as opposed to the price of a first-class stamp, but the U.S. Postal Service will give priority mail better attention. Your invoice will have a better chance of reaching its destination in a shorter amount of time. We could give many examples of delayed or lost mail. In general, we have seen first-class mail between Virginia and Wisconsin take as long as five to ten days. The priority mail packets usually arrive in fewer than five days—often in just two days. In addition, your client may give it special attention due to the packaging. If the invoice is for a large amount or you need to have it turned around quickly, skip the U.S. Postal Service entirely and send your invoice in a letter packet with your favorite private carrier.

e-Idea

Take advantage of any electronic billing system your client offers—no matter how magical it may seem, it will most likely ensure a faster turn-around than the post office process. If your clients do not mention the system, ask. Your client may advise you to contact accounts payable. Do so. It is always good to have that department on your side.

Monitor Accounts Receivable Methodically

At the end of every week, the bookkeeper on staff provides me with a cash-flow report. It identifies the amount in our checking and savings accounts, overdue invoices, and those due this month and next. The report also highlights significant expenses, such as noting that payroll will be taken out the following week.

Know Your Clients' Reputation for Prompt Payment

The payment strategy you have chosen will often define how readily your clients pay you. Most clients I work with pay within our thirty-day expectations. Some industries are notoriously late; some of your clients may be late on occasion.

For example, if you have decided that providing service to the federal government is your niche, find out what you are getting into. First, although there is a prompt-payment law, some agencies have a difficult time paying within thirty days. This is due not to a lack of funds but to a lack of efficient processes. As I write this, one of our organizations is two months behind in paying us due to some technicality, and another is awaiting money from a specific source. We know we will be paid, but we do not know when! These kinds of situations can be detrimental to your cash flow if you are not prepared for them. Second, government work is fickle.

Here today, gone tomorrow. Even with a signed contract, the federal government has the right to cancel at any time. As a taxpayer, I am fine with that. I don't want my tax dollars spent if they should not be spent. However, if you are the consultant whose eighteen-month contract has been cancelled prematurely, you may need to scramble to fill in the lost revenue.

Government work is fickle.

The federal government also offers you the choice of accepting payment for your services in the form of a credit card. The advantage is that you can be paid immediately upon completing the work. The disadvantages are that you will take a discount of approximately 5 percent and pay a monthly fee to the credit card company to maintain the service.

Serving government agencies, especially our Department of Defense clients, has always been a rewarding part of our work, so we don't want to eliminate it. Our strategy is to have government contracts generate a maximum of 35 percent of our revenue. This strategy has helped us balance working with great clients and maintaining a healthy revenue stream for the business.

Include Project Initiation Fees in Your Proposals

You can reduce cash-flow concerns by requesting a sum in advance to initiate the contract. Put an amount in your proposal, normally a few thousand dollars to cover initial out-of-pocket expenses, such as travel. Your contract could read, "$10,000 is due to initiate this project and to cover initial out-of-pocket expenses." We prefer to avoid this technique, because we want to always project an image of success—including financial stability. The technique, though perfectly legitimate and used by many successful firms to show commitment from the client, can suggest a shortage of cash. Your business philosophy will determine your decision about whether or not to use this business practice.

Offer a Prepayment Discount

Some consultants offer their clients a discount of 3 to 7 percent if they prepay. I have never done this, but those who use it like it. I admit that the reason I do not use this technique is that it feels amateurish. Others offer a 1 to 3 percent discount for early payment, say within ten days of the invoice date.

Refrain from Paying Client Expenses

Rather than paying for copying, research, or other direct client costs out of your pocket, send the invoices to the client. Paying for them yourself and then asking for reimbursement can tie up your cash for over thirty days.

Make Your Money Work for You

You can reduce cash-flow problems by ensuring that the money you do have is working for you. Few people think of a business as having a savings account, but the interest you earn is as valuable as working a few extra hours! Talk to your accountant for other ideas.

Bank on Good Advice

Selecting a bank and banker is second only to selecting your accountant. It is important that you keep separate accounts for your business. Commingled business and personal funds may raise tax or liability issues. Your banking needs may not seem critical initially, but you will find that a good banker can become a close and valuable partner. How do you begin? Ask your accountant and your attorney for recommendations. You benefit when the members of your support team know each other and work together. Next, meet and interview the key individuals from the bank with whom you will work. What should you look for in a bank?

- Is the bank federally insured?
- Does it offer the services you need—loans, checking accounts, money market accounts, advisory services, notary public, safe-deposit box, direct deposit, IRA or Keogh services?
- How experienced is the management?
- What experience have the bank managers had with consulting firms?
- Is the location convenient for your business? What is the bank's hours of operation?
- If you plan to work internationally, can the bank handle foreign currency and offer wire transfers?
- Can the bank help you set up payroll deductions for IRAs?
- What kind of fees will you pay for your checking account? Is it free with a minimum balance?

- Will the bank place a hold on your deposits?
- How soon will you need to order checks? How much will they cost?

e-Idea

Be sure to ask your bank if you can bank electronically. Also be sure to order checks that can be used by your accounting system and printed using your computer.

- What business advice does the bank provide, and in what format—for example, brochures, phone, or seminars?
- What networking capabilities does the bank have? Can it put you in touch with suppliers, potential clients, or other business owners?
- How well did you connect with the people you've met? How comfortable will you be discussing your financial needs with them in the future?

Obtain a Line of Credit for Your Business

As quickly as you can, talk to your banker about a line of credit. A good banker will understand the need and its connection to cash flow. During your start-up phase, you could use your home as collateral if your banker doesn't find equity in your company's reputation, accounts receivable, or contracts alone. A line of credit is invaluable during a tight spot. Generally a phone call to your bank will deposit the amount you request into your account the same day. You can pay back the loan on your terms, sometimes paying only the interest each month.

Use a Business Credit Card Wisely

A business credit card can allow you to delay a payment for up to forty-five days. For example, let's say your credit card billing period runs from the first of the month to the end of the month. You purchase office supplies on the third of the month. The credit card company doesn't send your bill until the thirtieth of the month, and you have two weeks before it is due, on the fifteenth of the month. You have delayed payment for forty-two days from the date you purchased the supplies. This period can be longer if your credit card company gives you longer to pay or shorter if you make your purchase later in the month. No matter what the dates, a credit card can help cash flow. One word of caution: the best way to use a credit card is to pay the balance every month to avoid the huge interest rates of 14 percent, 18 percent, or even 21 percent. Don't run a credit card bill up so high that you are stuck paying these high interest rates.

Compare Leasing and Purchase Rates Carefully

I have always been a "buy it with cash" kind of person to avoid the interest rates. In fact, I was in business for ten years before I even considered leasing equipment. One year we needed a new copier and were short of cash. I studied the leasing agreement. It compared favorably to a cash purchase when I considered the maintenance agreement and the outright purchase option at the end of the leasing period. Since that experience, I always make the comparisons.

Play Up Your Small-Business Status

If you are a small business, you can type "Small business. Please expedite payment" at the bottom of your invoices. We've never used this technique, but have been told that it works with empathic accounts payable departments.

Act on Late Payments Immediately

Even when you stay on top of invoices and send them out in a timely way, late payments will create a cash-flow issue. How do you deal with late payments? First, determine why the payment is late. It can be for any of the following reasons:

- The client did not receive the invoice.
- One or more of the organization's processes caused a delay.
- The client may be deliberately paying late to manage cash flow or for other reasons.

Begin by calling the organization's accounts payable department to learn whether the invoice was received. If the organization is notoriously late, you may wish to call one week after you send it to ensure that it is in their hands.

Next, call the client for whom you completed the work and ask if your work was satisfactory. Assuming that the answer is yes, say that the reason you were asking is that the payment is past due, and you were wondering if it was being held up for anything for which you were responsible. This will usually result in your client's taking some action to help expedite your payment.

Last, submit a second bill that includes a new date, a statement that this is a "second bill," and a late-payment charge identified on the bill. Often consultants want to give the client another chance and not add the late-payment charge. You may if there was an unusual processing problem. You should if the bill never arrived. However, if the payment is more than a week late without good reason, submit a second invoice with the additional late fee added.

Act on late payments immediately.

What amount should you charge for the late payment? Charge 1 to 2 percent per month. The very last line on our invoices reads, "A late payment charge of 1½ percent will be assessed for all bills over 30 days." Some consultants use a ten- or fifteen-day payment schedule. If you choose something other than the conventional thirty days, it should be spelled out in the agreement or contract you have with the client.

How can you mitigate the impact of late payments? If you have had experience with a late payer, you may wish to request staggered payments for long projects including a start-up fee, a midproject fee, and a completion fee. You could also try billing more frequently, perhaps twice a month rather than once. You may wish to offer a prepayment discount as suggested earlier in this chapter. And, as Laurie Lewis (2000) states in *What to Charge*, "Do not accept more work from a client who owes you a bundle!" Make it your company "policy" that you do not accept new work from clients who are late in paying.

Pay Bills When They Are Due, Not Before

Have you ever received a bill to renew a magazine when the subscription still had four months left? This is a common practice. Watch the due dates on bills for professional organizations, magazines, clubs, and others whose process is to bill you three or four months before the due date. You can file the bill you receive for later payment or even toss it! My professional organization bills me four times before they really expect payment.

Compare Actual Expenses to the Budget Every Month

As I will be discussing further in the next section, it is critical that you keep informed about the status of your expenses: what's been paid, what's due this month, and which categories are ahead or behind budget. The budgeted amounts may be a real guessing game your first year, but projecting your budget is a learning tool. The amounts for the second year will be more accurate if based on your first year's actual totals.

e-Idea

If you have not selected your accounting software, speak with your accountant first. Life will be easier if your software is compatible with your accountant's software and if your accountant is familiar with the package. Accounting software commonly used by small businesses includes Quick-Books Pro, One-Write Plus, MYOB (Mind Your Own Business), and Peach Tree. These packages are reasonably priced. If you are not familiar with accounting software, have your accountant help you set it up so that you will be able to manipulate the data to produce the most useful reports for you.

TRACK EXPENSES

Where is all the money going? If you are not good at the details of bookkeeping, find someone else to do it for you. Although you are a consultant, you must also consider yourself a business owner. Tracking every expense is imperative. You may be lax about requesting and saving all those $4 parking receipts when you visit the library each week. Indeed, $4 does not seem like much. However, if you visit that library once or twice a week for resources, your parking receipts could easily add up to $200 worth of expenses. If your total state and federal tax bracket is 40 percent, you've just thrown away $80!

Now think about how many other things you might "forget" to record, such as tolls, business-related books or magazines, client gifts, mileage, seminar supplies you purchase on-site, office supplies you pick up on the weekend, light bulbs, cleaning supplies, or paper products you bring into the office from home.

What's the solution? Develop an easy way to gather and track expenses. For example, our consultants use envelopes for tracking expenses and for filing receipts. The 9"×4" business-size envelopes identify the consultant, the client, the date, and a list of the expenses. We had a printer print several thousand for a very reasonable cost. They serve several purposes: They serve as a place to put the receipts while we are collecting them; they provide a method for tracking expenses by client, even if we are in the same city for two separate clients; and they are neatly stored by project for easy retrieval at a later date if necessary. I use the same envelope system to store office supply or repair receipts for the month.

In Chapter Four we listed items that might be in your monthly budget. These same budget line items are your expenses. You will want to track them for two reasons.

First, you will want to study them. Your expense record will provide the most information about your financial situation. It will tell you where you might cut back if you need to save, what you can expect in upcoming cash flow, and what you could prepay if you show too large a profit at the end of the year. (Perhaps the last item is surprising after the discussion about tight cash flow. You should assume that you will be so successful that you will face that problem in a year or two!)

The second reason you will want to track your expenses is to ensure that you can easily compile your records prior to filing your taxes. You will want to claim as many legitimate deductions as possible because it reduces your tax bill. Poor record keeping takes cash out of your pocket.

Poor record keeping takes cash out of your pocket.

The monthly expense record in Exhibit 6.1 will be valuable for tracking your monthly expenses. The following categories identify where your money will go.

Accounting, Banking, and Legal Fees. As we discussed in Chapter Four, finding an accountant is one of your first tasks. Good accountants will save you five times what they cost. There is no way (unless you are an accounting consultant) that you can keep up with all the tax law changes. For example, whenever new retirement

Exhibit 6.1. Monthly Expense Worksheet and Record.

Account	Budget	Jan	Feb	Mar	April	May	June	July	Aug	Sept	Oct	Nov	Dec	Total
Accounting, banking, legal fees														
Advertising and marketing														
Automobile expenses														
Books and resources														
Clerical support														
Copying and printing														
Donations														
Dues and subscriptions														
Entertainment														
Equipment leases														
Insurance														
Interest and loans														
Licenses														
Meals														
Office supplies														
Pension plan														
Postage														
Professional development														
Professional fees														
Rent														
Repairs and maintenance														
Resources														
Salaries														
Seminar expenses														
Taxes														
Telephone														
Travel														
Utilities														
Total														

The Business of Consulting, Second Edition. Copyright © 2007 by John Wiley & Sons, Inc. Reproduced by permission of Pfeiffer, an Imprint of Wiley. www.pfeiffer.com

plans are offered or changed, my accountant informs me and helps me decide whether I should maintain the plan I have for me and my employees or switch to a new one.

You will have few legal fees beyond your initial incorporation, but you will likely have some minor monthly banking charges.

Advertising and Marketing. Initially, you will have the expense of creating a website and printing a brochure or introductory piece to let people know who you are and what your capabilities are. I started out with a simple one-page introduction printed on high-quality stationery. I never have completed a "mailing" of our corporate brochure, but it is useful as an introduction piece or as something to leave when I visit a potential client. Expenses here may include a special announcement mailing, books or articles you purchase to send to clients or potential clients, or any marketing firm expenses you incur.

Automobile Expenses. Establish a good tracking system for your automobile expenses. If you use the same vehicle for personal and business use, you will most likely track mileage only. The best way to handle this is to keep a clipboard with a form like the one in Exhibit 6.2 that allows you to track the date, destination, purpose, beginning and ending odometer readings, and total mileage. Remember, you cannot deduct mileage going to and from your office. If you visit a client first, you cannot count that first leg of your trip either. Your accountant will assist you with the nuances of mileage.

Books and Resources. Keep up on the latest books in your field. A good library is a real time saver when it comes to developing new materials or writing proposals.

Copying and Printing. If you do not purchase or lease your own copy machine, build a good relationship with the employees at your local copy center. There will be days when you will need a rush job!

Donations. Your business may make monetary or equipment donations to local charities. We donated a lettering machine to our local Head Start and old computers and software to the Salvation Army and a nursery school. The items were in good condition, but we had outgrown their use.

Exhibit 6.2. Mileage Log.

Name: _____   From: _____   To: _____

Date	Destination	Odometer Begin	End	Business Purpose	No. of Miles
				Total Miles This Sheet	

e-Idea

Be sure to purge any confidential or sensitive information from your computers before donating them to charity or anyone.

Dues and Subscriptions. Dues to professional organizations and subscriptions to professional journals are tax deductible.

Entertainment. Although you can deduct only 50 percent of the expense incurred when you take a client to dinner, you must still track it and maintain receipts. Track the full amount. Your accountant will take care of the reduction.

Equipment and Furniture Purchases. You may think these are only one-time purchases, but you may upgrade computers or need a new desk sooner than you think. Depending on the amount you purchase or on your financial situation at the end of the year, your accountant may suggest that you depreciate the expense over several years to capture the greatest tax advantage.

Equipment Leases. Be sure to check the advantages of leasing against purchasing. Sometimes it's just a matter of preference, but there also may be savings with one or the other.

Insurance. This is a broad category and may include fleet insurance if you own a company vehicle, fire and theft if you rent or own an office, group health if you have employees, business liability insurance, disability insurance, and a number of others. Again, your accountant is the best source for determining which would be better as business expenses and which would be better as personal expenses. For example, we have group health insurance for employees, but the law does not allow me to include my insurance as a business expense. Although my employees do not need to claim the premiums as income, as the owner, I do.

Interest and Loans. You may have taken out a loan to start your business. The interest is tax deductible. Although the principal is not a deductible expense, the interest and any payments you make to reduce the principal will still affect your cash flow. By the way, even if you loaned yourself the money to start your business, you should track it.

Licenses. Check into state or city licenses that are required to do business in your city.

Meals. Local meals are tax deductible when they are business related. Keep all receipts for food when you travel. Again, as with the entertainment category, only 50 percent of the actual cost is tax deductible. Your accountant will assist you with this process at tax time.

Office Supplies. This category includes paper supplies, ink cartridges for your printer, rubber bands, pens, paper towels, glass cleaner (to clean your copier's glass), floor mats, light bulbs, and anything else you need to keep an office operating.

Pension Plan. Excellent plans exist for small businesses. Check into them soon, even if you don't think you can afford one. Your accountant may demonstrate to you that you can't afford *not* to invest in a plan.

Postage. This is of course the cost of sending proposals, marketing materials, and other correspondence using the postal service or private carriers.

Professional Development. Stay current with the changes in your field. This category includes the costs for conferences, training, or local professional meetings you may attend.

Professional Fees. This category is for subcontractors you may hire to assist you with larger projects.

Rent. Track your office rent expense in this category.

Repairs and Maintenance. Often these expenses are included in an office lease. However, you may need to hire your own cleaning firm. In addition, if you own your computers, copier, and fax machines, their repairs will be tracked in this category.

Salaries. Pay yourself first. You've heard that advice before. This category also includes anyone else you have hired, such as your secretary, receptionist, assistant, or professionals who are on your payroll.

Seminar Expenses. You may need to purchase a DVD to use during a training session. You may have some materials that you use in your sessions. For example, I use crayons, play dough, clay, jump ropes, and other toys in my creativity sessions. Sometimes it is easier to purchase these on-site than to ship them.

Taxes. This category includes local business taxes, personal property taxes, unemployment taxes, self-employment taxes, FICA, and other payroll taxes.

Telephone. Telephone calls, fax transmissions, and your email expenses are listed here.

Travel. Travel expenses include taxi fares, airfares, hotel rooms, shuttle buses, parking, tips, and other costs incurred as a result of getting to and staying at a site to conduct business. The expense report in Exhibit 6.3 will help you track travel and other out-of-pocket expenses you incur throughout the month. The "Employee Tax Record" section tracks salary and associated taxes for you and each of your employees.

Utilities. Electricity, water, heat, or air conditioning may be included in your office rent. If you are working out of your home, your accountant will assist you in determining what percentage of the total you can consider a business expense.

Breaking expenses into categories like this creates a system that makes it easy for you to track expenses, manage cash flow, and predict revenue needed for next month as well as next year. In addition, the structure will pay dividends in time saved when preparing your tax statement.

SET ASIDE PETTY CASH

If you find yourself digging into your own pocket to pay for postage or other small purchases during the month, you may want to create a petty cash fund. Having cash on hand eliminates the need for you to record every little expense for reimbursement. To establish the fund, write a check out to petty cash. Keep the money in a safe place separate from your personal money. The form in Exhibit 6.4 provides an easy way to track these expenditures.

⊙ Exhibit 6.3. Time Sheet and Expense Report.

Name: _____   Work Period: _____

Date	Activity	Mileage			Other Travel Expenses*			Employee Tax Record
		Destination	Miles	@.50	Travel	Lodging	Meals	Gross =
								– State Tax
								– Federal Tax
								– SS Tax
								+ Expenses
								– Deductions
								Net =

Miscellaneous*

Specify	Amount

Totals

Signature: _____   Date: _____   *Attach Receipts in Expense Envelope   Expense Total: _____

The Business of Consulting, Second Edition. Copyright © 2007 by John Wiley & Sons, Inc. Reproduced by permission of Pfeiffer, an Imprint of Wiley. www.pfeiffer.com

Exhibit 6.4. Petty Cash Record.

From: _____ To: _____

Date	Paid to Whom	Expense Account Debited	Deposit	Amount of Expense	Balance
Balance Forward ⟶					

e-Idea

Although many financial tracking forms are on the CD accompanying this book, most forms will also be found on the accounting software you select. Become familiar with the software so that you can customize the forms to make them begin working for you right away.

CHARGE YOUR CLIENT

In general, we consultants are not very confident about what we charge our clients. Perhaps this is due to the many jokes and cartoons making fun of consultants and our fees. I remember how difficult it was to state my fee when I first raised it to $1,000. "I charge one th-th-th-thousand dollars a day," I would stutter. Certainly the exercise in Chapter Three showing how easily a $1,500 daily charge can be accounted for should allow you to feel more confident. Although it is important that *we* know that our prices are fair, it is even more important that *our clients* be satisfied that they receive value for their investment.

If we have difficulty stating our fees, we have even more difficulty ensuring that our clients know what we did for them. Granted, much of our work can be elusive, intangible, and invisible, but that does not mean that it is not valuable. Keep your work in front of your clients—not bragging, but informing. Try these suggestions:

- Itemize your invoice to include specific accomplishments.
- Itemize things you did without charge and specify the amount as $0.00. We often list books we have provided at no extra charge or an unscheduled meeting.
- Submit your invoice in person, discussing what it covers.
- When on-site, save the end of your day to update your client about recent activities and their results.
- Submit a brief ongoing status report if visits are not practical.
- When your client requests something special, follow up personally with the results.
- Keep the client informed of what is happening behind the scenes. What should the client expect to see or hear?
- If there are extended time periods between your activities or site visits, make a phone call to stay in the loop and to show that you care.

- Send books or articles. We all come across things that we think would be perfect reading for a particular client. Make it possible by sending it!

Each of these ideas ensures that you keep your client informed of the value you are adding to the organization.

Invoices

As mentioned previously in this chapter, issuing invoices should be one of your top priorities. You should submit them as soon as the project has ended. If the project's duration is greater than thirty days, bill monthly or every two weeks for deliverables you have completed, plus the expenses incurred. This is best for you and for your client. You prevent cash-flow problems, and your client will find it easier to pay several small invoices each month than one large one after four months. The invoicing summary in Exhibit 6.5 provides an easy method to track the date you invoiced the client, what services you invoiced for, and the date the client's payment was received.

Your invoice should provide all the information necessary for a client to quickly approve payment. Include these items:

- Your corporate name, address, and telephone number. (During start-up, use your stationery rather than have actual invoices printed.)
- A numbering system for tracking invoices.
- The billing date.
- The address and the name of the person to whom the invoice is sent.
- An itemized list of the tasks completed, dates, and hours if appropriate.
- The name of the person completing the tasks.
- A list of the expenses incurred.
- Total of the entire invoice.
- Terms of the invoice, such as due date and consequences of late payments.
- Your federal taxpayer ID number or your Social Security number.
- The name of the person to whom questions may be addressed (optional).

In addition to the invoice, attach copies of receipts for expenses incurred—for example, a hotel bill, meal receipt, or copy-center invoice. Although your client may not require these receipts, I believe it builds trust and is a good practice. Exhibit 6.6 is a simple yet complete invoice format.

Exhibit 6.5. Invoice Summary.

Work Date	Organization	Consultant	Invoice Number	Billed	Paid	Facilitator Fee	Materials Fee	Expenses	Total Fee
Total									

The Business of Consulting, Second Edition. Copyright © 2007 by John Wiley & Sons, Inc. Reproduced by permission of Pfeiffer, an Imprint of Wiley. www.pfeiffer.com

Exhibit 6.6. Invoice.

INVOICE

100-000111-20XX

TO: Mr. Dale Woodward
Gilbert Manufacturing
333 Ridge Road
Anywhere, NY 10000

Invoice Date: January 24, 20XX

For: "Talent Management Applied: Learning from
Our Experience" for Gilbert Manufacturing
on January 23, 20XX.
Elizabeth Drake, Facilitator
Facilitator Fee . . . . $ 4,000.00

EXPENSES: Mileage Round Trip to Airport:
80 miles @$.50 per mile . . . . $ 40.00
Airfare $710.00
Airport parking . . . . $ 30.00
Lodging $190.00
Books . . . . $ 0.00
Expense Total . . . . $ 970.00

Amount Due: . . . .$ **4,970.00**

Terms: Due upon receipt

Payable to: ebb associates inc
Box 8249
Norfolk, VA 23503

Federal ID# 33-5333XXX

2 percent late fee charged per month for accounts due over 15 days

e-Idea

Once you have an invoice format that meets your needs, save the template on your computer to make it easier to invoice each time.

The Clients' Expenses

For what expenses can you expect the client to be responsible? In almost all cases, the client will reimburse all travel expenses incurred when you are away from home: airfare, taxis, mileage to and from the airport, parking, reasonable lodging, meals, and tips. If you have agreed to it, a client may also cover material costs, audiovisual equipment and supplies (for example, LCD or high-definition DVD recorder/player rental and CDs or DVDs), seminar supplies, room rental, and refreshments. Depending on the industry you serve and your pricing structure, your client may also reimburse you for telephone expenses, overnight mail, computer time, or computer program development. We consider telephone calls and express shipping a cost of doing business and include them as a part of our overhead.

*Keep your client informed of the value
you are adding to the organization.*

Do not expect a client to cover laundry, dry cleaning, liquor, upgraded hotel rooms, entertainment, or unrelated phone calls when you travel. Local travel and meals are not reimbursable. Postage is not generally reimbursed, unless you have a large mailing to send as a part of the contract.

In any event, all reimbursables should be clearly spelled out at the beginning of any contract.

PROJECT REVENUES

As important as tracking expenses is projecting revenue. We project revenues by the month. This works for us because we have been able to adjust our accounting processes so that we pay bills only once each month. You may wish to track revenue weekly, especially if cash flow is a concern. The revenue projection form in Exhibit 6.7 can be transferred to a spreadsheet so that you can keep a running total by month as well as by organization.

Exhibit 6.7. Revenue Projections.

Organization and Project	Jan	Feb	Mar	April	May	June	July	Aug	Sept	Oct	Nov	Dec	Total
Total Revenue													

DEAL WITH BAD DEBTS

Bad debts occur when your clients do not pay you for the services provided. They occur infrequently in the consulting business, but when they do, they can be devastating to a small business. Although we have never experienced a bad debt, we have heard that professional firms can experience bad debt rates from 5 to 30 percent.

If you should have a bad debt, you may want to use a collection agency to assist you. In some cases, you may choose to take the matter to your local small claims court, where you will generally find well-informed and helpful people.

KEEP AN EYE ON YOUR NUMBERS

Although you are a consultant, you should never forget that you are running a business. Businesses exist to make a profit. The numbers will spell profit or loss for your business. You must establish processes for gathering the numbers and then keep an eye on them. As a good business owner, you will want to know where you stand financially at any given time, which means that you must read the numbers and know what they mean. Have there been increases? Decreases? You must also compare the numbers to those for the last project, the last month, the last year. Are they better? Worse? Finally, you have to play with the numbers: What if you invested in a new computer system? Prepaid bills before the end of the year?

*Never forget that you
are running a business.*

What specifically can you look for when you are studying your numbers?

Expenses

Certainly you should compare your actual expenditures with your budget. Are you over? Under? Both are worthy of investigation. If the actual amounts are over the budget, look at the detailed report. What pushed you over the limit? Is it likely to occur again? Should you adjust your budget to account for the difference? What about being under budget? That's good, so don't worry—right? Wrong! If you have budgeted for something and the money wasn't spent, you need to examine this as well. Perhaps a marketing mailing you budgeted for was not done. This may affect income several months down the road.

Businesses exist to make a profit.

It could mean something worse. Once I discovered an extra $400 in the budget. First I felt smug, then I became curious. When I finally discovered what had caused the difference, I panicked. The fire insurance on our new office building had not been paid! Remember, being under budget can be as bad as being over budget.

Value

Compare some of your expenses to the time invested to determine if the value received warrants the expense. For example, you have hired two associates to help you deliver services. Your receptionist is stretched, yet you cannot justify hiring a bookkeeper. So now you find yourself doing the payroll every other week. Check into the payroll services that abound. They do it all: figure salaries, compute the taxes, write the checks, deposit the taxes, and provide monthly as well as year-end reports and W-2s. And they do it for a reasonable fee. Consider the time you are investing in payroll or any other administrative task. Is it the best use of your time? Is this where you should invest your value?

Growth

You will certainly be comparing income to expenses, but you should also watch the overall growth trend. Is the number of projects increasing? Is your gross income growing proportionately? Are expenses growing at the same rate, or are they higher or lower than you would expect? You might think that growth is always desired. That isn't so. It is not desired if you have overscheduled yourself. It is not desired if you have decided not to hire employees. It is not desired if the projects are less profitable. And it certainly is not desired if you are working harder and enjoying it less.

Exhibit 6.8 is a form for you to track time and materials used on individual projects. Exhibit 6.9 provides a method for recording and comparing the profitability of various projects. This can assist you in determining which projects are the most profitable and in bidding on new projects.

Exhibit 6.8. Project Time and Expense Record.

Date	Team Member	Task Performed or Materials Used	Hours or Expense	Salary or Cost

Exhibit 6.9. Program Development Costs Versus Revenue.

Program Title	Company	Work Date	Production Hours	Production Cost	$ Charged

Certainly, growth can be exactly what you desire and what you have planned for. Given that, there is still one more thing to watch for. Fast growth can lead to cash-flow issues. You may need to invest in new projects up front that are not in your budget. Check the cash-flow suggestions earlier in this chapter and keep an eye on the numbers.

e-Idea

Place your spreadsheets on a memory stick. Update the memory stick every time you update the data on your office computer. This way you are not taking up space on your laptop, and you can easily refresh your data and keep them current, as well as have the data at your fingertips.

PROTECT YOUR CAPITAL INVESTMENTS

You are running a business. That means you have capital investments, and with them comes responsibility. If you own equipment, put each item on a preventive maintenance schedule. Clean phones, computers, copiers, printers, and other equipment regularly. You will benefit in the long run. Equipment will last longer, and it will not be "down" just when you need it to complete the last-minute details of a program you will conduct the next day!

Your library is a capital investment that can easily walk out the door without your vigilance. We have a complete library that can easily compete with any area library in the training, business, consulting, leadership, talent management, creativity, and communication categories. Many of our local clients and other consultants, as well as employees, borrow volumes from it. Although we want to share the resources, a library sign-out sheet allows us to do so without worrying about unreturned books. Exhibit 6.10 is a copy of that form.

This chapter should have driven home the importance of tracking and monitoring your income and expenses. You could be the best consultant in the world, but if you do not make money, you will not remain in business, and the world will never know about your consulting expertise.

Exhibit 6.10. Library Sign-Out Sheet.

Book	Borrowed By	Date	Will Return By	Returned

chapter
SEVEN

Building a Client Relationship

Hold yourself responsible for a higher standard than anybody expects of you. Never excuse yourself.

Henry Ward Beecher

You started your business to serve clients. Serve them well! You can do this only if you are continually aware of building the relationship you have with each of your clients.

Your initial contact with a new client is more important than you can imagine. Your comfort with one another and your ability to communicate clearly and candidly are critical to starting on the right foot.

The success of your interactions and the results of your project will establish and build your relationship and help you maintain a client for a long time. There is an interesting phenomenon that the longer you have clients, the longer they will continue to be clients. Now mind you, this is not about building a client's reliance on you. It is about a client who thinks of you whenever a new project comes up. With the frequent changes that businesses go through today, that can be often.

You started your business to serve clients.

179

In these relationships, you become too valuable to lose. Your knowledge of the organization, your rapport with key managers, and your experience with the political and operational factors of the organization cannot be replaced—at any cost.

Why would you want to encourage repeat business? Here are a few good reasons:

1. Repeat business means you will not need to expend time marketing your services. The client knows you—knows your capabilities and how you might help. Also, because you know the client, there will be less lag time between the time the client hires you and the time you begin the project.

2. The client will call you regularly to assist in many different situations. Each will build on past projects, and you will continue to increase in value. We are frequently referred from department to department or from division to division.

3. You will have a leg up against your competition. You have already built a relationship with the client. The trust you have built will count heavily on your side when the need arises.

4. You will not lose clients during difficult economic times. In fact, your expertise may be readily called on to help them through.

5. You will develop a valuable marketing vehicle. A client's referral is the most potent marketing tool you can have. If your project is successful and you have built solid relationships, your clients will refer you to others. Our clients market us to other organizations. This happens because we pay attention both to doing the job with quality results and to building the relationship. I am firmly convinced that without the effort we put into building the relationship, this marketing by our clients would not occur.

So how can you get to a point at which your clients market you? First, you must identify the project; your first meeting will most likely determine that. Next, you must build the relationship. Every interaction, every product, and every result will make a difference. Finally, you must maintain the relationship. The project ends, not the relationship. Your follow-up will maintain the relationship.

The project ends,
not the relationship.

THE FIRST MEETING

Your initial meeting is critical. It sets a tone for the rest of the relationship, which is why it is important to be yourself in this meeting. Many consultants come prepared for their initial introduction with a "dog and pony show"—a slick PowerPoint presentation, materials in a bound folder, and a precisely worded presentation. If that's your style and it works for you, continue doing it. We try to create a conversation with the client; that's our style. It's natural, and it sets the tone for the rest of the relationship. How do we fare? We are regularly pitted against the top consulting firms in the United States—many of those listed in Chapter One. We are awarded the work a much higher percentage of the time than not. Be yourself. That way, if you land the project, you won't struggle to continue some charade you used to get it.

The skills you need for this first meeting read like an Interpersonal Skills 101 class:

- Read the client to determine whether to make small talk first or get right down to business. Attending to the client's communication style will lay a foundation for the rest of the discussion.
- Listen for understanding, especially to determine the critical points. Sometimes clients will not be clear about what they want. Read between the lines and interpret meaning or structure the content to make sense of the situation. Remember that every statement has at least two messages: the content and the intent.
- Ask pertinent and thought-provoking questions. Before you attend the meeting, develop three to ten questions based on what you know about the situation. Three well thought out questions will usually start a discussion. You will probably not have time to ask ten questions, and if you have more than ten, it will be difficult to prioritize while you're trying to focus.
- Put others at ease by remembering and using their names, showing interest in their needs, and balancing the discussion appropriately in a group. Ask for a list of attendees and their positions for your first meeting. Study the names before the meeting. After you are introduced, subtly make a seating chart as a reference. Then use people's names throughout the meeting.
- Exude self-confidence without arrogance. You will display your self-confidence with your body language as much as anything, so use good eye contact, a pleasant demeanor, and confident posture. The client will want to know about your past

experience. Providing examples or relating similar situations should be a natural part of the discussion. Take care to avoid bragging, giving too much detail, or sounding as if you have rehearsed a rote speech.

• Project a professional image. First impressions count. A firm handshake, appropriate attire, and genuine interest in the client and the organization you are visiting will help you make a great first impression.

As I said in Chapter Two, your personality, not your expertise, will land most contracts. That may disappoint you, but it is the truth. Sure, you must have the basic skills in place, but that's a given. Your wit, charm, sincerity, professionalism, or interpersonal skills will be the deciding factor at this stage.

Your personality, not your expertise,
will land most contracts.

A quick measure of how you're doing can be determined by how much you are talking. If the clients are doing the majority of the talking, it's a sign that they feel comfortable with you and that you are asking appropriate questions. If you are doing more talking, more selling than listening, your chances of successfully landing the contract are decreasing.

FOUR PHASES OF BUILDING A CLIENT-CONSULTANT PARTNERSHIP

The relationship you begin to establish during the first meeting lays the groundwork for a solid client-consultant partnership—one in which both the client and the consultant are equal, contributing counterparts in an effort to accomplish a mutual goal.

Building a partnership with your client may be similar to building a friendship or a team. Let's explore building a client-consultant partnership in four phases: (1) finding the right match, (2) getting to know one another, (3) being productive, and (4) creating independence.

Phase I focuses on finding the right match and deciding whether you and the client can work together. When you are introduced to someone, you make decisions about whether you want to pursue a relationship. Even though you and your client may already be discussing the project, a final decision about how to move forward has not been made. I have been in this phase for as little as ten minutes and as long as a couple of months.

Phase II focuses on getting to know one another. At this point a commitment exists to move the project to the next level. The relationship is moving forward as well. Both parties are learning everything they can about one another and how to work together effectively.

Phase III occurs when you and your client are productive. The project is in full swing. If you and your client have worked on the relationship, your partnership is in full swing as well.

Phase IV focuses on helping the client become independent. The project is coming to a close. By focusing on the client's independence, you ensure that the organization continues to be successful. Equally important, you ensure that your relationship continues to be healthy.

Phase I: Finding the Right Match

During this phase, you will focus on two areas: obtaining information and setting expectations. Both lead to a final decision about whether to move forward with the project.

Getting Information. Prior to meeting someone of interest, you may ask questions and try to gather information about that person. Prior to meeting a client, you may choose to obtain the best public information available about the organization and the industry. How? Ask people. Go to the client's website. Visit the library. Check the industry journals. Obtain a copy of the client company's most recent annual report.

If you are meeting someone from an industry that is new to you, become familiar with the general industry jargon. Reading several industry journals will help.

This is also the time to define the scope of the effort. Your client may not be able to answer all questions at this time, but it is important that you clarify the scope as much as possible. You may find that the project is larger than you want to take on.

We've found it valuable to discuss past projects for which the client used consultants. Answers to simple questions, such as "What went well?" and "What would you do differently?" provide information about how the client likes to work.

Your client will be obtaining information from you, too. Be prepared to provide references, and encourage the client to call them. Speaking with your former clients gives a potential client confidence in your abilities. Last, discuss your consulting fee and how you invoice.

Setting Expectations. Establishing expectations between you and your client lays a solid foundation for the relationship. The process is often referred to as "contracting."

Contracting is the process by which you and your client identify, clarify, and agree on the needs, wants, and expectations of both you and your client. Contracting is critical in the first phase, because it is here that you and your client will begin to build your partnership, clarify the project, and understand and appreciate one another's principles, styles, and values.

In his best-selling classic, *Flawless Consulting,* Peter Block (2000) explains contracting as the process to reach "an explicit agreement of what the consultant and client expect from each other and how they are going to work together." Your contracting discussion should explore and come to agreement on the following:

- Your role, the client's role, and how they are related.
- The project's time frame.
- The expected outcome of the project.
- The support, resources, and information you will need from the client.
- How this project fits into the larger organizational picture and the organization's vision.

As a result of this discussion, you should have a better idea of the client's ability to support the effort and the organization's support for the project; you should also have a sense of some of the values that you share and where you differ, the client's vision for the project, and your desire to complete the project.

In addition, you should have determined who your primary client is. The primary client is most often the individual who hired you for the project, but on a few rare occasions, one department—human resources for example—may actually bring you in and provide the budget for work you conduct in another department.

You will also have secondary clients and stakeholders. They are the individuals who are affected by your work, but are not directing it.

Exhibit 7.1 is a list of questions you can use in two ways: as a reminder before the contracting meeting of all the things you must discuss during the meeting, and as a means of evaluating your behavior after the meeting.

Exhibit 7.1. Contracting Checklist.

Evaluate the contracting meeting with your client.

Did I:

		Yes	No
1.	Do my homework before the meeting?	❏	❏
2.	Determine the primary client?	❏	❏
3.	Determine the secondary clients and stakeholders?	❏	❏
4.	Define the scope of the effort?	❏	❏
5.	Elicit the clients' specific needs and expectations?	❏	❏
6.	Identify shared values and differences?	❏	❏
7.	Evaluate the client's expertise and ability to support the effort?	❏	❏
8.	Discuss my rates and consulting approach?	❏	❏
9.	Clearly state my needs and expectations?	❏	❏
10.	Obtain a sense of client commitment to the effort?	❏	❏
11.	Provide references?	❏	❏

Asking Questions. Questions are the means by which the client and consultant determine if they have found the right match. Either you or the client may find the following questions helpful:

- What are your mission, vision, and guiding principles?
- How would you define your organization's culture and values?
- What values are most important to your organization?
- What resources are available (time, people, space)?
- What observation opportunities exist (consultant in action, meetings, work processes)?
- How will we conduct a front-end analysis, and what type should it be?
- What options are available to work through a relationship problem?
- What logistics do we need to clarify (shared copyright, scheduling, reporting)?

Additional questions you might ask to learn more about the organization include these:

- How do you feel about my being brought into the organization?
- What's it like to work here?
- How will this organization be different as a result of this intervention?

Phase II: Getting to Know One Another

When you build relationships with individuals, you spend time getting to know them. You can do the same thing with your clients. This phase is typically considered the data-collection step in consulting. It is natural that as you build the relationship, you learn everything you can about the client. You learned things about the client in Phase I, but now you are on-site, asking questions, touring plants, observing meetings, interviewing employees, or eating in the corporate dining room.

As with a personal relationship, the more you know about the organization, the better you will understand its people, its problems, and its culture. Every time you interview key employees of the organization, you influence the relationship. You will be gaining information about the organization's attitudes, skills, and climate.

During this phase you have the opportunity to invest in the relationship by modeling appropriate skills. Every interaction is an opportunity to model good communication, teamwork, and high-quality work. The relationship benefits in two ways: you gain respect from the client, and the client has an opportunity to observe professional skills.

Initial planning takes place during Phase II. You will provide an analysis of the situation, recommendations, and a plan for proceeding. You will reach consensus around the plan as well as agreement about how to keep the client informed. Provide ample opportunity for milestones, progress reports, and other communication that will keep the client informed of progress. Maintaining an open line of communication will continue to build the relationship. If you spend the time getting to know the people and the organization, you will begin to build a trusting relationship.

Phase III: Being Productive

Several books have been written about how to manage an external consultant. Chances are good that your client has not read any of these books and will be expecting you to manage the project and the relationship. During this implementation stage, you have the opportunity to continue to build the relationship through what you deliver and how you deliver your services.

What You Deliver. All clients I have worked with believe that they are special and that their business is unique. Perhaps that's human nature. Although you will find plenty of similarities from client to client, you must still study the situation with an open mind. Look for the differences. That allows you to create customized solutions for the client more easily.

You will probably need to conduct one-on-one coaching sessions. Be honest and helpful. Building the relationship does not mean that you will agree with everything the individual does or says. In fact, once individuals reach a certain level, they rarely receive candid feedback from anyone within the organization. How many employees give feedback to the president?

Become an active member of the client's team. You can do more as a part of the team than by maintaining your separateness. Become involved. Be aware of the "magic wand" syndrome. Some clients may believe that you have arrived to "fix things." Permanent fixes occur only if you and the client work together in a partnership.

Things will go wrong. You will uncover things you wish you had not. The unexpected will occur. In every instance, be honest, candid, and timely about issues, problems, and concerns. Don't be afraid to say, "It's not working." Keep the right person informed. Your honesty and candor will be respected by everyone.

While you're in the thick of implementation, it may be difficult to focus on the day when you will no longer be involved in the project. However, this is the ideal time to plan for the skills your client will need to ensure continued success. Your client will brag about you if you make this happen. That means you must attend to it now, through coaching, teaching, and mentoring. Continually create ways to promote the client's independence.

Communicate, communicate, communicate! Keep everyone informed. You will not be able to communicate too much. Guaranteed! Find many ways to keep employees informed, such as memos, email, posters, telephone trees, town meetings, presentations, Q&A sessions, and paycheck stuffers. Help your client develop a communication plan.

How You Deliver Services. As in any business, how you deliver your services is as important as the service you provide. Build your relationship with your client by providing superb service. As with any business, the following eight commonly accepted elements of service apply to your consulting practice:

1. *Time.* How much time are you spending on the project? Too little and your clients will wonder what they are paying for; too much and your clients will wonder if you have moved in! Don't forget to plan time to build the client relationship. It's a key element in delivering high-quality service.

2. *Timeliness.* Do you do what you say you are going to do when you say you will? Do you return phone calls promptly?

3. *Completeness.* Do you do everything you say you will? Do you do everything you should do? Always?

4. *Courtesy.* Do you treat everyone in your client's firm respectfully, politely, and cheerfully? Do you greet the receptionist with the same positive attention with which you greet the CEO?

5. *Consistency.* Do you provide the same high-quality services to all clients and to every department and to everyone within each organization?

6. *Convenience.* Are you easy to reach? Are you able to turn on a dime to meet special needs that may come up?

7. *Accuracy.* Do you provide your service right the first time? Do you aim for "flawless consulting"? Do the results demonstrate the level of quality that was expected initially?

8. *Responsiveness.* How quickly do you respond if something goes awry? Do you accept the responsibility for problems?

Phase IV: Creating Independence

As the excitement of the project winds down and you complete your final tasks with the client, you may not feel as enthusiastic about the project as you did when you started. This is natural, something like the postholiday letdown that sometimes occurs. Some consultants avoid this unpleasant feeling by focusing on their next clients. They just drift away. This is unfair to the client. Finish the project completely. Maintain your standards of quality.

You still have work to do. Although you should have been building your client's independence throughout the project, this is the time to confirm that the client has the tools and skills to continue without you. You may want to ensure that trainers are certified to teach ongoing classes, that supervisors are comfortable using the new computer program, that the project manager knows where to obtain additional information and support, or that the internal coaches know how to use the resources you designed for them.

You will want to ensure that the client knows to contact you with questions or concerns after the project has ended. We tell our clients that they can't get rid of us! What we mean by that is that our initial consulting fee grants them the privilege to call us at any time with questions, when they need ideas, if they need advice, or if they just need to vent.

There is a fine line between making the client dependent on you and providing help when it is really needed. After you have worked with a client and know the organization well, it's easy to provide additional ideas and support.

During this phase you will want to discuss continued communication. Identify who will be the best point of contact for future communication or follow-up. Let your client know that you will continue to maintain contact by sending articles, books, or notes and with periodic phone calls. Find out what the client's needs are as well.

Celebrate the project's success with your client. Celebrations are a great way to establish closure to the project. You could take the client to lunch or give a small gift that represents the partnership you have developed.

When you return to your office, don't forget to send a follow-up note thanking your client for the business and the opportunity to provide service.

Exhibits 7.2 and 7.3 provide two client-consultant partnership checklists—one for you and one for your client. These can serve as reminders for what you can do during each phase to build the relationship or can serve as discussion starters for you and your client during the early part of your relationship.

Exhibit 7.2. Client-Consultant Partnership: Consultant Checklist.

Phase I: Finding the Right Match

- ❏ Obtain the best public information available about the organization and the industry.
- ❏ Learn general industry jargon.
- ❏ Define the scope of the effort.
- ❏ Require that the client specifically define expectations and who does what.
- ❏ Evaluate the client's ability to support the effort.
- ❏ Identify shared values and differences.
- ❏ Identify the client's vision for the project.
- ❏ Provide rates and anticipated invoicing plan.
- ❏ Obtain feeling for the organization's support.
- ❏ Provide references.
- ❏ Discuss the efforts and biases of previous consultants.

Phase II: Getting to Know One Another

- ❏ Learn everything possible about the client.
- ❏ Get inside the organization to understand its culture.
- ❏ Interview key people.
- ❏ Develop baseline information about attitudes, skills, and climate.
- ❏ Model skills at every opportunity.
- ❏ Provide an initial plan.

Exhibit 7.2. Client-Consultant Partnership: Consultant Checklist, Cont'd.

❑ Build consensus around the plan.

❑ Plan for milestones, progress reports, and communication.

Phase III: Being Productive

❑ Study the situation with an open mind.

❑ Create customized solutions.

❑ Conduct one-on-one coaching sessions.

❑ Become an active member of the client's team.

❑ Determine the client's self-sufficiency needs for the future.

❑ Be aware of the "magic wand" syndrome.

❑ Be honest, candid, and timely with issues and concerns.

❑ Continually create ways to promote the client's independence.

❑ Communicate, communicate, communicate!

Phase IV: Creating Independence

❑ Validate self-sufficiency.

❑ Develop a system of continued communication.

❑ Determine the best point of contact for future communication or follow-up.

❑ Continue to maintain contact by sending articles, books, or notes and with periodic phone calls.

❑ Celebrate success with the client.

**Exhibit 7.3. Client-Consultant Partnership:
Client Checklist.**

Phase I: Finding the Right Match

❑ Request a proposal to ensure that the consultant understands the situation.

❑ Learn about the consultant's company.

❑ Contact references and past clients.

❑ Obtain information: how long the consultant has been in business, the consultant's background and general reputation, the type of clients the consultant has served, and whether or not the consultant has repeat business.

❑ Observe the consultant in action, if possible.

❑ Check the consultant's experience in your industry.

❑ Identify shared values and differences.

❑ Determine capabilities versus needs.

❑ Determine the flexibility and availability of the consultant.

❑ Clarify specific expectations and who does what.

❑ Identify your desired time frame.

❑ Discuss limitations (money, time).

❑ Discuss known or suspected roadblocks.

❑ Think in terms of a long-term relationship: Is rapport evident? Is there a personal fit?

Phase II: Getting to Know One Another

❑ Choose one person as point of contact.

❑ Include the consultant on the team.

Exhibit 7.3. Client-Consultant Partnership:
Client Checklist, Cont'd.

❑ Ask the consultant to help identify the problem as well as the solution.

❑ Provide the consultant with telephone directory, rosters, and list of email addresses.

❑ Add the consultant to the in-house mailing list for newsletters and updates.

❑ Add the consultant to the distribution list for pertinent teams.

❑ Provide feedback on employees' initial reactions to the project.

❑ Discuss risk factors.

Phase III: Being Productive

❑ Establish regular feedback sessions.

❑ Develop a tracking system to ensure continuity.

❑ Be honest and candid with information and concerns.

❑ Communicate, communicate, communicate!

Phase IV: Creating Independence

❑ Validate self-sufficiency.

❑ Ensure that a system of continued communication is in place.

❑ Ensure that management is aware of next steps.

❑ Continue to provide news and success stories.

❑ Keep the consultant on the mailing list.

❑ Request advice if issues arise.

❑ Plan a success celebration.

HOW TO IMPROVE THE RELATIONSHIP CONTINUOUSLY

A sale is not something you close; it closes itself while you are busy serving your customer. Having a positive relationship with your client makes it easier to close your next sale, thanks to referrals. Do such a good job of completing the project and building the relationship that your client brags about you.

---

*A sale is not something you close;
it closes itself while you are busy
serving your customer.*

What can you do so that your client will brag about you? The following ideas will help you start. Then think of twenty more that are unique to you.

- Deliver more than you promise.
- Make opportunities to meet as many employees as possible.
- Request copies of the organization's newsletter and telephone directory.
- Learn something personal about your most frequent contacts.
- Keep everyone informed; publicize project status as appropriate.
- Keep both company and individual information confidential.
- Arrive early and stay late.
- Adapt your work style to that of the organization.
- Meet all deadlines.
- Find ways to build trust.
- If you cannot meet a deadline, inform your clients as soon as you know and tell them why.
- Invite the client to shadow you when appropriate.
- Make the client feel like the "only" client.
- Send articles and share books that would be helpful to individuals.
- Be tough on the problem, but supportive of the person.
- Openly offer information about yourself.
- Explore a non-business-related topic you both enjoy discussing.
- Discover common acquaintances.

e-Idea

At your off-sites, use your cell phone or digital camera to take pictures of the participants and their work. Email them back to the clients after the session.

- Discover locations where you have both lived or visited.
- Discover common experiences you have had.
- Write thank-you notes and how-are-you-doing notes.
- Call frequently when not on-site.
- Be available when not on-site.
- Follow through on special requests from individuals.
- Provide treats for special meetings or if they're not in the client's budget.
- Offer and provide resources.
- Assist with developing outlines for future needs that support the effort.
- Send surprises, such as puzzles, posters, cartoons, or tools to make the job easier.
- Be prepared to help your client deal with the stress of change.
- Support your clients. Find positive aspects in situations that they may not see.
- Avoid internal politics.
- Discuss the organization's successes, but also discuss your objective thoughts about what could be done better.
- Discuss small problems before they become big problems.
- Be prepared to deal with unplanned delays—cheerfully.
- Openly discuss delays caused by the client that may prevent you from meeting deadlines; resolve them with the client.
- Plan and work as partners.
- Give the client credit for success.
- Attend the organization's social functions.
- Coach on an individual basis.
- Teach by example.
- Ask for feedback.
- Apologize.
- Smile.

e-Idea

My husband is a pilot. Recently we took the plane up to photograph our house. One of my clients had recently built a new complex, so we also took pictures of his buildings. The pictures turned out so well with the digital camera that we emailed the photos to the company president. We also enlarged three of the best and had them matted and framed. Too far-fetched for you? Remember, you are looking for ways to get your clients to brag about you. What do you do or have access to that is unique?

Decisions

Building a solid client relationship may create situations that require you to make decisions. One such situation is difficult: it is possible to become too friendly with your client. This prevents you from maintaining your objectivity. When that happens, ethically you will need to sever the professional relationship. This is definitely a drawback to building a solid client-consultant relationship and has happened to me several times. I've always decided that the long-term friendship was worth more than the business I lost.

Another decision you may need to make is of a more positive nature: you may receive job offers. If you are good at what you do, it's going to happen. A client respects your professional approach, admires your results, and enjoys working with you. These are the ingredients that lead to a job offer. This is the kind of validation that consultants appreciate. Do you want a job, or do you want to continue as a consultant? The decision is yours.

Communication

Even if you are being paid to give advice, listening is the most critical communication skill, both for completing the project and for building the relationship. Learn and use good questioning techniques so that you are asking the right questions in the right way. Neither a wimp nor an interrogator be! Learn and use paraphrasing, summarizing, and clarifying techniques.

Remember the critical role that nonverbals play in the communication process. You may wish to pair up periodically with someone who can give you feedback about the nonverbal messages you may be sending.

IT'S THE PEOPLE

Perhaps the most important aspect to remember about building a strong client-consultant relationship is that it's all about people. You are not really building a relationship with the client organization. You are building a relationship with the individuals within the organization.

You may be working on a project *for* ABC, Inc., but you are working *with* individuals like Jack and Ilona. ABC, Inc., may pay your consulting fee, but president Francis and receptionist Lee will determine whether you earned it by adding value. You may receive a referral from ABC, Inc., but Jose will write it.

Build a relationship with everyone in the organization. They are all important to the company. Building a relationship with all employees is equally as important as building a relationship with the president. Kowtowing to the president will be observed by the employees—and by the president. Don't do it.

For me, building a relationship with my client is equally as important as completing the project and exceeding the results my client expects. It is part of my philosophy of doing business. If building relationships is not a part of your business philosophy, you may want to review the beginning of this chapter. Reconsider the business value of building relationships.

HOW TO MAINTAIN THE RELATIONSHIP AFTER THE PROJECT IS FINISHED

It would be foolish of you to ignore a relationship you have spent months to build. Many of the ideas in this chapter can be used to maintain a relationship after the project ends. Continue to stay in touch with your clients. You will find ways to maintain the relationship. Let me share some of the ways I do this:

- I purchase article reprints and books that will be interesting to my clients and send them on a regular basis.

- I stay in touch. I continue to send notes and cards. Usually I've learned a great deal about clients' likes, dislikes, pet peeves, hobbies, and interests. I may find items or reading materials about any of these. I find reasons to call clients.

- If I find that I will be near a previous client's location, I will call the client and plan to have breakfast, lunch, dinner, or just a visit. I drop in and visit clients' business locations when I can.

- I encourage my clients to call at any time. I enjoy helping them find resources or materials. I enjoy helping them track down a bit of information or someone who could help them. They call to ask if I know of available jobs or people to fill job openings that they have. They call for recommendations about conferences or books. It is a sign of a solid partnership to have requests coming my way regularly.

e-Idea

Use your network to conduct small-scale research for your clients. I recently had a client who was wondering about the amount of time it took to design an hour of classroom and online training. I emailed a dozen people, and ten responded. Their information was consistent enough for me to pass on to my client. I was able to do this in less than a week.

- I sell my clients to others regularly. I find new customers for them. I recommend them to serve on boards. I sell their products. For example, Land O'Lakes is one of my clients. If a restaurant uses Land O'Lakes butter, I never hesitate to compliment them on using the best butter in the world.
- I also call clients if I need help. I call them if I know of available jobs. I may call them to serve as a resource for someone else or to ask if I can use their names as references. Always ask permission before you use a client as a reference for another project. Even this continues to maintain the relationship.

Maintaining the relationship can be whatever you decide it should be. We have lots of repeat work. I believe that is primarily due to providing high-quality, results-oriented consulting. However, I believe that a solid relationship makes it easier for clients to remember us when new projects evolve.

We have other clients with whom we simply enjoy staying in touch. There is little chance that additional work will ensue. That isn't our primary reason for maintaining the relationship. We do it because we like to.

MORE VALUE FOR THE CLIENT

A successful client-consultant relationship provides more value for the client than the client expected. Think about how delighted you are when you receive more than what you expected: fresh flowers in your hotel room, a complimentary mug with your breakfast buffet, a free chocolate sample with your bakery purchase, or a free car wash with your oil change. A relationship focus makes it easy to remember to add extras that have value to the client but cost you little.

You'll know that you've built a solid client-consultant relationship with high-impact results when two things happen. First, you complete the job on time, within budget, and with the highest quality possible. Second, both you and the client would be pleased to work on another project together. You create value for the client in three ways to ensure both of these outcomes. These three differentiators transform your work "from good to great."

1. You customize the solution for the client. No stale answers, no been-there-done-that solutions, no Band-Aid approaches. You add value when you search for an original answer that addresses the client's unique needs. Although there is a place for best practices, a great consultant provides fresh advice and distinctive solutions that build on best practices.

2. You challenge the client. We consultants are paid well because our work is not easy. We push back, we force clients to crawl out of their boxes, and we push them out of their comfort zones so that they can see themselves—both personally and organizationally—as they really are. We do this to help clients see that it is not usually the "situation" that is the problem. Instead, in many cases the individuals or the organization may be the roadblock to success. Once clients see themselves as they are, there is a better chance for them to envision how they could be. A great consultant builds a trusting relationship as a foundation on which to provide constructive, candid, and, at times, difficult advice.

3. You create the client's independence. You are not there to make your clients dependent on you, but to ensure that clients receive the maximum return on their investment. Your work has a lasting impact only if you ensure that your clients have the competency required to sustain lasting impact. Before walking out the door, the great consultant ensures that the client owns the solutions. The great consultant inherently knows that this is the best way to be invited back.

Building the client-consultant relationship is a process that takes time and energy. Building the relationship is equally as important as your expertise. Do it because you care. Caring—truly caring—is a powerful business advantage.

HOW MANY CLIENTS DO I NEED?

Just how many of these client relationships do you need as an independent consultant? It depends on a lot of things: how long your typical engagement lasts, what percentage of face time or billable time you have with the client during the engagement, how many days per month you intend to work, and how much you are charging. All of these create a formula for the number of clients you have.

I currently have nine clients. I work with one of my clients every week on-site. I work with another once every month. I coach one on a daily basis. Two are periodic, but I do intense work with them for at least five days at least every other month. The other four are at different levels at different times. These clients will change throughout the year. One or two projects will end and then a new client will come on board, or a client from five years ago will call with a project. This number seems about right for me.

Take care that you do not end up with only one or two clients. A change in the economic climate or the industry or even a change in leadership could end a project abruptly. The average consultant (if there is such a person) will work with five to ten clients at a time. This allows for the gentle shifting of the client tide as one moves out and another moves in.

Keep in mind that this also means that while you are serving your five to ten clients, you are also marketing so that you have clients ready to move into the empty spots when you complete one of your projects.

ENSURE SUCCESS

If you see yourself as a business owner first—not simply as a consultant—you are on your road to success. You own a business, and you must act like a business owner, or you will be out of business—no matter how good a consultant you are. Observe the following principles to be a successful business owner:

Commit to consulting. Do what you love. Owning your own business isn't a hobby. It's a lifestyle. Sticking with it takes a strong commitment. Most successful consultants work long hours as they start their businesses—sometimes it may seem like 24/7. They miss family gatherings; they skip vacations. Starting your own business is risky; running it is challenging. If you really love it, it's worth it. If you don't, you will most likely fail. Success takes commitment.

Understand the value of your services and price accordingly. The biggest mistake made by new consultants is that they underprice their services. The purpose of your business is to make money. Make sure you price your services high enough so that you make money, stay in business, and as a result can continue to help your clients. Too many consultants underprice their products because they are hungry for the work or timid because of lack of experience. The result is that they don't make the profit necessary to pay their taxes and have cash for continued improvement in the company. Have confidence in your ability to deliver value. Don't be shy about charging for that value.

Strengths—know what yours are and build on them. Don't try to do it all yourself. Be honest with yourself about what you're not good at, and hire it out. This frees up your time for the things you excel at and love doing. Isn't that why you went into business for yourself in the first place?

Team—build a strong one. Small business owners can't do it all themselves, even though they want to sometimes. Build a team of smart professionals who know more than you do about their areas of expertise. Your team should have an accountant, attorney, banker, and insurance person. Choose wisely. You must be able to trust the advice they give you. Don't hire cheap! Hire the best people you can afford, give them a goal, and get out of their way.

Observe others to perfect your people skills. Your potential customers want to do business with someone they like. Charisma and people skills are so important. People want to do business with those who excite them and exude confidence. As a consultant, you do not have a tangible product that delights your customer. You have *you*. Your success is directly related to your ability to build and maintain relationships. Clients hire personality over expertise every day.

Measure and monitor every aspect of your business. The most successful business owners I know have a one-page numeric "snapshot" of their business—sales, receivables, payables, trends, profit averages—something that fits on one page. Monitor these data against your business plan to know when things need tweaking. I monitor using (1) monthly profit and loss trends; (2) an actual versus budgeted P&L statement for the current month and year-to-date; (3) a forecasted cash flow and profit analysis; and (4) balance sheet trends. Know your numbers.

E xpect to succeed. Why just hope your business will succeed? Decide that it will. Those who succeed know they will succeed. When things are going wrong, it takes drive from within to push forward, no matter the consequence. Those who expect to succeed believe they can make it happen. Without inner strength, few would be able to stomach the roller-coaster ride of starting a business. Many people want to start small businesses. A much smaller percentage actually do—and from that percentage, the ones that make it to the next step do so because they expect success. They know they can do it—and that's the difference.

R ecognize the importance of your clients. Cater to your customers. Your services improve people's lives. Period. No amount of venture capital can help a business if it doesn't at least do that. Successful business owners make every effort to understand why customers do or don't come back. It is a natural part of their culture that goes beyond an annual survey. They put themselves in their client's shoes. The ability to empathize with the customer helps them understand the real value in what they do.

This list spells CUSTOMER—the center of every successful business. Without customers you will quickly be out of business. Taking care of your customers and adhering to each of these principles will ensure your success.

Caring—truly caring—
is a powerful business advantage.

Growing Pains

A goal is a dream with its feet on the ground.

Anonymous

All business owners reach a point at which they begin asking themselves questions about growth. Let's explore a few of the many opportunities for growth.

Perhaps the first question is, "What does growth mean?" We can probably assume that it at least means more income. Does growth also mean more people in your organization? In what capacity? Do you want someone who replicates your skills? Complements them? Do you want a staff?

Are there ways to increase income other than increasing the number of bodies? Do you need to figure out how to level the peaks and valleys of your business cycle? Do you have products that you could market? Could you offer other services? For example, if you are a trainer, do you also want to offer to be a keynoter at conferences? Or perhaps it is simply time to increase the fee you charge.

Think long and hard about this step. Once you change the makeup of your business, it will never be the same. You have dozens of options and combinations of options to consider. For example, when I decided that I wanted a partner in my business, the two of us sat down and came up with the following list of possibilities for the business configuration:

- I own; you're employed.
- You own (buy me out); I'm employed.
- Equal partnership.
- Unequal partnership.
- I own the primary business; you own a subsidiary.
- We both own the primary business (equally or unequally); I own a related subsidiary.
- We create a franchise arrangement.
- You start your own business; we share overhead.

We were creative and tried to identify all the possibilities. You should do the same. Before you make the move to grow, think hard and long, do all your homework, and talk to others who have done what you are thinking about doing. If growth is still on your mind, this chapter presents several options for you to consider.

ADDING PEOPLE

Because increasing the number of people is usually the first thing people think about when the issue of growth comes up, let's begin there.

Should You Hire Staff?

Beth was the first person I hired. I hired her part-time to be in my office when I wasn't in to answer the telephone. This was in the early years of answering machines and voice mail. An answering machine was a dead giveaway that you were new to the business and probably working from your kitchen table. In the early 1980s, working from your home was not regarded as professional.

After I hired Beth, things started to snowball. I hired Beth for her telephone voice. I knew she would be great with clients. In addition to having a great voice, Beth also loved computers. She immediately started to do some of my word processing. That freed me up for more billable days. I took on more clients with more sophisticated needs. Therefore, we needed a better computer and a copying machine.

To pay for the new equipment, I started to take on larger projects. I was unable to provide the highest-quality services by myself, so I started to hire other consultants. Beth could no longer keep up with the demands of additional clients, so we hired additional administrative staff for support. Of course that meant we needed more computers and a larger office. To pay for the additional equipment . . . well, you get the idea.

Once you begin to hire staff, have a clear plan in place for exactly how much growth you desire and how you will fund this growth. I have read that a consulting firm must have seven or eight people before it truly turns a profit, provides the same flexibility an independent consultant has, and is worth the effort and investment. I have no hard data to back this law of diminishing returns, but I can tell you that I've been through it, and I agree.

Advantages. The greatest advantage to hiring staff members is that they will be a part of your organization. Clients will see that you are growing. Some clients will be impressed with the number of employees you have. I am asked on a regular basis, "How many employees do you have?" I have noticed that clients' interest level rises in direct proportion with the number of employees we have.

A larger staff affords you the luxury of pursuing larger, more complex projects, and it is usually easier to manage several large projects than many small projects.

As staff members become a permanent part of your organization, you will become familiar with their talents and limitations. That means you will be able to more knowledgeably match them to the project, the client, and the industry.

Disadvantages. The greatest disadvantage of hiring staff is the ongoing payroll commitment. When our company was at its peak, I thought about how many people, roofs, tires, braces, and dogs were dependent on the success of the company.

More administrative tasks are required. As soon as you hire one person, you become an employer, and the paperwork mounts: you need unemployment insurance, new federal and state tax configurations, an "office" where they can work, and a dozen other employee-related items.

Another disadvantage is one that you might think is an advantage: if there are other people in the organization, they can do more of the client face-to-face work, and you can do more marketing. Wrong! It has been my experience that clients will want you to do the work. You have the reputation, and it's your name on the door. No matter what you do, clients will still want you. The only way to keep all the demands from falling on you is for the consultants in your organization to generate their own work. They need to make face-to-face contact with clients and also do their own marketing.

So if having additional consultants on staff was your solution to freeing yourself up from the grind of billing, go back to the drawing board. Unfortunately, it won't happen.

> *No matter what you do,*
> *clients will still want you.*

Exhibit 8.1 explores additional advantages and disadvantages of hiring employees. If you are considering this option, take time to add your own thoughts under each item. When you have finished, review what you have written. Which side appears to be the stronger for you?

Should You Enlist a Partner?

I had a partner for five years, and I would do it again if I could find another exactly like him. We were alike in some respects and very different in others. We communicated well, trusted one another completely, made decisions effectively, and complemented one another's skills. I've heard it said that taking on a partner is more like a marriage than marriage itself. So the choice of whom to partner with is not a simple one.

> *Taking on a partner is more like*
> *a marriage than marriage itself.*

According to small business owners, the single biggest mistake entrepreneurs make is choosing a partner too casually. You would be wise to establish a trial relationship to explore the likelihood of a successful permanent one. I highly recommend an arrangement that allows you and your potential partner to work together for six to twelve months before making the relationship permanent.

How to configure your partnership is a second concern. We decided that although we were going to be partners, it made more sense for us to incorporate legally as a subchapter-S corporation. (Chapter Four describes the advantages of this legal entity.) We also decided that because I had more equity and eight years in the company, I would maintain slightly more than half of the ownership. We agreed that we would draw the same salary after the partnership was formed. The split of dividends, of course, is governed by law. We would each receive an amount proportionate to the percentage of ownership.

Exhibit 8.1. Building a Firm.

Advantages	Disadvantages
Increased ability to serve more clients	Increased time necessary to educate new employees
Increased availability and types of services	Increased time in managing others could decrease time to serve clients
Increased earning base	Increased overhead
Security of backup in emergency	May invest time in those who will leave and compete with me
Spread my philosophy and increase name recognition	May have different values

Prior to becoming a partnership, my partner and I agreed that he would work for at least one year at a reduced salary. The salary not taken was his way of buying into the company. We established several other parameters. One was that he needed to show that he was generating an equal amount of work.

Dividing responsibilities and roles is often the most difficult task. If you can be as lucky as I was, you can have roles and titles that clearly define the responsibilities. For example, a founding partner can focus on work with major clients and maintain the corporate vision, while a managing partner can manage the daily operation of the company, including taking over responsibility for sales and profitability. In our case, we were separated geographically: my office was in Wisconsin, and his office was in Virginia. Each of the offices was responsible for different aspects of the business—for example, invoicing clients, bookkeeping, or producing client materials. Each of us had responsibility for an office.

Exhibit 8.2 is a tool for generating discussion and for getting a sense of you and your potential partner's compatibility. Each partner completes the questionnaire. The two of you should set aside at least half a day to discuss your responses. The discussion will uncover concerns and issues that could create problems within the partnership. Take care of them before you form a legal entity.

Advantages. Consulting is a lonely business. Often the thought of having a partner seems like the perfect answer. There would be someone to bounce ideas off of (consultants like to bounce ideas) and someone to cover for you if you are ill.

A partnership broadens your business capabilities, expertise, skills, and experience. This is one reason for partnering with someone who is unlike you—someone who complements what you bring to the business.

A partnership sends a message to the world that you believe the person you have elected to partner with is at least your equal. This is important if your present clients are to accept the person as a qualified substitute for you.

From a business perspective, there is someone to share the responsibilities or the cost of doing business—someone with whom to share the decision making.

Disadvantages. The greatest disadvantage to having a partner was already listed as an advantage: you must share the decision making with someone! Depending on your agreement, each of you will probably need to check with the other before making a move. If you like independence and not having to ask permission to do

Exhibit 8.2. Partnerability.

Each potential partner completes this questionnaire. Set aside at least half a day to discuss your responses.

Rate each item on a 1–7 scale: 1 = low and 7 = high.

	Low	High

1. The importance of my title 1 2 3 4 5 6 7
    My ideal title would be . . .

2. The importance of salary 1 2 3 4 5 6 7
    My ideal salary would be . . .

3. The importance of responsibilities 1 2 3 4 5 6 7
    The responsibilities I want are . . .

    The responsibilities I do not want are . . .

4. My commitment to this partnership 1 2 3 4 5 6 7
    Because . . .

5. My willingness to challenge you 1 2 3 4 5 6 7
    Because . . .

6. My level of trust with you 1 2 3 4 5 6 7
    Because . . .

7. My willingness to take risks 1 2 3 4 5 6 7
    Examples are . . .

Exhibit 8.2. Partnerability, Cont'd.

8.   The strengths I bring to this partnership are . . .

9.   The liabilities I bring to this partnership are . . .

10.   My five-year vision for this partnership is . . .

11.   My "must haves" or things I will not budge on are . . .

12.   My philosophy about travel expenses is . . .

13.   My philosophy about quality of work is . . .

something, shared decision making could get in the way of your relationship. In addition, it may take more time to make decisions.

You will need to share resources. This can be a concern, especially if one of the partners is either generating or billing a greater proportion than the other.

Should You Consider a Practice?

I think of a *practice* as having one key person (you) with others on staff in assisting roles, and a *firm* as having numerous people who can do the same thing (many you's!), plus support staff (receptionists, administrative assistants, or word processors).

Advantages. The greatest advantage of a practice is having dedicated support. Someone is there to help with the ordering, scheduling, typing, copying, cleaning, filing, billing, packing, and dozens of other things that need to be done. Someone is available to pick up the slack and share the administrative stress. If you're on the road and need something, someone is available who can fax or mail it to you.

Disadvantages. The greatest disadvantage of a practice is having someone on payroll who is not billable and cannot generate income. This means that you are working to support two people. If you decide to hire someone, make sure that it is worth your while. Will the person free up enough of your time that you can easily make three times the individual's salary? If not, it is not a worthwhile pursuit.

Do You Want to Hire Subcontractors?

If you accept a project that is too big for you to handle alone, you may choose to hire subcontractors. It is an excellent idea from a tax perspective because you can add people on a temporary basis.

Subcontracting is on the increase. In addition to being helpful for large projects, the arrangement allows consultants to tap into one another's expertise. This allows you to seek projects for which you may not have all the qualifications.

Although I prefer to work on a handshake, if you have a large project for which you will use multiple subcontractors, we recommend that you use a subcontractor agreement. The more people involved, the higher the chances that there will be mistakes, misunderstandings, and disagreements. Exhibit 8.3 is an example of a subcontractor agreement; the subcontractor expense record in Exhibit 8.4 can be adapted for your use.

Agreement

Whereas ebb associates inc, Box 8249, Norfolk, VA 23503, has entered into a contract with the Client to provide materials and facilitation for a series of team-building sessions titled "Building Your Team" (which shall be described as "sessions"); and whereas _____ (Facilitator) desires to and ebb associates desires to have Facilitator facilitate these team-building sessions; therefore, in consideration of the premises hereof, ebb associates and Facilitator hereby agree to the following terms and conditions:

I. Statement of Work

The Facilitator shall use the materials provided by ebb associates to facilitate the sessions for the Client at the locations and dates to be determined by Client.

II. Facilitator

Facilitator agrees to the following:

A. Facilitate the sessions using the material provided by ebb associates in a manner that ensures consistency of content, detail, and method of presentation.

B. Contact the Client team leaders before each session to ensure that content addresses unique team issues. The Facilitator will customize the session for each team. The Facilitator will verify all unusual requests from the teams with ebb associates.

C. Become familiar with the nature of the Client's business, team needs, and environment. This includes reading the Client's strategic plan.

D. Distribute and collect Client Evaluations at the conclusion of each on-site segment. All evaluations shall be mailed to ebb associates.

E. Summarize in writing the results of the Client session using the Facilitator Evaluation as a guide at the conclusion of the facilitation. Write a brief report describing the session and relevant information collected during

Exhibit 8.3. Subcontractor Agreement, Cont'd.

group discussions, including any significant events that the Facilitator considered either supportive of or detrimental to the success of the session and the ability of the team to be successful. Include comments about the logistics, facility, appropriateness of the training for the actual audience, and any other noteworthy considerations.

F. Mail the invoice, expense records, and evaluations as appropriate within fifteen working days after each on-site segment.

III. ebb associates

ebb associates agrees that it will:

A. Coordinate the schedule of training dates and locations with Client.
B. Perform final design, editing, proofing, printing, and preparation of the session materials for submission to Client.
C. Provide a Facilitator Manual and materials required to deliver the sessions.
D. Work with Client to ship participant materials to the training site.

IV. Period of Performance

A. The initial period of performance shall begin after award of the Client contract and extend through September 30, 20XX.
B. Potential session numbers and dates for delivery are outlined in Exhibit 1 and are made a part of this contract. Client and ebb associates may request a change or cancel any of the dates set forth in Exhibit 1. The rescheduling of any such changes will be by mutual agreement of all parties. ebb associates and Client will be obligated to pay only for services provided.
C. Facilitator cannot be guaranteed a minimum number of billable days.

V. Facilitator Remuneration

A. For providing services for the session, ebb associates will pay the Facilitator eleven hundred dollars ($1,100.00) for each day of facilitation. Payment of fees will be made only if Facilitator submits an invoice and

Exhibit 8.3. Subcontractor Agreement, Cont'd.

expense record to ebb associates and after full payment is made by Client for said expenses. In no event, however, will Client reimburse at a rate higher than allowed by Joint Travel Regulations summarized in Exhibit 3.

VI. Billing Instructions

A. Submit your invoice, including the following information: Name, address, Social Security Number or Employer Identification Number, dates of facilitation, session number, fee at $1,100.00 per day, and total travel costs.

B. Invoices shall be submitted in original and two copies to:

> Lorraine Kohart
> ebb associates inc
> Box 8249
> Norfolk, VA 23503

VII. Copyrights and Other Rights

A. All written materials provided by the Facilitator in the session shall be appropriately documented as to their original source (author).

B. Unless Facilitator gives ebb associates written notice in advance that any part of Facilitator's contribution to the session is not or would not be Facilitator's original work and unless ebb associates approves in writing the use of any material that is not original, Facilitator hereby warrants that Facilitator's contribution to the session shall be Facilitator's original work and shall not infringe on the copyright or other property rights of any person, business, or corporation.

VIII. Miscellaneous Provisions

A. The parties understand and agree that all provisions of this Agreement and all rights and obligations arising hereunder are conditioned and contingent on execution and parallel performance of the Client Contract, including performance of each corresponding provision in the Client Contract.

Exhibit 8.3. Subcontractor Agreement, Cont'd.

B. A specific waiver by ebb associates or Facilitator of any provision of this Agreement on any particular occasion for any reason will not be deemed to be a basis for any automatic waiver of the same or any other provision hereof in the future.

C. This Agreement shall not be deemed to create an employment relationship, a partnership, or joint venture and shall be interpreted according to the laws of the Commonwealth of Virginia.

D. Facilitator agrees that all requests for training and consulting services to be performed by Facilitator made by Client subsequent to this Agreement shall be scheduled and invoiced through ebb associates.

E. This Agreement may be modified only in writing and with the consent of both parties. It is intended to bind only the parties hereto and their corporate successors and may not be assigned by either party without the express written consent of the other.

F. This document contains the entire agreement between the parties and embodies all the terms of any prior agreements, understandings, or representations, whether oral or written.

ebb associates inc   _____
                                       (Facilitator's company)

By: _____   By: _____
         (PRINT)   (PRINT)

Title: _____   Title:_____

_____   _____
       (SIGNATURE)   (SIGNATURE)

_____   _____
        (DATE)   (DATE)

Exhibit 8.4. Subcontractor Expense Record.

Contract _____   Invoice # _____

                                        Invoice Date _____

Consultant Name _____

Session Number and Location _____ Dates _____

Team _____ Number of Team Members _____ Billable Days _____

Travel Costs   *To be completed by Facilitator. Attach receipts for all (*) items.*

Airfare*/Train*/other. . . . . $_____

Rental Car* $_____   Fuel* $_____ . . . . Total $_____

_____ Taxi*/Shuttle* from _____ airport to hotel . . . . $_____

_____ Taxi*/Shuttle* from session to _____ airport . . . . $_____

Meals* (itemize) . . . . $_____

Hotel* . . . . $_____

Airport parking* . . . . $_____

Local Privately Owned Vehicle # miles _____ × $.50/mile or

   Taxi* from residence to airport . . . . $_____

Local Privately Owned Vehicle # miles _____ × $.50/mile or

   Taxi* from airport to residence . . . . $_____

                                                   Total Travel Costs $_____

Session Costs *This section to be completed by ebb associates inc*

Facilitation fee $_____

Other $_____

(explain)

                                          Total Session Costs $_____

                         Total (Travel and Session Costs) $_____

Advantages. Subcontractors can be hired on a per-project basis. That means that there will be no ongoing payroll expense. You will not be required to withhold income taxes or pay any share of their Social Security or Medicare taxes. Generally, you will hire people who are skilled and professional. Subcontractors increase your flexibility, as you are able to hire the talent you need on a project-by-project basis.

Because they are independent, they know how important it is to produce high-quality work. They will work hard to satisfy your needs because it could lead to repeat work for them. They also require less administrative overhead. Your only obligation is to send completed 1099 forms to them by the last day of January.

Disadvantages. The greatest disadvantage is actually only a potential one. The IRS has adopted common-law rules for differentiating between an independent contractor and an employee. The rules cover such things as whether you have the right to direct the person's work, whether you supply the person with tools and a place to work, whether you establish the hours of work, and whether you have a continuing relationship with the individual. Even if you have studied the guidelines and are complying with the law, the IRS could tie you up in an investigation for months. As an independent consultant, you can imagine what this might do to your business.

e-Idea

For additional information about the difference between subcontractors and employees, go to www.irs.gov/businesses/small and select "Online Classroom." View the lesson 6 webcast, "What you need to know about federal taxes when hiring employees/contractors."

Subcontractors are not always available when you need them, and because they most likely substitute for other consultants, they will not know your projects well and may not understand your consulting preferences. This means that you may need to spend almost as much time bringing them up to speed for a project as you would if you had done the job yourself. You can only hope that the investment of time will have a payback in the future.

Subcontractors may also become your competitors. Ethically, subcontractors represent your company when they work for you. Further, they are not supposed to discuss their own business, nor are they to market themselves to your clients while on your project. Even if they do not, however, your client may discover the arrangement and want to hire them directly to save money. This can be uncomfortable for everyone, especially you.

Can You Use Graduate Students?

University graduate students may be hired as interns for project work under arrangements similar to those of subcontractors, but you must still follow all IRS guidelines. You could also hire them as part-time employees, in which case you provide a payroll for them.

On occasion you may be able to locate a student who will work for credit only. If you have a thriving practice that provides true learning opportunities, this may be an option you should check into. Call at least the business and communication departments of your local campus. There may be other specialty departments to call also.

Advantages. Graduate students usually are interested in the experience more than the salary. That means you can find lots of talent at a very good price.

You can complete projects that you have been unable to tackle in the past due to a lack of time. For example, you may assign a student to one specific project, such as developing a new seminar based on materials you have collected.

Disadvantages. The greatest disadvantage is that graduate students usually lack experience. They may have lots of knowledge, but not the practical hands-on experience that your clients expect. Even if they work as support staff, they may have little experience with running a copy machine, creating computer graphics, or answering a telephone.

University students are generally short-term employees. That means you will not often have them for more than a school year—and usually for just a semester.

Due to class schedules, they may not be available when you need them the most. Sure as heck, they will have a big exam scheduled when you have a major project due for your best client.

GROWING WITHOUT ADDING PEOPLE

As soon as you hire your first employee, you change the complexity of your business. You no longer have choices about where, when, and how much you will work.

You now have a responsibility to another human being. Before you take that big step, consider growing without employees. How can you increase profits yet maintain your practice as a sole employee? First, consider using your local temporary services to help you out on occasion. Second, try several configurations involving other consultants: subcontracting for or collaborating with another consultant, joining a joint venture, offering other related services, or selling products that are related to your consulting work.

These are all viable options. Consider the advantages and disadvantages of each.

As soon as you hire your first employee,
you change the complexity of your business.

Could a Temporary Service Meet Your Needs?

One of the fastest-growing industries in the nation is temporary services. Corporate America is outsourcing almost every kind of job. We use temporary services when we have repetitive tasks or simple processes to complete. Temporary services are useful when we have huge mailings (envelope stuffing, stamping, labeling) or need a large amount of word processing or copying.

We find temporary employees to be especially helpful when everyone in the company is busy with a huge project, and we need someone to serve as a receptionist.

Advantages. Temporary services can provide the specific skills necessary for repeat work. You pay a reasonable price for short-term prequalified support. If you are in a bind, temps can fill in at the last minute.

Disadvantages. The disadvantage of temporary employees is that the individuals have to be trained each time you are sent someone new. It is highly unlikely that you will be able to use the same person more than twice. If the person is good, he or she will be offered a permanent position.

Another disadvantage is that you will not always have the best person from the agency if there were many requests ahead of yours. Also, no matter how clearly you define the task, the person who shows up may not be able to live up to your standards of quality.

Do You Want to Subcontract?

You could become a subcontractor for another firm, offering your services directly or perhaps completing design and development behind the scenes. Remember that as a subcontractor, you must be seen by the client as an employee of the firm for which you are doing the work. Many consultants' egos will not allow them to do that.

Advantages. As a subcontractor, you could continue to run your own business while subcontracting with others. This provides an opportunity for you to fill in the gaps when you don't have billable work. If you have been offered a long-term project, it could provide a steady income.

A big advantage is that you will be able to work for or with other professionals. This will certainly give you experience and knowledge that you might not acquire any other way.

Disadvantages. The greatest disadvantage to subcontracting is that you will most likely make one-third to two-thirds of your daily fee. It is possible that you may need to turn down a full-paying project to fulfill your subcontracting responsibility.

You may have a difficult time working under someone else's business name—especially if you have had your own consulting business for any length of time. As stated earlier, we consultants typically have healthy egos that may create dissonance within ourselves.

Have You Considered a Joint Venture?

Some use the term "virtual partners" to describe a temporary arrangement, usually aimed at completing one project at a time. The parties involved are usually separated geographically, but that is not a requirement. The partners in the joint venture may work under a name that represents the group. That name may remain while partners come and go, depending on the project.

Typically no legal agreements are made. However, you should not become involved in a joint venture without some written agreement among all parties. This will save you time and energy should something negative occur.

Advantages. A joint venture is a temporary arrangement. This allows you to work with others on an experimental basis. It allows you time to determine if you would like to create a more permanent arrangement with some or all of these individuals.

The individuals have a shared responsibility for the outcome of the project, for completing the work, and for the financial success of the project.

Disadvantages. Because the joint venture operates under a loosely drawn up agreement, it is likely that something will be forgotten. The temporary arrangement exacerbates the situation, as individuals in the venture may not be as dedicated to its success as they would be if they were in for the long term.

One of the biggest disadvantages is that the decision-making process may become convoluted—especially if more than two people are involved.

Do You Want to Collaborate with Another Consultant?

A collaborative arrangement is a fashionable growth option. You may hear a number of terms, such as "alliance" or "coalition" or "consortium," to describe a loosely formed arrangement of shared resources, clients, and decisions.

Although a collaborative agreement is similar to a joint venture, there are some key differences. A joint venture is project-oriented; a collaboration is relationship-oriented. Membership in a joint venture is temporary and ends when the project ends; a collaboration is a continuing relationship and is maintained whether or not there is a project.

Collaborating is similar to a partnership but has fewer legal ramifications. Sometimes consultants collaborate with one another as a way to determine if they would like to form a partnership or corporation. Although the consultants may have good intentions, using the arrangement for that purpose is rarely a good idea. The loose agreement between two collaborating consultants is not the same as truly working together under a legal description that encourages individuals to make the best of any situation.

Before becoming involved in a collaborative arrangement, scrutinize the other individual(s) and the arrangement. Does the person's image reflect favorably on you? His or her values, ethics, expertise, experience, and reputation should be similar to yours. In addition, you will want to ensure that there is value to you in the relationship. For example, you will gain exposure to a new client base, a different industry, or distinctive content not readily available to you.

Working in a collaborative effort will most likely result in a greater investment of time than you may have originally thought. It will take longer to make decisions. It will require long, time-consuming communications. Sorting out support mechanisms and staff issues will take time. Planning will take longer. There are some common elements that should be in place for a successful collaborative effort to flourish:

- *Trust.* The effort should be based on trust between both consultants.
- *Value.* Each party must recognize the value he or she brings as well as the value the other consultant brings. In addition, each must clearly articulate the added value that neither of you would create if working alone.
- *Risk.* Both consultants must recognize the risk and the pros and cons of that risk.
- *Alignment.* Both parties must determine the degree to which they are aligned in mission, goals, values, and priorities and to what extent the differences may prevent success.
- *Guidelines.* All must agree on the guidelines, which will cover communication, responsiveness, the ability to withdraw, financial support, and so on.

Advantages. Some of the greatest advantages are for your clients. Collaborating with someone allows you to add services to those you presently offer. The collaboration means instant growth in your customers' eyes. Another advantage to your clients is that you will have backup if something should occur that prevents you from being available on a scheduled date.

Another advantage is that the collaborating parties have more for less. The collaboration allows two consultants to share support staff and to pool resources for efficiencies in marketing, product development, and other high-ticket items.

A collaboration also increases opportunities for you to learn from another professional.

Disadvantages. Time becomes one of the greatest problems in a collaborative effort. Joint activities usually take more preparation time than solo events because you must discuss and plan as a team. Sometimes the projects each party continues independently get in the way and limit the time for joint activities. It is difficult for the individuals to give up these projects, as they are loyal to their clients, and the projects provide income. In the end, it becomes difficult to find time to generate collaborative efforts.

Lack of a legal agreement causes continued separation, which can prevent the collaborating parties from learning to work together. The logistics may cause problems if the individuals live a distance apart. If they rarely see one another, they may not find the time to begin to meld their businesses together. If your values clash and you are not working together, the collaboration is doomed.

As with most things, money can create problems. Because the collaborative arrangement keeps the individuals separate, they may not make final decisions about how much to charge, how to share revenues, how to determine required investments, and a host of other issues.

If the two individuals are working in the same field, there may be crossover of clients. If this creates a competitive situation, the collaborative arrangement will end.

Do You Want to Offer Other Services?

If you are a trainer, you might consider offering keynote addresses for conferences. Keep in mind that the two require very different skill sets. You could offer other services. For example, a computer consultant could teach evening computer classes. Consultants can also write newspaper or journal columns, write and sell articles, tutor college students in their professions, or create and sell subscriptions to a for-profit newsletter.

e-Idea

Consider selling "add-on" products and services via the Web. For example you could offer webinars (web-based seminars) for individuals or on a subscription basis. They could be synchronous or asynchronous.

Before you decide to take on a new service, decide what effect, if any, it will have on your business image. You may decide that it will have a positive effect and will enhance your consulting business, or that it will engulf your consulting business or be detrimental to your image.

Advantages. The advantage of offering other services is that you broaden your skills and capabilities. There is always the possibility that you may discover another career that you like even more than consulting!

Disadvantages. The greatest disadvantage is that you may spread yourself too thin, taking on too many different things. You may not focus well. You may also become so tied up in a new venture that you will not be available for a consulting project when it comes up.

e-Idea

> Have you considered coaching? Most of the work can be conducted through email and telephone calls. Most successful businesspeople have had coaches, even though the field of executive coaching has officially been in existence for only about two decades. Today it's not just the executives who have coaches; people in other key positions also avail themselves of coaching. I recently met a director who had several field office managers reporting to him. He stated that he has learned a great deal from his coach, whom he has never met in person. All of his "coaching" is conducted using the phone and email.

Most other "regular" jobs, such as teaching at a college or writing a newspaper column, require you to meet a consistent schedule—for example, to show up every Tuesday and Thursday to teach. This does not fit into the erratic schedule of a consultant. You will need to determine whether two different services can coexist within your vision.

Can You Expand into the Product Market?

If you have been in business for a number of years, you probably have enough potential products in your files to fill a small library: Questionnaires, activity pages, surveys, survey results, reading lists, topic papers, quotes, checklists, tests, quizzes, summary sheets, games, puzzles—books' worth of things you have used once. Could they become products to sell to clients?

The members of the National Speakers Association (NSA) are truly experts at turning their content into products. They take the best quotes from their speeches and turn out planning guides, pins, T-shirts, plaques, posters, CDs, tapes, workbooks, newsletters, and special reports! They may sell such products in the back of the room or to the client who distributes them after the presentation.

e-Idea

A blog is a Web journal that contains dated entries on a given topic or theme. It may include searches, feedback from readers, and links to other sites. Making money from a blog is possible and isn't even difficult anymore. Make money by putting ads on your pages (check out BlogAds or Google's Adsense). Use affiliate marketing, whereby a company agrees to pay you a commission for selling its products (Amazon, Linkshare). Get sponsored by a company; deals range from including obvious advertising to adding a company's name, logo, and brand to an existing blog. Or get hired by a company to keep its blogs going. Finally, you can sell your own and others' intellectual property through your blog.

As a consultant, you don't want to open a store, but surely there is one book among all your stacks and files. Turn your favorite workshop into a how-to book for managers. How about a collection of self-evaluations or ten activities that will improve [you name it]. An interesting phenomenon occurs after you are a published author (even if you self-publish). You become an "expert." This automatically gives you the authority to increase your fees!

How about taping your next presentation and selling it? You could arrange to have it both videotaped and audiotaped. People seem to have less time to read books these days, and books on CD and audiotape are increasing in popularity. Many listen to audiotaped books in their cars during a long commute to work each day. Perhaps the next book they listen to will be yours!

e-Idea

And as long as you are taping content, consider podcasts. Podcasts are a way to distribute an audio or video episode via the Internet for playback at any time on any MP3 device or PC. Podcasts allow training about new product information, negotiating ideas, recorded speeches or other events, or even new employee orientation that can be delivered on demand to anyone anywhere.

Before you start taping your first podcast, consider these suggestions for success: keep them about ten minutes long, plan a series to be released on a specific schedule, script them just as you would any video show, incorporate music, focus on one succinct idea, maintain professionalism, and archive your old podcasts.

Perhaps you are a sales training consultant. Wouldn't it be great if past training participants could download one hot tip every Monday morning to get their week started? The cost could be included in your original fee as a featured benefit for choosing you over your competitor, or you could sell the podcast as an add-on component.

If you are an expert in a specific area, you could develop a series of webcasts. They could be live or on demand. If you do decide to do this, contact someone like Thompson NETg to help you get started.

e-Idea

If you decide that taping (videos or webcasts) is a profitable outlet for you, be sure to check with the experts about what to wear. Access this Web address: http://w3app.ilearning.com/alt_files/traininggateway/Best-Practices/whatToWear.html. It takes you directly to the best information.

Before you jump up and grab your video camera, think about distribution. Who will sell your products for you? You could approach some of the large training product catalogues or publishers. Distribution requires specific knowledge and special skills. For minimal sales, you could advertise on your website.

Product possibilities are endless. Here's a list that may pique other ideas:

- Sell an electronic book.
- Publish and sell a newsletter (electronic or hard copy).
- Print and sell articles to clients.
- Publish and sell instruments or surveys.
- Sell articles to magazines and trade journals.

- Syndicate your articles electronically.
- Conduct research, compile the results, write a white paper, and sell it.

Advantages. The advantage of producing products is really twofold. First, you have ways to make money while you sleep; you could be selling an asynchronous webinar on the other side of the world at the same time that you are consulting for a client in your own city.

Products may help even out the uncertain income dips of consulting. Products can provide not only an additional revenue source but a *steady* revenue source.

Second, your products keep your name out there. They market your skills and services while earning money for you.

Disadvantages. Products take time and an investment of cash to produce. Then you must distribute them and let people know that you have them for sale. Products won't do you much good sitting in your garage. You must put them into potential buyers' hands.

Again, this is something you should discuss with others who sell products to determine if it is a viable option for you to consider.

EXPAND YOUR GEOGRAPHICAL MARKET

If your business has always been located in the same geographical area, consider whether you want to expand your horizons.

Do You Want to Expand Domestically?

You might ask your current clients for references to other similar organizations. Sometimes clients have locations in other cities, but they assume that you do not wish to travel. Let them know that you do.

You could also select cities or other states to which you would like to travel, and identify several organizations to which you would like to provide services. Contact these organizations using the same process described in Chapter Five. If you live in Minneapolis, Dallas probably sounds like a great place to go in January. Remember, however, that if you do acquire work, it is doubtful that it will be seasonal; and you will need to travel to Dallas in the middle of July's heat as well as the middle of January's welcome relief from Boston's blizzards!

Do You Want to Expand Internationally?

Perhaps you are interested in building business in Europe or Asia. How can you do that? One of the best ways to begin is to attend international conferences, such as IFTDO (International Federation of Training Development Organizations) or IODA (International Organization Development Association). Consider networking with the international attendees at domestic conferences. Many will have an international room set up for guests; visit them and exchange business cards. Of course, submit a proposal to speak at these conferences as well. You may meet foreign businesspeople who need someone to distribute their material in your country. This may grow into a two-way partnering. Let your clients who have global sites know that you are interested in working in their offices in other countries. Offer to provide similar services in other regions of the world.

e-Idea

For more information about IFTDO and IODA, check their websites at www.iftdo.org and www.iodanet.org.

Note that there is nothing we do in the United States that is unique or better than what is offered in many global locations, the residents of which have the advantage of understanding the culture. Unless you are a well-known "guru," it might be wise for you to work with a local firm or your own client organizations located elsewhere in the world. Read all you can about the culture before you go; talk to people who have lived and worked there. Plan your trip so that you will have time in advance to meet with your local "coach," who can give you some guidance on the culture and specific organizational issues. Ideally, that same person will sit in on your session and provide feedback to you at breaks.

e-Idea

Two Dallas-based training companies—PodTraining (www.podtraining.us) and Language of Life—have partnered to design a series of iPod and DVD language programs. Check them out.

If you want to work internationally, the most important thing of all is to think of yourself as being a learner. You will be of the greatest value to your clients if you are a student of each culture that you visit and remember that no matter how competent you may be in your own fields, you are a beginner at the art of working, living, and learning in that new place. The rewards of being "at home" in the world are great. It all starts with being a learner and developing relationships that will make you a welcome visitor wherever you go.

International work brings two distinct advantages. The first is greater credibility among peers and clients. The second is that you will most likely be able to charge more for your services when working in foreign countries. By the way, always request payment in U.S. dollars and ask to have the funds wired directly into your account. As an alternative, request U.S. funds drawn on a U.S. bank. Fees for collecting from a foreign bank can be 20 to 25 percent of the transaction.

e-Idea

Once you land a job in a foreign country, gather advice about appropriate business etiquette, customs, protocol, and behaviors. Several websites can help you: www.ExecutivePlanet.com, www.businesstravelogue.com, and www.cyborlink.com.

DO EVERYTHING YOU CAN TO GROW YOUR CURRENT BUSINESS

Ask yourself whether you have done everything you can to grow the business you now have. Sometimes we are so busy we forget the basics of the business we are in. The following questions will jog your thinking about what you may be able to do with what you have:

- Have you recently studied your numbers? Have you compared them with past data? Have you conducted a reality check with another consultant to determine if your expenses are in line? If your income is reasonable?

- How closely are you following your business plan? Is that good? Or not? Just because you have a business plan does not mean you should shut your eyes to anything but what you have in the plan. Stumbling onto success is just as good as planning for it. However, you do need to assess and redirect.

- Have you become overly dependent on one industry? Is it time to expand or at least to explore other industries?

- Have you expanded the coverage of your market area? Can you serve clients in the next state? On the other coast?

- Have you selected clients who hire you for the kind of projects you prefer? Who can provide repeat work? Who can pay the rate you charge?

- Have you evaluated your consulting rate? Is it time to increase it?

- Have you kept up with technological advances? Are you current with how they affect your work? Have you incorporated them into your projects appropriately?

- Have you built relationships with your clients? With other consultants?

Your answers to these questions may contain some interesting ideas for growth.

FINAL THOUGHTS

How can you determine the best way to grow your business? First, define what you mean by "grow your business." Next, review your strategic plan: think about the kind of consulting you conduct, how your clients define your brand, and what makes your products and services unique. Also identify your ideal client. Third, determine the options for growth and the pros and cons for each, and narrow your choices down to three or four. Then speak with consultants who have grown their businesses using these methods. Last, consider the implications for the bottom line, your time, and the added responsibility. Is making the change worth it?

One of the advantages of being a consultant is that there are so many other avenues open to you. As you consider all your options, take care that you do not trap yourself into a financial commitment that you cannot support. If you decide to add individuals to your present business entity, consider the responsibility you have added and how it will affect you and your present business.

The Ethics of the Business

Have the courage to say no. Have the courage to face the truth.
Do the right thing because it is right. These are the magic keys
to living your life with integrity.

W. Clement Stone

One of our founding fathers, Thomas Jefferson, said, "In matters of principle, stand like a rock! In matters of taste, swim with the current!" In your work as a consultant, your principles are always on the line, and your principles contribute to the ethics of the profession. Perhaps Thomas Jefferson could easily tell the difference between a principle and a taste, but it's a bit more complicated in the consulting profession.

One consultant will say it is appropriate to charge the full per diem for expenses, even if it's not used, because the organization budgeted for that amount. A second consultant will say it is inappropriate to charge for what was not spent.

One consultant will justify varying the fee charged if a client cannot pay the full amount. A second consultant will say that is absolutely wrong. Anything can be justified and argued for with facts.

Even though consulting is a high-paying, high-profile job and 50 percent of people in M.B.A. programs flirt with the idea of becoming a management consultant, jokes abound about consultants. Did you hear the one about the consultant who is asked the time by a client? The consultant asks for the client's watch and then says, "Before I give you my opinion, perhaps you could tell me what time you think it is." One of the best ways to ensure that consulting is not a joking matter is always to provide services in the most ethical manner, to build relationships with the highest level of integrity, and to run your business with the highest principles.

Your reputation as a consultant will be created by thousands of actions, but can be lost by only one. It is imperative that you always model your high standards with clients, other consultants, and the general public.

---

*Your reputation as a consultant
will be created by thousands of actions,
but can be lost by only one.*

This chapter focuses on ethics in the consulting field. It will address the ethics issue from three relationship perspectives: consultant to client, consultant to consultant, and client to consultant.

We take a fairly hard stand with regard to ethics, for two reasons. First, we believe that the reputation of the consulting profession has been tarnished by past practices and that taking a tightly focused approach may help polish it to a reputable shine. Second, and more important, is that the practices we espouse here are those that we follow and strongly believe are right.

If you intend to join the consulting ranks, support the profession by maintaining high ethical standards. You will benefit everyone associated with the profession.

CONSULTANT TO CLIENT

Let's first focus on the consultant's relationship with the client, because that's the one that probably concerns you the most at this time. We will discuss consultant-to-client ethics in two categories—delivery of services and business aspects.

Delivery of Services

Some pointers for delivery are given in the following paragraphs.

Deliver Only the Highest-Quality Products and Services. You have been paid to produce the highest-quality products and services, at a reasonable price, on time, every time. Provide quality first, last, and everything between.

Accept Only Projects for Which You Are Qualified. Ethically, you must be willing to turn down a job that is beyond your competence. This does not mean that you should not accept projects that are a stretch or during which you can learn something. However, you should be able to contribute significantly to the client.

Learn on Your Own Time. You will always need to learn something about the project or a new client, and there is often a hazy distinction about who is responsible for the investment. Our rule of thumb is that we will invest 5 percent of our time learning about our clients. That is, if we have a contract that is about twenty days in duration, we will spend at least one day learning about the client without charge.

Turn Down Projects That Are Inappropriate. If you are asked to do something that is inappropriate from any standpoint, say no. As I related in Chapter Five, in the middle of the data-gathering step for a team-building session, I learned that the manager who had hired me actually wanted me to collect data that would support firing a specific individual. I ended the project the same day.

Cease Work If the Client Is Not Benefiting. Do not continue to work under a contract if you do not believe the client continues to gain from your involvement. You may have completed the project earlier than anticipated, or the client's circumstances may have changed, preventing the client from appreciating any further benefits.

Place the Client's Interest Ahead of Your Own. This means that you will not take advantage of your client in any way—large or small. At the large end of the continuum, it means that if you overbid the project, you do not charge the full amount. At the small end of the continuum, it means not taking a limo when a taxi will do. You are charged with monitoring your own performance, as these are usually things that may never be uncovered.

Be Willing to Say "I Don't Know." Consultants must feel comfortable responding honestly, even when the answer is "I don't know." Some consultants think that they look weak if they do not have all the answers. Being honest with a client will gain more respect than will "faking it."

Accept Only Work That You Can Manage with High Quality. Consulting is notorious for having peaks and valleys. Therefore, consultants become nervous in the valleys and take on more work than they can manage. They may fall behind on deadlines or cut corners to meet everyone's needs.

Accept Work Only from Organizations You Respect. When you work for organizations that you do not respect or whose business purpose may undermine your own values, you are hurting your own reputation. Watch for clients who may not appreciate your high standards of consulting or who try to reduce your quality. An advantage of being a consultant is the ability to choose your work.

Hold All Confidential Information Close. Never divulge any proprietary information or information about your contract. Although the reasons for it may not be obvious, doing so could give some other company a competitive advantage.

Avoid All Conflict of Interest. If you have the potential to benefit personally from any information you gain, you should not accept the project. For example, if you know that you will be in competition with the client in the future, do not accept the project.

Accept Your Social Responsibility. Accept responsibility for the fact that your work may alter the lives and well-being of people within your client organization. Act with care and sensitivity.

Create Your Clients' Independence. The goal of every consultant should be to go into organizations, complete the work, and leave the clients better able to take care of themselves. An ad for a seminar titled "How to Build and Maintain Your Consulting Practice" appeared in several newspapers recently. I was appalled to see that it touted "How to build your client's dependency!" A few more ads like that and most consultants will not need to worry about their reputations!

Repay Any Loss You Cause the Client. Inform the client immediately when problems arise or errors occur. No matter what the error, if you are responsible for it, own up to it and rectify it. This is not only an ethical issue: you may be held legally liable if anyone is hurt or if the business is damaged in any way as a result of your error.

Complete All Work Yourself. If you find yourself in a bind and unable to complete an assignment, go to the client before you turn the project over to someone else. There could be another solution. Perhaps the client can take on more responsibility or was hoping to delay the project but did not want to change the agreement. You will never know unless you ask.

Avoid Working with Competing Clients at the Same Time. Due to the sensitivity of information to which you may be exposed, it is likely that sharing such information with the competition, even inadvertently, could have negative consequences. We take this one step further. Due to the size and nature of many of our contracts, we will not work with clients' direct competition for a full two years after our last contact with them.

Conduct Regular Self-Examination of Your Practice. During and after consulting engagements, assess your progress and results. Learn from the experience.

Continue to Provide Excellent Services That the Client May Never Comprehend. Someone will notice. Even if no one does, you know you did what was right. We conducted the same workshop for a large manufacturer for eighteen months. Near the end of the contract, a participant said she signed up specifically to meet us. She was from accounts payable and said she wanted to see the only trainers who were not gouging the company on expenses!

Always Give Credit Where Credit Is Due. Never pass off someone else's work as your own. Obtaining permission to use someone else's work is easier than you can imagine. Tom Wood, owner of Watershed Associates, one of the best negotiating consulting firms in the world, is frustrated by other consultants who make excuses for why they did not get permission to use someone else's material: "It's not a big deal—I'm only going to use two minutes," or "I'm promoting the movie by showing the clip!" Tom uses several movie clips in his seminars and is proud to have obtained permission to use all of them. He says it feels good to be "squeaky clean"!

e-Idea

Get permission to use almost anything from www.copyright.com. Tom Wood gets permission to use his movie clips from Motion Picture Licensing Corporation, 800-462-8855. The company's website is www.mplc.com.

Business Aspects

Some ways to be more businesslike are given in the following paragraphs.

Adhere to a Consistent Pricing Structure. If you followed our advice in Chapter Three to establish a fee structure and stick with it, you have already created an ethical foundation for your business. We said there that you should identify a clear and consistent pricing structure for all your clients. Your structure should clearly spell out any differences among clients, such as nonprofit groups or government agencies; kinds of work; or work locations. Be consistent.

I once hired a subcontractor with whom I needed to establish a daily rate. When I asked him what his daily rate was, his first response was $1,200 to $1,600. When I asked what constituted the difference, he could not give me a specific or measurable definition. Two weeks later, he came to me and proposed that I take 15 percent and he take 85 percent of some arbitrary daily fee. I responded that we all needed to try to give clients as much for their money as we could. He finally agreed to accept a fee that ranged from $850 for writing, data gathering, and phone interviews to $1,100 for on-site strategy development. It appeared that the subcontractor sensed that the client had deep pockets, and he intended to charge as much as he thought the client would pay. The client was able to accomplish about 30 percent more for the same amount of money.

Charge for the Work That Needs to Be Done. It may be tempting to charge more just because you know the client has more in the budget. Don't do it. You will never feel good about it. Also, don't add on services that the client really does not need.

What if you have quoted an amount and the project actually takes less time and effort? It's your call. You can justify charging the full price, or you can buy surprised respect from your client by charging for only what was required. A number of years ago, our company returned money to a large firm. The company called us to say that there was no process for putting the returned fee back into the system!

Charge Only for Reasonable Expenses Actually Incurred. Expenses are petty little things that can easily lead to a distrustful relationship. The easiest way to deal with them is to build telephone calls, express mail, and such into your daily fee, so that you neither need to track them nor present them to your client for payment.

Expenses are petty little things that can easily lead to a distrustful relationship.

Travel expenses should always be charged at cost and verified with receipts. Do not exaggerate mileage, and do not exceed reasonable expenses. The question you should ask yourself is "Would I spend this if I were at home?" For example, "Would I eat this $78 lobster dinner if I were at home tonight?" If the answer is no, it is probably not a legitimate expense.

Double dipping, or charging two clients for the same trip, is one of the worst ways a consultant violates the trust between consultant and client.

The Bottom Line

Your fee structure, your expense report, and how you deliver your product are all important aspects of building an ethically strong relationship with your client. The bottom line, however, is that the ethical overtones will be dependent on the personal and professional relationship between individuals.

How can you determine if you are doing everything possible to build this relationship? Ask your client. Discuss it. Your client may not be aware of your standards or what you do to maintain them. This kind of discussion will build respect for you.

CONSULTANT TO CONSULTANT

A consultant's relationship to other consultants is critical. You will want to maintain your reputation among your peers. Let's discuss this first with regard to subcontracting relationships and then other situations that you may experience.

Subcontracting

Subcontracting is a special relationship. The following paragraphs describe some guidelines for subcontracting.

Subcontractors Shall Represent Themselves as a Part of the Primary Consultant's Organization. Most clients feel nervous when they believe that a group of independents, a hodgepodge of consultants, will come in to work on their delicate problems. Thus it is important to present a united front. As a subcontractor, you give up the right to represent your firm or to discuss it. You give up that right in exchange for steady work.

Subcontractors Shall Not Market to the Client. Even if the client approaches you, the client belongs to the primary consultant, who has invested in marketing to this particular client. Report any offers you receive to the primary consultant. Perhaps the two of you can work something out, such as one or the other of you providing the service and the other receiving a percentage of the fee. Some firms have their subcontractors sign "noncompete" agreements. We do not do that. We state what we believe is right and then trust the subcontractor to do the right thing. We believe that a client is not fair game for a subcontractor until at least two years past the final contract date.

Subcontractors Shall Not Speak for or Represent the Client. Subcontractors should not speak for the client in contractual matters, changes in the delivery, or anything else. The primary consultant must take care of all issues and questions. The subcontractor should never discuss money with the client.

Subcontractors Shall Be Positive and Supportive. Subcontractors must support in word and deed the delivery of services. The subcontractor's responsibility is to enhance the primary's performance. This is sometimes difficult. Egos get in the way. One tries to outguess the other.

Primary Consultants Shall Clearly Identify All Issues of Pay, Time, and Expectations Up Front. Be completely honest and candid. State doubts you may have about any aspect of the project, even if it has not been stated by the client and is only your gut feeling.

Primary Consultants Shall Keep Subcontractors Informed. Subcontractors are very similar to employees, and you have the same ethical responsibilities to let them know if you have any concerns about the original plan. For example, let a subcontractor know if a project will be extended or shortened.

Other Consultant-to-Consultant Experiences

You will find yourself in other situations that test your ethical stamina. Here are several.

Give to Your Colleagues More Than You Get. I believe there is very little new under the sun. I will always give credit to anyone from whom I get a new idea, and I never think that my ideas are so unique that they cannot be shared. Therefore, anytime I can help someone, I do. I will send a book on request or give advice or recommend another consultant. If someone asks permission to use my materials, I always grant it—but I do expect someone to ask.

I am not alone in my belief that collaboration sustains the consulting profession. Julie O'Mara, for example, is a world-renowned diversity consultant. I recently sent her this email:

> I am working with a client who has had a couple of attempts at diversity efforts and they always fizzle out. They mean to do well, but just don't "take the time" to get the support from the senior leaders. In the past they have had 5 years of external consultants who spent 4–5 days per week at the organization and have had a diversity council, but just don't seem to make any headway. Consultants have been gone now for 3 years. The organization has a new diversity coordinator but she

doesn't know where to start. Can you provide me with a bit of direction? Is there a book or plan or something that I can hand them—or work with them to create—that will get them started? If the answer is too long, or if what they really need is *you*—just say so. I am not looking for free consulting. Hope this explains it. I am sure it is a story you've heard before.

Julie, the quintessence of professionalism and a diversity expert, responded immediately, saying, "Not a simple answer. I have some thoughts. I have an hour long drive to a client. I can call you from the car and would be glad to share some ideas. I'll be in the car from about noon until 1:15 PDT. Will that time work and what number can I call? I have other times to talk, but that would be the easiest. Attached are two documents that I'll refer to."

Julie spent an hour with me on the phone laying out the entire plan, what I needed to do, how the client needed to be involved, how to design the intervention, and what to do next. I followed up with a handwritten note and a thank-you puzzle. The client is now headed in the right direction.

Contrast this with another professional, who asked me to share an hour's worth of content. I did so willingly at 9 P.M. However, nine months later when I asked for similar support, he stated that his content was proprietary and that he could not discuss it with me. I went to his website, where the information is publicly displayed, to get my question answered.

Asking for Help Is Okay, but Don't Expect Others to Do Your Work. As I said earlier, I will always assist where I can, but I can't do your job for you. A man whom I had met briefly on one occasion emailed me in desperation asking me to help him with a consulting project: "I am enclosing the five PowerPoint slides and hope that you can suggest activities from the *Pfeiffer Annuals* or develop activities that I could use with this client—at least one for each of the five slides." He was in effect asking me to design his training session.

I wrote back,

> I am sorry that I cannot help you. Coaching is not my area of expertise. It may seem like a simple request, but I do not select activities as you presented. It would seem to me that you need to design a full-day coaching course. If the slides you presented me are all the materials

you have, you will probably need at least four days worth of design. Then you will design the activities as a part of the holistic design. I rarely use the activities from the *Annuals* exactly the way they are, but customize them for every situation and every audience. So you see I do not have enough information to make a decision. Good luck to you!

He emailed again: "I thought I had the course designed, but the clients changed their mind. I have to redesign the material to fit the audience as much as possible. Is it possible to send me the list of activities for the 2002, 2003, 2004, 2005, 2006, and 2007 *Pfeiffer Annuals* (for both the Training and Consulting)? Then I could decide what might fit."

I wrote back, "I am on the road for the next week. I am with a client from morning until about 9 P.M. each night. I do not have access to email once I go into their secured office space, and my office manager, Lorraine, is out until next Tuesday. So I am afraid we are no help to you. Check for the Table of Contents to the twelve *Annuals* on the Pfeiffer website. You know, sometimes you just say 'no' to the client too. . . ."

He emailed *again:* "Thanks for telling me where to look. Actually I still have a week if you could tell Lorraine to contact me in addition. The last time I checked, they did not list the table of contents." (In fact, the tables of contents are listed on the Pfeiffer website.) There were several more emails back and forth, plus a fax to him of about forty pages.

In the end we never heard how his problem was resolved. He never acknowledged our support or thanked us.

Thank Your Colleagues. Although it may not be an ethical issue, do not forget to thank your colleagues. At the least, take a couple of minutes to send an email. Even better, buy a cool thank-you card (you can find ones that sing!) and write a couple of personal words inside. Thank those who support your success. If you don't, they may feel used, and they aren't likely to forget.

Do Your Part. Consultants are like mailmen: "through rain or sleet or falling snow. . ." No matter what, you do not let your colleagues down by being a no-show when you have agreed to support them. There is always a way. Find it.

Be Positive. When you discuss other consultants, it is unprofessional to criticize them. Take care with your nonverbals as well; those around you may observe subtle signals. If you do have serious reservations about the competence or behavior of another consultant, you are ethically responsible for confronting that individual. As professionals, we must regulate ourselves to ensure high standards and ethical behavior.

CLIENT TO CONSULTANT

Although you have no control over your client's behavior, you should be aware of some of the things clients may do that can undermine your relationship with them. I'd like to believe that some clients simply do not know better. In those situations, it is our responsibility to educate them. If we all inform them of the effect any of their behaviors have on us, we will improve relationships for all consultants and clients.

In other cases, the client may have an agenda that does not meet your standards. Typically you would learn about this during the early stages of the relationship. Turn the project down and find something else.

Sometimes the client's agenda is not apparent until later in the project. You may see warning signs along the way. The client may have unrealistic expectations of you or may begin to withdraw commitment from parts of the project. Be honest and candid with the client to resolve your concerns. If the client will not move back on track, you can either work within the boundaries you have been given or quit.

What unethical actions might you encounter? Here are a few. *Prior to contracting with you, the client:*

- Wants to "pick your brain."

- Offers you lower pay than you quoted in your proposal.

- Has asked for your proposal in order to have the minimum number of quotes, without any intention of giving you the job. (Many clients have no idea that it takes four to twenty hours to write a good proposal.)

- Requests samples of product from several consultants, then puts them together and develops a program based on information that came from the consultants.

- Already has decided what the answer is to the problem.

During the project, the client:

- Fails to provide data and information as promised.

- Is slow to approve work.

- Is slow to approve invoices.

- Shifts gears in the middle of the project.

- Refuses to remove barriers for you, such as difficult staff.

- Ignores your recommendations.

- Presents your ideas to management without sharing the credit.

- Requests that you omit information from a report.

CODE OF ETHICS

Most professional associations that represent consultants—such as the Institute of Management Consultants (IMC), the Academy of Professional Consultants and Advisors (APCA), and the American Society for Training and Development (ASTD)—have codes of ethics. If you do not know what your association's code is, call the customer service line and ask that it be sent to you.

e-Idea

To view the IMC's code of ethics, check the website at www.IMCUSA.org.

As an independent consultant, you will establish your own code of ethics. You will develop a set of ethical standards that you choose to abide by as you do business. That is both a privilege and a responsibility. It is a privilege you have been given. As an independent consultant, you do not need to live by others' ethics. It is a responsibility you must accept. As a consultant, you have the ability to increase the public's respect and trust for the consulting profession.

e-Idea

Subscribe to an online ethics newsletter. *Ethics Today Online* is a forum for exploring a broad range of organizational ethics and character development issues. It is published monthly and is available at www.ethics.org. The Society for Business Ethics is an international organization engaged in the study of business ethics; the Society's newsletter is available at www.societyforbusinessethics.org. Both newsletters are free.

If you have the courage to face the truth and do what is right, you will always feel good about the services you provide, and you will do what is best for the profession. Place a high value on your talents and your high-quality service. Think highly of yourself. Do not sell out on your integrity; do not negotiate your reputation away. In your work as a consultant, your principles are always in jeopardy. When your name is on the project, your reputation is on the line.

When your name is on the project,
your reputation is on the line.

Exude Professionalism

If we did all the things we are capable of,
we would literally astound ourselves.

Thomas Edison

What does it take to be a true model of success and professionalism in the consulting world? Probably the same things that it takes to be a model professional in any vocation, whether it's ballet, football, chemistry, landscaping, teaching, or writing. I once read that most people achieve only a third of their potential. Successful professionals in any position achieve much more than a third of their potential because they work at it.

Most people achieve only a third of their potential.

What are the traits of professionals? Let's look at a few:

- Professionals compare where they are with where they want to be or where their customers expect them to be.

- Professionals continue to learn. They realize the value of expanding their knowledge and skills to develop the expertise expected of them and to evolve.

- Professionals improve their processes continuously. They deliver services and products to their customers that are always on the cutting edge of industry trends.

- Professionals balance their lives and their businesses. They know the value of rejuvenation and renewal. They make conscious choices about how to spend their lives.

- Professionals manage their time. They are busy people who have learned ways to invest their time in the things that count.

- Professionals motivate and inspire others. Their authenticity paired with their enthusiasm sparks excitement and encourages others to aspire to a higher level of expertise.

- Professionals give back. No one "makes it" without the help and support of many others. True professionals give back to the profession, the community, their families, and their friends.

MEASURING UP

Successful professionals step back and take stock of where they are and where they want to be. They determine some measure of success, drive a stake in the ground, and head for it.

The next few paragraphs will help you assess where you are as a consultant. Many ways exist for you to measure how well you are doing. The following consultant competencies can help you start thinking about what you stand for as a consultant, where you are, and where you want to be.

Competency 1: Professional Standards

Establish standards for yourself that are high enough to keep you on your consulting toes; position the bar such that it encourages continual reaching.

Establish standards for yourself that are high enough to keep you on your consulting toes.

Guarantee that your services will be of the highest quality your clients have ever experienced. If you have employees, help them understand how important quality is to your business reputation. Put quality and your clients ahead of everything else—including profitability. What kind of a remark is that?! Especially from someone who has just written a book telling you how to run a financially sound business!

It may very well be one of the best pieces of business advice in this book. The project will end; your relationship will not. You will learn from pricing mistakes, and you will not make them again. Poor-quality service mistakes will follow you and your reputation for life. A project that goes in the red is a small price to pay for a lifetime reputation. You are only as good as your last client says you are.

Set your standards high and never compromise them. Our standard is "Quality: first, last, and everything in between."

Competency 2: Professional Awareness

Stay on top of the profession by having a clear understanding of consulting, its practices, and where it's going. This includes knowledge of the state-of-the-art practice as well as the fads of the day; knowledge of the industry and consulting gurus as well as their philosophies; and knowledge of the professional organizations, journals, and newsletters that can help you stay abreast of the field.

One of the best ways to stay in touch with the field is to be an active member of your professional association. I often hear consultants say they "can't afford the dues." They have it all wrong. They "can't afford not to join"! Your ability to keep up with the profession is dependent on staying in touch. It is an investment in *you*. If you won't invest in you, who will?

If you won't invest in you, who will?

Whether you have chosen the IMC, ASTD, or ISA, do more than just write the check for your annual dues. At a minimum, attend the organization's annual conference. Volunteering for a committee is also a great way to stay in touch with the profession. You will be involved in the work of the profession, communicating with other professionals, and working with colleagues in your profession. It's an enjoyable way to stay up to speed!

Competency 3: Consulting Skills

Your ability to do the work is a basic requirement. A professional consultant knows the basics of the consulting process: defining a business need, clarifying expectations and reaching agreement (contracting), gathering data, recommending options, and implementing change. Continue to learn techniques and strategies that move you from being an apprentice toward becoming a master consultant.

In addition to becoming an expert at the consulting process, you will need skills in other areas, such as problem solving, managing meetings, designing surveys and materials, team building, and facilitating.

Certification or accreditation is available in many fields as a way of learning and of achieving a professional standing in your profession. The accreditation could be related to your profession, such as a Certified Public Accountant (CPA) or a Certified Electrical Engineer (CEE). It could also relate to your specific consulting area, such as a Certified Professional in Learning and Performance (CPLP), Certified Speaking Professional (CSP), International Coach Federation (ICF) credential, Certified Professional Facilitator (CPF), Registered Organization Development Consultant (RODC), or a Certified Management Consultant (CMC).

e-Idea

> Check these websites to learn more about certification. Go to
> www.nsaspeaker.org for a CSP; www.coachfederation.org for a ICF
> credential; www.imcusa.org for a CMC; www.iaf-world.org for a CPF;
> or www.cplp.astd.org for a CPLP.

Competency 4: Communication Skills

The skill that goes awry the most often in any situation is communication. Therefore, you are probably not surprised to see communication skills listed as a competency. Your abilities to listen, observe, identify, summarize, and report objective information are important for a productive working relationship with your client. Equally important are your abilities to persuade, offer empathy, solve problems, and coach others.

Communicating authentically, or stating what you are experiencing in the moment, is, in Peter Block's words (2000), "the most powerful thing you can do to have the leverage you are looking for and to build client commitment." This statement indicates how important authenticity is to your relationship with your client. Authenticity means that you are able to express clearly who you are and what you are feeling, without being inappropriately influenced by those around you. Authenticity is honesty, candor, and clarity, combined with sensitivity to others.

Each of these and many other communication skills are requirements for a successful consultant.

Competency 5: Professional Attitude

Attitudes are elusive. They cannot be measured or clearly defined, but we all know they are there. A professional maintains a positive attitude under all circumstances, asking, "What's good about it?" when something goes wrong.

Professional consultants are self-confident, open minded, and flexible; they believe in people and can cope with rejection. Professionals take responsibility for their actions and are accountable to their clients.

Your attitude about consulting will permeate everything you do. If you love the work, enjoy helping your clients, get a high from the challenge of difficult projects, and find consulting to be an outlet for you as a person, you have probably found your niche in life. In *The Consultant's Calling*, Geoffrey M. Bellman (2002) suggests that you "Pursue this work as a personal calling, bringing who you are to what you do."

Love what you do. I am delighted that I stumbled into the consulting field nearly thirty years ago. I love the work, and it shows. I believe you should not get up and go to work in the morning; you should get up and go to play. I am fortunate because I am allowed to play every day—and in the process make a good living. Consulting offers a good income, but if you are in it only for the money, you may not succeed.

You should not get up and go to work in the morning; you should get up and go to play.

Competency 6: Business Development

Generating work provides the steady flow of projects essential to staying in business. You must know enough about sales and marketing to be able to analyze your present situation, clarify a marketing strategy, set measurable goals, and select marketing tactics to accomplish those goals.

You must know how to develop an annual marketing planning calendar and how to monitor your results. You will want to determine how to even out your work load and income. Your ability to sell yourself and your services is the competency that keeps you in business.

Competency 7: Business Management

Staying in business is less dependent on how good a consultant you are than on how well you run your business. To stay focused, refer to your business plan on a regular basis.

Take care of the details of managing your business. Selecting a team of professionals to assist you (accountant, attorney, banker); tracking expenses and projecting income; invoicing in a timely manner; studying your data to learn how well you are doing; developing contracts and proposals; understanding office technology, systems, and equipment; dealing with suppliers; managing your money; scheduling, informing, and tracking clients and projects; and a myriad of other details are required to run a business. You will need to attend to these details to stay in business.

Competency 8: Building Relationships

Whether you are working with clients, other consultants, or your employees, your success as a consultant is directly related to your ability to build and maintain relationships.

As a consultant, you do not have a tangible product that delights your customer. You have a service—one that may at times be difficult to define. Your service is invisible to the human eye; if you are truly doing your job, someone else may actually take credit for what you do. This helps explain why building relationships is imperative.

Your Competency Level

Set time aside each year to assess how you are doing as a professional consultant. Your future success is dependent on how well you are doing today. Exhibit 10.1 is a professional checkup to determine how you are doing.

You may also wish to assess yourself on each competency. Go back to each competency described earlier and rate yourself on a 10-point scale. Think of a 1 as representing a "beginner" level and a 10 as representing a "master" level.

Exhibit 10.1. Professional Checkup: How Am I Doing?

Think about your skills and behaviors as a consultant and respond to the following:

When working with clients, do I:

1. Develop a positive working relationship?

2. Communicate candidly, completely, and in a timely way with all stakeholders?

3. Maintain focus on the effort?

4. Respect all confidential discussions, comments, and information?

5. Create candid discussions about client responsibility and role in the effort or project?

6. Avoid internal politics and maintain an open mind?

7. Respect the organization's limitations of time, budget, and other resources?

8. Encourage the client's independence?

9. Provide regular progress reports that clearly identify the benefits of my work?

10. Ask for feedback on how I am doing?

11. Regularly evaluate my competence?

12. Upgrade my skills and knowledge beyond just what is needed?

The Business of Consulting, Second Edition. Copyright © 2007 by John Wiley & Sons, Inc. Reproduced by permission of Pfeiffer, an Imprint of Wiley. www.pfeiffer.com

It is likely that you will be high in some competencies and lower in others. It is also likely that you may have been higher in some areas in the past than you are today. For example, several years ago you may have been highly involved in your professional organization, but more recently you have had little involvement, and your reading may have dropped off a bit. Two years ago you may have rated yourself as a 9, but today you may rate yourself as a 3.

After you have completed your self-assessment, you will want to create a professional developmental plan. The next section will help you with that planning.

CONTINUING TO LEARN

You have an obligation to your clients to improve your knowledge and skills continually. The rapid changes in the world today can turn today's expert into tomorrow's dolt if the person fails to keep up. The professional identifies a developmental plan for continued growth. Let's consider several strategies.

Attend Learning Events

At a minimum, attend your professional organization's annual conference. It may be expensive, but you owe it to your clients to invest in yourself. I can think of no more enjoyable way to learn than to go to a great location, meet new people, renew past acquaintances, and attend sessions in which presenters discuss new ideas and approaches. To top it off, you may very likely go home with a fistful of business cards belonging to potential clients.

You have an obligation to your clients to improve your knowledge and skills continually.

To get the most out of your attendance, be sure to network. Don't sit on the sidelines or retreat to your room during breaks. You will not gain all the value that you can. Instead, go where the action is. Be the first to say hello. Introduce yourself to others and be interested in who they are. Identify common interests and experiences. Trade business cards. If the person has asked you for something or if you want to follow up after the conference, jot a note on the back of the business card as a reminder.

Attend virtual learning events. My email box is filled with offers to "attend" webinars, teleconferences, and webcasts. Many are free; the rest have a small price tag. All will stimulate learning, produce knowledge, and encourage thinking.

Go back to school. You may not need an M.B.A., but courses at the graduate level are critical. Take courses in finance, marketing, human performance technology, or organizational change. Take a class to bring yourself up to speed in the area of technology.

Ask Others

Ask for feedback from others on a regular basis. Ask for it from friends, colleagues, and clients. I usually conduct an exit interview to ask clients what they liked about my work on the project and what they wish I had done differently.

Ask clients about their most pressing concerns. Although this is not related to you specifically, the learning may be fascinating, and this will enhance your relationship.

Join an Association or Group

Affiliation with a national professional association or group is critical to maintaining your professional awareness. Through the group, you will be kept informed of learning events.

Sometimes a professional organization will provide a networking list designed to provide you with contacts in your geographical area. If not, form your own network. Networking is one of the best ways to continue to learn or, at the very least, to learn what you ought to learn!

Study on Your Own

Reading is one of my favorite methods of learning. The suggested reading list at the back of this book is a place to begin if you are interested in learning more about the business of consulting.

If you have not yet read the two books I have referred to several times, you must put them on your immediate to-do list: *Flawless Consulting*, by Peter Block, and *The Consultant's Calling*, by Geoffrey M. Bellman.

Subscribe to and read your professional journals. Read general business magazines, such as *Fortune, BusinessWeek*, or the *Harvard Business Review*. Read the same publications your clients read to keep yourself informed about the industry.

Read the cutting-edge journals, such as *Fast Company*. While working on another project, I learned that consulting professionals are voracious readers. Dana Robinson, for example, reads half a dozen journals each month, and Jack Phillips subscribes to almost forty publications.

Read your junk mail. You will learn what your competition is doing, how to write more effective marketing letters, and how to design brochures. Realize that you will observe and learn from both good and bad examples!

Listen to tapes while driving longer distances.

Identify Resources

Visit your local technology training organization. Check out the classes they offer and other available resources they can lend you.

Visit your local bookstore. Browse the shelves looking for trends in the industries you serve and in business in general. Thumb through all new books about consulting to determine if they should be on your bookshelf.

e-Idea

Sign up for an online service. The World Wide Web is a dynamic source for professional development resources. Sites provide information as well as link you to other related sites. Sign up for newsletters and webzines in your particular field. The *New York Times* and your other favorite newspapers will deliver each day's headlines to your computer if you subscribe.

Co-Consult or Train with Others

Consulting with a colleague is a unique way to learn from someone else in the profession. It allows you to observe someone else, elicit feedback, and learn from the experience of working together.

Invite colleagues to observe you during a consulting or training situation. Ask them to observe specific things. Sit down afterward and listen to everything your colleagues say. Ask for suggestions.

Create Mentoring Opportunities

Meet with other professionals to discuss trends in the consulting profession. Some consultants form small groups that meet on a regular basis to share ideas, discuss trends, and help one another.

Identify someone in the consulting field whom you would like as a mentor, then ask the person if he or she is willing to act in that capacity. My mentor and I meet for breakfast four to six times each year. I pay for our meals. This has become the best $20 investment I've ever made. I'm investing in myself.

Develop coaches in your key client industries. This requires effort on your part, because you may not cross paths with these folks on a regular basis. For example, several years ago I found myself working with several utility regulatory bodies. I remembered that my cousin had a friend who held a management position in the same industry. I called my cousin and set up a meeting with her friend so that I could learn more. He became a good friend as well as a resource, and now he calls me for coaching!

Identify where the experts hang out. Then go there. Sometimes this is a related association or an informal group. More seasoned people and those with different experiences can offer you priceless advice.

Aspire to the Best of Your Knowledge

Your clients expect you to be on the leading edge, regardless of your field. You have an obligation to them and to yourself to learn and grow. Learning is an ongoing process, even if you are at the top of your profession. Often it is what you learn *after* you know it all that counts!

---

*Often it is what you learn **after** you know it all that counts!*

BALANCING YOUR LIFE AND YOUR BUSINESS

Many people I meet think of consulting as an exciting, high-powered career: flying from coast to coast, meeting with publishers in San Francisco and executives in New York City, staying at the Madison in Washington or the Ritz Carlton in Dallas, eating at a bistro in Manhattan or a coffee shop in Seattle. I make a good living, dress well, land large contracts, hobnob with the influential and famous. But that's only the first layer.

My friends know what my life is really like: getting up at 4 A.M. to catch a flight for a noon meeting, spending six hours in an airport because of delayed flights, calling to cancel dinner plans, and finally arriving home at midnight. It is also about eating poorly prepared restaurant food, writing proposals until the wee hours of the morning, and losing a contract due to a technicality. Most of all it is about long hours.

Although you have the freedom to set your own schedule, the truth is that the hours are long. Projects demand your immediate and sustained attention. When you are putting food on the table, you may find it easier to stay glued to the project than to break away. In today's fast-paced world, no one finds balance an easy task. It becomes even more difficult when you are dependent on the success of the project your family now expects you to hold at bay while you attend the annual family picnic in Pauquette Park.

Although you have the freedom to set your own schedule, the truth is that the hours are long.

One of the most challenging issues facing consultants today is achieving a balance between the competing priorities of their lives and their businesses—balancing their families and their work.

Joel Gendelman (1995), author of *Consulting 101,* says, "I actually installed a lock that had to be opened with a key—a key that only my wife had. She opened my office in the morning and closed up shop before dinner. The rest of the time, my little company was closed."

How can you achieve balance? What can you do?

Identify the Imbalance

Geoff Bellman leads an exercise in which he asks you to identify the three things you value most in life. Write them down. Now scan your checkbook and calendar. Do the choices you see there match the three things you value the most?

Next ask your spouse, a colleague, or friend what he or she believes you value the most. Did that person choose the three things you chose?

Now begin to make real choices. What do you need to do to demonstrate the value you place on the three things you chose?

Make Your Own Rules

A business takes creativity and energy, so draining yourself becomes counterproductive. Of course, sometimes you stay late or work a weekend simply to meet a deadline, but do not make that your standard way of working. Establish a rule that helps you put your business in perspective. Tell yourself, for example, "If it's not done by 6 P.M., it will wait until tomorrow."

Enjoy the Doing

Don't hurry through each project just to get to the next one. If you love what you do, you may be missing some of the fun! Much of the pleasure may be in the doing.

Take Time Off

It is very important to take a break from your business. Go on vacation, even if you just spend a week at home. Invigorate your mind, rejuvenate your body, sleep late, relax, and read something that has nothing to do with work.

Identify Other Interests

Join a book club. Learn golf. Try embroidery. Fly a kite. Collect something. Visit an antique store. Try hiking. Read catalogues. Solve a cryptoquote. Learn to paint. Take a cooking class. Write poetry. Work crossword puzzles. Refurbish a classic car. Study your heritage. Go for walks. Develop your family tree. Write a letter. Plan a trip. Do it with your spouse, your children, or a friend.

Take Advantage of Being at Home

If you work from your home, find ways and times to get away from it all. Go for a walk at noon. Visit the gym a couple of times each week. Read the morning paper in your kitchen or eat lunch on the deck.

Issues of balance become more acute during transitions. Therefore, if you are planning to transition to consulting, plan the transition. Focus on all the important areas of your life: social, family, spiritual, business, education. Identify how the balance might shift initially, and determine how you want it to change and how soon.

To some extent the issue of balance in life is really one of time management. Don't mistake busy-ness for business. You must prioritize deliberately, based on what you want out of life. Add a few of the following consultant time-management tips to those you already use.

Don't mistake busy-ness for business.

MANAGING YOUR TIME

Time is the one thing we all have access to equally. We all have exactly twenty-four hours in every day. The truth is that we cannot save time. Time continues to march on no matter what you insist. You cannot save time, but you can *shave* time—shave time from some of the things you must do that are less enjoyable. As a consultant, you can shave time in two primary areas—running your business and planning your travel. Try some of the following to shave time from each of these areas.

Business Time Savers

Here are some of the ways I've found for saving some time for myself and for managing my business.

The Big Jobs. Work on several large projects rather than dozens of small projects. You invest a great deal of time moving from one client to another, getting up to speed, flying from one coast to the other, reminding yourself of all the personalities, and remembering names.

Prevent Scope Creep. Scope creep occurs when a project slowly grows larger than the original intent. This is certainly one of the greatest ways consultants misuse time. Unless you are paid by the hour, scope creep will erode your profits and consume your time. Prevent scope creep by establishing clear, measurable objectives and specific, identifiable timelines and deliverables. Then stick to them.

e-Idea

If you need to conduct a survey for your clients, subscribe to one of the online survey tools. Several to consider include the following: www.confirmit.com offers an industrial-strength tool; www.performancedriver.com gets great reviews from my colleagues; www.zoomerang.com costs about $600 for a one-year subscription; www.sensorpro.net and www.surveymonkey.com are others that might meet your needs. Online surveys will save you time conducting and compiling surveys.

End-of-the-Year Tickler File. I keep an end-of-the-year tickler file for my accountant. It's labeled "Take to Stephanie" and reminds me of all the things that have occurred during the year that I need to remember for tax purposes and personal desires. When something happens, I write a quick note or copy the necessary document and slip it into the file. It's a guaranteed method to ensure that I have everything I need when tax time comes and that I am not at the last minute rummaging through stacks of paper trying to locate an IRS notice or a question from my attorney.

Invoice Ease. Keep an invoice format on your computer for clients who will incur repeat billings. When it's time to bill them, just pull it up, fill in a new date and numbers, and print it. When I can accurately predict the billing date and amount, I complete the invoices when I initially schedule on-site dates. Early on in my career, I could return to my office, add a stamp to the envelope, and mail the invoice. Now I email my staff upon completion of the project, and they mail (or email) the invoice immediately.

e-Idea

Many companies use electronic payment systems. Check on it when you land your first job with a new client. You may be able to invoice electronically, and the company may deposit your payment electronically. In some instances (for example, with some federal government agencies), you may also be able to track the progress of the invoice or identify a payment date. This process eliminates concern that your invoice made it to the right place, removes worry about "lost in the mail" issues, eases cash flow concerns, and, most important, saves time.

Card Contact. Keep a bundle of note cards in your briefcase. When you are on a plane, stuck in a waiting room, or have a canceled appointment, you can pull them out. Use them to keep in touch with friends, colleagues, and clients.

File Tips. Develop a system that works for you. You must keep up on the filing so you can move through your office, of course; more important, you also want to find what you filed! We use different colored files to distinguish what's inside: blue for project files, yellow for office files, red for client resources, orange for originals, green for volunteer activities, and so on. We have separate cabinets to separate resources from client work.

e-Idea

Make smart choices for filing your work electronically as well. Establish a system as soon as you can. Think about the best way to file your documents so that you can find them. We have five large categories: client work, proposals, accounting, books, and miscellaneous. Client work is all filed by topic area first, then client name, and finally date. We file this way because when I have a new "cultural change" project, all the files for that topic are together. We keep proposals separate from the client work. When I am ready to compose a new proposal, I do not want to sort through content to find them. This may not work for you. You need to be logical about it and determine what will save you the most time.

Phone Time. Calls can break your concentration and interrupt more urgent activities. If you want to stay focused, accept or return phone calls at a specific time. If you have a number of calls to make, make them in sequence. If the person is not there, leave a time when you can be reached: "I'll be available from ten to twelve today."

Travel Time Savers

Travel can be hectic, but I have developed some ways to reduce the hassle and gain time for other activities.

Cash Stash. I have become almost entirely dependent on my credit card. However, there are still some times when I need cash. I keep $31.00 in the side pocket of my briefcase. If I'm traveling and do not have enough cash in my wallet, this amount will allow me to take a cab, buy a snack from a street vendor, or buy almost anything else that I cannot purchase with a credit card. One dollar is in quarters, which are handy for plugging a parking meter or a vending machine.

One Travel Agent. We use one travel agent. We get fabulous service from Ginger and her gang. They know our preferences for services and carriers. We email information about our trips to them, identifying times, destinations, and anything special. They email an itinerary back for our approval. They have all our frequent traveler numbers and enter that information as well. In addition, they track any itinerary revisions, alert us to changing airline rules, and remind us of expiring frequent flyer mileage. You cannot beat service like that!

Double Trips. Use a trip to work with one client and visit another potential client. Add a minivacation when your work with a client takes you to a special location. In this case, you will, of course, pick up all additional expenses.

Your Travel Bag. If you travel a great deal, keep the basics packed. I have two of everything: curling iron, hair dryer, makeup kit, toothbrush, and so on. When I return from a trip, I replenish anything that I used or emptied, such as pantyhose, underwear, deodorant, or whatever. This tactic ensures that you will never forget any of the basics and makes packing for the next trip a breeze.

Classic Time Savers

You will never *find* time for anything; if you want time, you must *make* it. The following list is a reminder of time-management tips you have always known, but may not be practicing. Try them. They work.

---

*You will never **find** time for anything;*
*if you want time, you must **make** it.*

- Set your priorities first thing in the morning or the last thing at night for the next day.
- Read *The Consultant's Calling* for Geoff Bellman's perspective on how a consultant can enjoy time.
- Address your top priorities first.
- Tackle large projects in stages.
- Identify your "best" times—that is, your best time for writing, best time to make telephone calls.
- Use your waiting and travel time productively: make lists, listen to tapes, write a postcard, balance your checkbook.
- Carry 3 × 5 cards or a small notebook to write down ideas or reminders.
- Handle each piece of paper once.
- Have a place for everything.
- Set deadlines.

e-Idea

Program phone numbers and other information into your cell phone as soon as you obtain the information.

- Make decisions in a timely way. Indecision is a time thief. Not only does indecision waste time, but it creates worry, which can be so destructive that you may be tired before starting the day!
- Always ask, "Is this the best use of my time right now?"
- Set a schedule. Stick to it.
- Take short breaks often.
- Have something to do when you are put on hold.

Exhibit 10.2 is a time-management log. Although keeping the log is not a way to manage your time better, you must collect data to find out where you are spending your time. The log is divided into quarter-hour increments. Track your time for two weeks to obtain a good sample. Diligently record what you were doing and for how long. Next, determine your key job categories. You might include marketing, consulting, administration, and professional development. Add a category for personal things.

After you have the data, determine what percentage of your time you spent in each category over the two-week period. Is that what you expected? Did you spend too much time in some categories? Too little in others? What can you do to change?

Two time-management tools that I cannot live without are my month-at-a-glance calendar and a session planner for each event. The calendar has room for almost everything that I need to keep myself organized. In addition to meetings and appointments, there is room to include telephone numbers, departure and arrival times for my flights, important monthly reminders, and social engagements. I color-code time spent with clients. I need to see the full month to have a feel for how things flow from day to day and week to week.

The session planner in Exhibit 10.3 has all the details for a successful event. I start it the day the project is scheduled. It initially serves as a memory jogger to ask all the right questions. Later it helps our staff know what needs to be prepared and packed. On-site it provides all the location information. It also tells staff how to get in touch with the consultant. Rework the session planner until it works well for you to help you manage your time and your engagements.

Exhibit 10.2. Time-Management Log.

Name: _____ Date: _____

Hour	15-Minute Intervals			
12:00 A.M.				
1:00 A.M.				
2:00 A.M.				
3:00 A.M.				
4:00 A.M.				
5:00 A.M.				
6:00 A.M.				
7:00 A.M.				
8:00 A.M.				
9:00 A.M.				
10:00 A.M.				
11:00 A.M.				
12:00 P.M.				
1:00 P.M.				
2:00 P.M.				
3:00 P.M.				
4:00 P.M.				
5:00 P.M.				
6:00 P.M.				
7:00 P.M.				
8:00 P.M.				
9:00 P.M.				
10:00 P.M.				
11:00 P.M.				

Daily Summaries

List task categories after each letter code (for example, meetings, telephone calls, marketing, consulting, administration, planning, and so on). Then put the corresponding letter into the block that was dominated by each task. Do not allow more than one hour to pass before updating this log. Multiply the number of blocks by 15 minutes to find out how much time was spent on each task.

Code	Task	#	Total Time
A.	_____	___ × 15 =	_____
B.	_____	___ × 15 =	_____
C.	_____	___ × 15 =	_____
D.	_____	___ × 15 =	_____
E.	_____	___ × 15 =	_____
F.	_____	___ × 15 =	_____
G.	_____	___ × 15 =	_____
H.	_____	___ × 15 =	_____
I.	_____	___ × 15 =	_____
J.	_____	___ × 15 =	_____

Exhibit 10.3. Session Planner.

Date: _____ Company: _____

Topic: _____

Contact Person: _____ Phone Number: _____

Purchase Order: _____ Fee: _____

Speaker/Presenter/Consultant: _____

Time Held: _____ Number of Participants: _____

Where Held: Address: _____

  Building: _____

  Room: _____

  Directions:

Travel: Hotel: _____

  Daytime Phone: _____ Nighttime Phone: _____

  Directions:

Equipment: ___ Computer   ___ DVD Player

  ___ LED Projector and Screen   ___ Flip Chart(s) and Markers

  ___ Other: ___ Other:

Room Configuration: _____

Confirmation with Company: [ ] By Phone   [ ] By Email
  [ ] Date   [ ] Number of Participants   [ ] Address/Location
  [ ] Hotel Arrangements   [ ] Equipment Needs   [ ] Room Configuration
  [ ] Consultant Arrival Time   [ ] Purchase Order Number

Materials: Binders: [ ] Type: _____
  Folders: [ ] Type: _____
             [ ] ebb Seals   [ ] ebb Business Cards
  Unbound: [ ] 3-Hole Punch   [ ] Staple   [ ] Other: _____

Supplies: ___ Table Tents   ___ Name Tags   ___ Markers   ___ Trainer's Manual
  [ ] Other: _____

Special Instructions:

Manage your time well—it is your most valuable resource. Guard it jealously. Once it is gone, you will never get it back.

Manage your time well—
it is your most valuable resource.

GIVING BACK

You have received assistance, advice, and ideas from others as you have advanced in your career. Now you are probably asking for more of the same as you consider a consulting career. You may feel as if you owe many people. How can you pay them back? By doing the same for others. You should always be ready to give back—give back to clients, give back to the profession, give back to your community, and give back to individuals.

Try some of these ideas:

- Mentor someone just entering the field.
- Volunteer your services to a social service organization.
- Volunteer services to a civic group.
- Volunteer to help a children's group.
- Serve on local government or civic boards.
- Provide pro bono work for a local nonprofit organization.
- Send a thank-you card.
- Volunteer to assist inner-city programs during their summer sessions.
- Volunteer to serve on a committee for your professional association.
- Volunteer to speak at your local professional chapter meeting.
- Speak at your local high school's career day.
- Start a scholarship fund.

A PERSONAL CHECKUP

Earlier in this chapter you conducted a professional checkup. You have now read additional thoughts that relate more to the personal sphere, including ideas about managing time and giving back to the profession. If you are one of the readers who have been in the consulting field for at least a year, you may want to consider the personal checkup in Exhibit 10.4.

Exhibit 10.4. Personal Checkup: How Am I Doing?

Think about your personal life.

As a well-balanced professional:

1. Have I determined what I value most?

2. Do I know what I stand for, and have I ensured that my business is aligned to those standards?

3. Have I tracked my time on a log and identified the imbalances?

4. How can I reestablish balance among the important areas in my life— social, family, spiritual, business, education, health?

5. How can I align my use of time with what I value most?

6. Does what I am doing still excite me? Am I having fun?

7. What adjustments must I make to the business to increase my satisfaction?

8. What role do my family and friends play in these changes?

9. How will I know if I have improved one year from now?

10. What can I do to continue to learn?

11. What can I do to give back to the profession?

12. How will I take better care of myself in the coming year?

If you're thinking about being a consultant, don't stop there. Be a *respected, knowledgeable, well-balanced* consultant! Be a *successful* consultant. Be a *highly professional* consultant. Be all the things that you are capable of being. *Astound* yourself!

Do You Still Want to Be a Consultant?

Life is either a daring adventure, or nothing.

Helen Keller

T he most important reason to become a consultant is because you want to do it. If you have read this far in the book and the disadvantages don't discourage you and the challenges excite you, you are ready to develop an action plan that will take you into the world of consulting.

The most important reason to become a consultant is because you want to do it.

This chapter provides an example of a week in the life of a consultant. It raises lifestyle issues that do not fit neatly into other chapters. One of the most salient reasons for becoming a consultant is that you can create the lifestyle you choose. Therefore, this chapter includes visioning exercises that will help you clarify your future.

If you answered the chapter's title question with a "Yes!" there is an action plan you can use to begin the planning and execution of your consulting practice. It provides a structure to take you from "I *want* to be a consultant" to *"I am a consultant!"*

If you are not quite ready to take the plunge into independent consulting, this chapter's Fast Fifty exercise will start you thinking about what you can do next to move "closer to ready."

A WEEK IN A CONSULTANT'S LIFE

It is Saturday afternoon, and I am completing this book on my laptop at home. I have written several books and recognize how crucial it is to get this book in on time. I am several hours behind my original schedule today because I was dealing with email for four hours this morning. It seems that most of my clients respond and initiate email around the clock, every day. Many things have changed in my personal life and in my professional life since I wrote the first edition of this book. Personally, I got married, bought a house on the Chesapeake Bay, and moved to Virginia. Professionally, I sold my Wisconsin office, wrote and edited two dozen books, conducted work with wonderful clients, and gained a different perspective on travel.

I will leave tomorrow, Sunday, on the 7 A.M. flight to California to conduct a Facilitating Organizational Change Certificate program for ASTD. Although the book isn't due until the end of the week, I must complete this manuscript today— or tonight, as I will be immersed in the seminar. If I do require more than today to finish, my husband will most likely attend a planned neighborhood gathering without me—again.

I could take the manuscript with me, but I have learned that if I do, I will not work on it. Therefore, if I am not near completion, I will call my neighbors and let them know I'll be absent tonight. I try not to do this too often, but when someone else is counting on me to come through—as my editor is on this book—I may need to be flexible.

I can look out my window to a beautiful view of the Chesapeake Bay, which is sometimes distracting and sometimes inspiring. If I look around my home office, I see the stacks that represent twelve major client projects I will complete over the next couple of months, two book projects I have started, a series of webinars I am recording for ASTD, and a book-writing retreat I will conduct.

In my briefcase I have a 3"×6" leather-bound annual calendar. It is scribbled full of notations, phone numbers, meeting dates, color-coded times for each client, and locations. I have about a dozen various colored files—each representing a different project.

There are seven blue files, each one representing a client project. One is a two-day team-building session that will be held in Houston. Four blue folders represent yearlong projects that I am completing with various private industry and government clients; the projects address learning, talent management, change, and Lean Six Sigma. I need to contact each of those clients this week. Because I will be in California and my clients are all on the East Coast, I will most likely make those calls at about 6 A.M. The last two files represent design projects with clients in California and New York. As I scan them, I am reminded that I need to design questionnaires and conduct interviews for both projects. I muse that those seven blue folders represent more work than I would have been expected to produce internally in a year. Politics, policies, meetings, and other things prevent internal employees from being as productive as I can be as an external consultant.

There are two green folders, representing two volunteer projects. I am moderating eight webinars that represent the areas of expertise for ASTD's Certified Professional in Learning and Performance (CPLP). The second volunteer effort is a presentation I will make in Atlanta titled "Squeeze More into Your Training Session."

A gray folder represents a special project. I am the consulting editor for the *Pfeiffer Training Annuals* and *Pfeiffer Consulting Annuals*. Because change management has become a staple in today's organizations, we decided to focus on that topic as a theme. I have a list of over ninety people I want to contact as contributors.

Pink folders represent marketing. One pink folder contains creative ideas for our Christmas mailing—one of our key marketing activities. The second folder contains the list of ninety trainers that contributed to *90 World-Class Activities by 90 World-Class Trainers*. We are designing a "worldly" gift for this stellar group.

An orange folder holds two proposals for which we are awaiting a response. I am carrying them with me in case one of the companies calls and wants something clarified.

The yellow folder contains my expense sheet, last week's financial report, the year's income projections, and the monthly expense and budget sheet. These four pages, combined with my calendar, contain enough data for me to make a number of decisions. I keep the spreadsheets on a memory stick as well in case I need more information while I am on the road. Also in the yellow folder are several real estate descriptions, as I am interested in investing in another piece of real estate.

I have also packed the latest issues of *Harvard Business Review, T+D, Consulting Magazine,* and *Fast Company,* and a copy of *Mayflower,* by Nathaniel Philbrick. These are all airplane reading.

Stuck among the folders is a small brochure advertising an e-learning conference. My thought process is something like this: "I should go. The fee is too high. But the lineup is great. I'm too busy. But I deserve a break. It's too late to plan anything around the trip. Some of my favorite people—Ken Blanchard, Elliott Masie—with be there. But I really should get that marketing campaign designed. The networking would be great for me. But I will lose a couple of billable days. I will gain the LMS knowledge I need to help my clients. I'll think about it on the plane."

Speaking of planes, my leather ticket folder is in the front of my briefcase, bursting at the seams with the printed itineraries for the next couple of weeks. It also holds my travel ID cards and a spare stash of business cards. My small wallet that holds everything I could ever need (I gave up carrying a purse more than twenty years ago) is also tucked in the front of my briefcase.

I have several lovely leather briefcases, but I continue to use my black nylon Lands' End model. It is light and easy to swing on my shoulder as I drag one or two suitcases on wheels through airports from coast to coast.

As an added thought, I stuff a dozen catalogues (Lands' End, Bloomingdales, Gumps) in my briefcase (you can always stuff one more thing in it). I like travel, and I like flying. Really!

Even with the new stricter travel rules, I like the hustle and bustle of busy airports. I like the takeoff; it gives me a surge of energy. I like the freedom to be unavailable so that I can read without interruption or distraction. I read books (fiction and nonfiction), catch up on my reading of professional journals, and shop. Shop? Yes. I love catalogue shopping and find that flights are a great time to thumb through catalogues and rip out pages that picture gift ideas. Later I'll make final decisions about which items to purchase for others or for myself.

I need to plan for the week. When I arrive in California I will set up the training room for Monday and Tuesday. It will take about three hours to ensure that everything is perfect for the participants. I will be up by 5 A.M., on the phone by 6 A.M. to clients on the East Coast, and in the training room by 7 A.M. The session starts at 8:30 A.M.

Tuesday night I will fly to Washington, D.C., on the red-eye. I try not to do this too often, though it was my preference in my early years as a consultant. I need to be with a client on Wednesday morning for a meeting that starts at 10:30 A.M. So I will drop my luggage off at the hotel, freshen up, and head to the meeting. Wednesday evening I will probably have dinner with someone from the company. It will be a late night—dinners with clients usually are.

Thursday morning I will work with another department in the same organization to coordinate a Lean Six Sigma project. I have worked with this organization steadily for eight years. I know a great deal about their people and their business, so they use me in many capacities. In the afternoon I will rent a car and drive to a small town in Maryland where I am working with another small consulting firm to design a negotiations participant handbook.

e-Idea

If you drive to most of your clients' places of business, you can always use MapQuest (www.mapquest.com) or Google Maps for directions. Even better, invest in a handheld GPS system (or one built into your car). Once you have it, you'll wonder how you ever lived without it. If you rent cars in other countries, a GPS system is a huge time saver. (Yes, it will speak English.)

I will fly home Thursday evening, stop at the office for an hour to better prepare myself for the next day, and arrive at my door about 10 P.M.

Friday morning I will enjoy the newspaper on the deck with a cup of chai and be at the office before 8 A.M. Friday is usually a catch-up day for me. I will return phone calls, proof proposals, finish old projects, start new projects, write letters, handwrite half a dozen notes to clients and colleagues, add my opinions about office issues that concern others, and just catch up on everything else. I will leave the office around 6 P.M., after making phone calls to the West Coast.

Sometimes I stay home on Fridays to work on projects that require more concentration and perhaps go into the office for an hour or two in the afternoon. A heavy travel schedule makes it difficult to schedule appointments at the dentist and doctor or even to have my hair cut. I count on my staff to make the calls to obtain the appointments. Traveling also makes it difficult to schedule social time with friends. I count on my husband to plan our evenings on the town or to know where the best jazz band is playing. If it were up to me, it would be too late to schedule anything, and our friends would all have plans with other people who do not travel.

After reading these paragraphs, you may have some questions. Let's tackle each of your potential questions, as each represents an aspect of the consultant's lifestyle that you may wish to consider before becoming a consultant.

- *Why is she writing a book, and why is she so intent on finishing it?* Consultants write books as a marketing tool, to demonstrate their knowledge and expertise, and to share something with the rest of the world.

I enjoy writing. Unless you have a best-seller, you will not make money from the book itself. Self-published authors claim that they do make money, but then you need to deal with distribution and other hassles I don't want. I am intent on finishing the book on time because I said I would. As a consultant, you will want to build trust with everyone you meet. Everyone is a potential client, and everyone is a potential reference for you. Why write a book at all? Being published is equated with expertise for some, which allows you to charge a higher fee. I am already charging what I consider the maximum fair client fee. I write for the joy of writing. As a consultant, you may write for other reasons.

- *Why can't she take her laptop and finish the book next week?* Consultants owe their clients their undivided attention when they are working for them.

When I work with a client, I am completely absorbed by the work at hand. I rarely think about the other projects in my briefcase. I am focused completely on the client for whom I am working. It's difficult to go back to a hotel room after focusing for twelve hours on one client and switch gears to write a proposal or even a letter, let alone a book! The long hours require some downtime. If you go out to dinner with a client, you can expect a late night.

- *Why did she spend four hours on email on a Saturday, and why is she traveling for business on Sunday?* Weekends may not always be free for consultants. They often see Saturday morning as a catch-up time.

I try to make myself available to all clients at any time. Everyone I work with is busy! I try to keep up with email myself when I can, and sometimes schedule telephone calls on the weekend. It is frequently impossible to find a time when two of us can meet in person or by phone. Some of my clients want to talk on weekends and evenings, though I try to discourage it. Other consultants prefer to talk on weekends more often. The Sunday travel is my choice. If I travel on Monday, I have lost another billable day. If I schedule a Monday-Tuesday assignment, I can still easily be available for a Thursday-Friday assignment if necessary. As a consultant, you will need to determine how working or traveling will affect your weekends and your lifestyle. You will also want to consider how you will choose to balance being available to clients and still respecting your personal lifestyle.

- *How often does she cancel social plans for work?* Consultants do not work a typical workday or workweek and may need to switch social and work times around.

I rarely cancel social plans after I make them. However, I must admit that it takes a concerted effort to schedule social activities. I have to think about them a week in advance and put them on my calendar. When I arrive back in town on Friday evening, it is usually too late to plan for weekend activities. On the positive side, I have the option to build social time into my workweek. I do not need to ask anyone for permission to take an afternoon off for a haircut. I can add a day to my New York trip for shopping. I can browse in a bookstore on a Wednesday morning as long as I choose. As a consultant, you will have total freedom to set your own schedule.

- *How does the setting affect her work?* Consultants choose where they will work.

My surroundings affect my work greatly. I need the sun and water and a view when I am creating, developing, or designing something new. As a consultant, you will be able to select where you want to live. As long as you are a short drive to an airport, you can live anywhere. One of the best things about my move to Virginia is a shorter drive to the airport. It takes fifteen minutes now, as opposed to an hour when I lived in Wisconsin. If you decide you do not want overnight travel, you will need to live near your clients.

- *How often does she work at home? What are the benefits? What are the drawbacks?* Consultants can choose to have an office and work only there, choose to work out of their homes, or any combination of the two.

I complete any work that requires creative input in my home office, where I have a separate room furnished with a desk, equipment, and supplies. My office is better equipped, however, and most of my resources are there. In addition, I have staff at the office to support me when I experience a computer glitch or need assistance. These factors sometimes make it easier to work at the office. I have a fax machine, printer, and copier in each location. I travel about 70 percent of the time. Of the remainder, I probably spend half at my office and half at home. You will need to determine how having an office in your home will affect your lifestyle. The benefit for me is that I have total privacy. The drawback is that I can easily be distracted by a half-dozen personal projects.

- *Why does she refer to the color of the folders?* Consultants are always on the go. They need to find ways to have an office-in-a-bag.

The colored folders display what I have to do at a glance: blue for projects, green for volunteer work, and so on. The color coding also simplifies filing and retrieval. Other things that round out my office-in-a-bag include a miniature stapler, Post-it notes, paper, pens, highlighters, small scissors (small enough to be acceptable on a flight), an address and phone listing of key contacts, a memory stick, cash, comb, breath mints, lipstick, an extra pair of panty hose, spare frequent-flyer coupons, and a disposable rain poncho. I think you can imagine why I need each item. As a consultant, you will determine how much time you will live on the road, out of your car, or at home. In any case, know that you will be busier than you originally expected. Decide how that will affect your lifestyle and what you can do to prepare for it.

- *Why does she use a paper calendar rather than an electronic schedule?* Consultants are usually bouncing from project to project; they need to find ways to be organized.

I like to be able to pull my calendar out in a restaurant, the back of a taxi, or anyplace else without plugging in a computer. I don't need my computer or a PDA to be organized. One calendar tracks both professional and social engagements. My friends are all over the United States, and I like to schedule visits with them in conjunction with my travel schedule. I like to see everything I'm doing in one month at the same time. That said, technology allows you more flexibility than you could ever imagine. You will want to determine how technology will affect your lifestyle and what you must do to keep yourself organized. Do what works best for you.

- *Why does she refer to her volunteer work?* Consultants can be role models for giving back to the profession and their communities.

I volunteer because it is good for my soul. I like to volunteer. I did not get where I am without hundreds of generous people giving me something—a lead, a reference, an idea, time, encouragement, or a chance. Volunteering and helping others enter the field are my ways of giving back to a profession that has given so much to me. Think about how some volunteer or pro bono work can fit into the lifestyle you are creating.

- *Why does she carry the financial information with her?* The financial data tell a consultant if the mortgage will be paid next month.

I carry it with me so that it is readily available if I need to make decisions. Besides, it really amounts to only four pieces of paper that are updated weekly or monthly. They are printed directly from the computer, and I toss old ones away as I receive updates. If I need additional data, they are available on the memory stick in my briefcase. You will need to determine how you will be able to fit data analysis into a schedule which dictates that you will not always be at your desk.

- *What's significant about the reading materials?* Consultants typically read a lot to stay on top of the profession.

What is significant about my reading list is what is missing, more than what is there. Although I have a good selection of professional reading, I typically pack a good fiction book for balance. My not taking a fiction book signals that this is a busy month. As a consultant, you must determine how you will keep up with all your reading.

- *Why can't she decide about attending the conference?* Consultants owe it to their clients to stay on top of issues and solutions.

I know that I need to attend a conference like the one described. As you read, there are always issues and events that will tug at you. Every argument is viable. You must determine how you will make decisions like this one. The lifestyle you choose will be a factor in helping you determine which is more important: feeding your brain or feeding your bank account, taking a break from work or catching up on work, capitalizing on an opportunity to hear leaders in the field or capitalizing on an opportunity to market to clients on your list.

- *Why the discussion about a briefcase, purse, and luggage?* Consultants have many things to juggle.

I try to simplify, simplify, simplify! That means ensuring that I have whatever I need wherever I go, but not one thing too many. Simplifying does not mean eliminating everything. If it rains and I don't have a poncho with me, I will need to scurry around solving that problem. Omitting necessities is not simplifying. I keep a suitcase packed with all the basics; I avoid checking luggage to save time and to avoid the hassle of lost luggage. New rules make it harder and harder to live with only carry-on luggage, but it is possible. See a later question for more details.

If I do need to check luggage, I always have what I need for the first twenty-four hours with me in my carry-on bag. I need wheels on my luggage so that I can cruise through airports and to a taxi without being dependent on a porter. You will want to look at the lifestyle you now lead to determine how consulting will add complexity or how it could simplify it. Ask yourself if you have the physical stamina for the rigorous travel that may be required.

- *How much equipment will she pack in her briefcase?* Many consultants carry laptops to use for development and research, PDAs for responding to emails, a cell phone, a DVD player, an iPod, and even a printer.

I have learned to travel most often with just my cell phone. But what about email, you may wonder? The greatest drawback of email is that people believe that you will receive it, read it, and respond to it immediately! This is not possible when I am with other clients, as I do not wish to take time away from them. Therefore I usually have my associate, Lorraine, monitor my email when I am with a client all day. Another option is to answer email from the hotel's business center. Many consultants use a handheld PDA for responding to email. PDAs can be very useful; some can be used as mobile phones, Web browsers, media players, and even as navigation equipment. Again, there are pros and cons to all the technological equipment available, and you will need to determine what you will require to be efficient.

---

*The greatest drawback of email is that
people believe that you will receive it, read it,
and respond to it immediately!*

---

e-Idea

Have someone you trust at your office monitor email while you are with a client. You owe it to your clients to be fully present when working with them. Yet others will expect an instantaneous answer. All your clients appreciate your focused attention when they are paying for your time.

I do not want to take my computer on every plane I board. I travel with my laptop if I need it for design or writing or for a presentation; otherwise it stays at home. Travel has become so inconvenient that I have limited the technology I schlep around with me. When I do take a laptop, I am more interested in saving my back than having a large screen. I have found a couple of laptops that weigh only two or three pounds and do not need their own separate case. They are wonderfully light and serve my purpose beautifully.

- *What's all the fuss about airplanes?* Consultants' travel can take up time, reduce productivity, and affect their personal life.

It is not uncommon for me to visit both coasts in one week. I am on an airplane every week, and because I do not live near an airport hub, I change planes for most trips. One trip often means four airplanes. Yes, I rack up frequent-flyer miles—over five million and still counting. But the drawback that will affect your lifestyle is the difficulty in maintaining balance. Consider two simple things: food and exercise. You really must work hard to eat a healthy diet and exercise while on the road. How will you approach travel in terms of its effects on your lifestyle?

Rules about what I can pack in my carry-on luggage have stymied my travel a bit. As I mentioned, I still take only carry-on whenever possible. Here's what I have changed. I have purchased the smallest size toothpaste (Did you know that baking soda and salt makes a good toothpaste in an emergency?) for travel and ask the hotel front desk for additional toothpaste upon check-in. I have stopped using lip gloss and switched to a solid deodorant and perfume stick. I also pack the fragrance samples found between magazine pages. I am a guest in two hotels almost weekly, so I have packed a small set of toiletries in a Ziploc bag, and they store it for me between visits. When I must, I drop in to the local drugstore to pick up hairspray and other items that are not available in a three-ounce container or do not have a dry or solid substitute.

- *Why are the details of her schedule significant?* A consultant's schedule is usually hectic.

The week that I described is pretty typical. I don't try to get my week down to forty hours. I don't think I will ever try. I love what I do, and I have created ways to build things other than work into my work schedule. Who do you know who can shop in New York City one week and in San Francisco the next? How many employees can take time off for a haircut or to browse a furniture store during the week? Who do you know who can work at home by choice? Who do you know who could take a stack of journals and sit next to the ocean to catch up on his or her professional reading? Although I may have worked about seventy hours in addition to travel time in one week, I will have many opportunities to balance those hours. Your lifestyle could change dramatically based on schedule alone. Will you have your family's support for such a dramatic change?

Your lifestyle is yours and yours alone. To thrive as a consultant, you will need to decide what you want your lifestyle to be like. The next section gives you some visualization activities to help you clarify what you want your consulting lifestyle to be like and to help you plant that lifestyle firmly in your mind so that you are more likely to create it.

e-Idea

You can take all kinds of information with you when you travel. Go to www.podcast.net and download all sorts of interesting topics before your trip.

VISUALIZING SUCCESS

A friend of mine was a high school state champion tennis player. Her coach required her to spend hours visualizing success. She visualized herself completing specific strokes perfectly. She visualized herself winning a match. She visualized herself as a champion. Coaches of many other sports use visualization as well. They ask athletes to close their eyes and visualize what the pass feels like leaving their hands, what the wind feels like against their faces, what the ball looks like going through the hoop, what the crack of the club against the ball sounds like.

You can do the same thing. You can be your own coach. Of course, before you do that you must have a clear picture of the kind of future you want. Turn to Exhibit 11.1. This exercise will help you determine how you want to live and work—how you want to spend your time. Find a quiet place—one where you are sure you will not be interrupted by a phone call, a visit, or a nagging chore. Take at least an hour to complete the exercise. Take more time if you can. Put it aside. Sleep on it. Feed your subconscious by thinking about it before you sleep. Then dream about it. Pull it out again and fill in more details. Now discuss it with your significant other. Make additions or deletions.

Place your visualization exercise in a safe place, perhaps in your end-of-the-year tickler file—or perhaps you want to give your dream one year. Make an appointment with yourself one year from now to review your desires. Realize that you may not have achieved all that you identified. Realize also that some of what you want may have changed. In any event, you will most likely learn much about yourself and what is important to you.

Create a "successful future" file to keep your ideal future in front of you. You may wish to place your Visualize Success exercise in the folder. However, because pictures speak louder than words, shout your future by collecting pictures and keeping them in a file. The following can give you ideas:

- Magazine pictures of people engaged in a hobby you want to begin.
- Snapshots of you and your family or friends having fun together.
- Pictures of the results of some activity you want to find time to do, such as a gourmet meal you want to try cooking or a handcrafted oak desk if you want to try woodworking.
- An advertisement for the condo you want to purchase.
- Cartoons that depict your special situation.
- A travel flyer advertising a vacation spot you want to visit.
- A picture of the scene you want to view outside your office window. (For years my picture was of the Chesapeake Bay!)
- A dollar bill with a larger figure written on it representing the amount you want in your savings account!

Periodically sit down with your file to remind yourself of what success looks like to you. It will keep you focused on your future. I guarantee it!

Exhibit 11.1. Visualize Success.

Take a few minutes to imagine a successful future for yourself. Think in terms of three to five years. Describe your successful future.

Part I. Professional

1. Describe your professional goals. (What is your title? What do clients say about your work? What do your colleagues say about you?)

2. Describe your interactions with your clients. (What are you doing? Where are you doing it? How does it feel? To whom are you talking?)

3. Describe your work more thoroughly. (How many people are around you? What is their relationship to you? What work excites you?)

4. Describe the logistics more thoroughly. (How much do you travel? Where? For how long? Why? What does your office look like? Where is it? What is the view outside your office window?)

5. Describe the results of your work. (What honors or awards have you received? What is your annual salary? What profit does your business make? How much is in your retirement account? Your savings account?)

6. What other professional dreams do you have? (What other professions? What other work?)

Exhibit 11.1. Visualize Success, Cont'd.

Part II. Personal

1. Describe your personal goals. (What are you doing? What percentage of your time is spent pursuing personal goals? Where are you? With whom?)

2. Describe your interactions with family and friends. (What clubs have you joined? What vacations have you taken? What are you doing? Where? With whom? How does it feel?)

3. What do you do when you are alone? (What are you reading? What are your daydreams? Where are you?)

4. What are you learning? (Are you taking classes? Did you earn an advanced degree? Where? How? Why?)

5. What personal skills have you acquired? (What hobbies are you trying? What sports are you participating in? With whom? How often?)

6. Describe the logistics of your personal life. (Where do you live? What is your living space like? What kind of car do you drive? How are mundane chores completed?)

TAKING ACTION

I subscribe to the belief that all of us should love what we do and do what we love. Money will follow in one way or another. Life is about passion. And if you fail? At least you failed doing something you loved!

I once heard a speaker say that only 2 percent of all Americans have the discipline to achieve their dreams. Of those who do not achieve their dreams, 23 percent do not know what they want; another 67 percent know what they want, but do not know how to make it happen. The remaining 10 percent know what they want and how to get it, but lack discipline to follow through. In which category will you be?

Exhibit 11.2 provides you with an outline to begin to put your plans on paper. Why not start today?

GETTING READY

Perhaps you have read this far in this book, and you're interested, but you are not quite ready to become an independent consultant. Perhaps you think you need a little more experience. Perhaps your financial situation is not stable enough to take the risk. Perhaps you are satisfied with the job you now have. But someday . . .

What can you do? Don't lose the spark. Turn to Exhibit 11.3 and list fifty things you can do to move closer to becoming a consultant. List everything that comes to mind as fast as you can, such as read another book, join a professional organization, interview a consultant, take a course, attend a conference, invent a name for your consulting practice, identify a client with whom you would choose to work. All suggestions are good. Don't pause to judge or prioritize them now. Just write. Ready, set, go!

What can you do with your fifty ideas? It would seem natural for you to begin to put a plan together for how to go from here to there. *The Consultant's Quick Start Guide* (Biech, 2001), another book in this series, can help you simplify the planning process by providing you with a series of questions, a list of ideas, and plenty of room for planning.

Remember, it takes as much energy to wish as it does to plan. So go ahead. Wish on paper, and it becomes a plan.

Wish on paper, and it becomes a plan.

⊙ Exhibit 11.2. Action Plan.

As you complete each step, check the box. The numbers in parentheses refer to exhibits in this book.

1. Do you know enough about the consulting profession?
   - ❑ Interview consultants you know. (1.1)
   - ❑ Read about consulting. Scan the reading list at the end of the book.
   - ❑ Compare your values to the requirements of consulting.

2. Are you a match for the profession?
   - ❑ Compare your skills and characteristics to those required of a consultant. (2.1)
   - ❑ Measure your propensity as an entrepreneur. (2.2)

3. Do you know enough about consultant billing practices?
   - ❑ Calculate your financial requirements. (3.1)
   - ❑ Read about consulting billing structures.

4. Are you ready to start?
   - ❑ Describe your business, its services, and products.
   - ❑ Identify your market.
   - ❑ Analyze your competition.
   - ❑ Assess your skills.
   - ❑ Name your business.
   - ❑ Determine your pricing structure. (3.2, 3.3)
   - ❑ Identify start-up costs. (4.2)
   - ❑ Select an accountant.
   - ❑ Determine your business structure.
   - ❑ Check on zoning laws, licenses, and taxes.
   - ❑ Select a location.
   - ❑ Develop a business plan (4.1) that includes the following:
       - ❑ Business description
       - ❑ Marketing plan (5.1)
       - ❑ Management plan
       - ❑ Financial plan (4.3, 4.4, 4.5)
   - ❑ Select a banker, attorney, and insurance agent.
   - ❑ Arrange for financing or set aside capital for a worst-case scenario. (4.6)
   - ❑ File documentation to register your business legally.

🔘 Exhibit 11.2. Action Plan, Cont'd.

5. Are you consistently marketing your services?
   - ❑ Complete and follow your marketing calendar. (5.2)
   - ❑ Identify potential client organizations and research them. (5.3)
   - ❑ Introduce your services with letters and telephone calls. (5.4)
   - ❑ Call on organizations in person. (5.5)
   - ❑ Maintain a client contact log. (5.6)

6. Do you have a handle on your expenses?
   - ❑ Maintain a monthly expense record. (6.1)
   - ❑ Track petty cash and expenditures. (6.3, 6.4)
   - ❑ Monitor invoices. (6.5)
   - ❑ Invoice clients in a timely manner. (6.6)
   - ❑ Project revenue. (6.7)
   - ❑ Track the time and costs expended on specific projects. (6.8)
   - ❑ Compare project profits. (6.9)

7. Are you building professional client relationships?
   - ❑ Clarify expectations during the contracting phase with each client. (7.1)
   - ❑ Continue to build a partnership with each client. (7.2, 7.3)

8. Are you ready to grow?
   - ❑ Explore various ways to build your business. (8.1, 8.2)
   - ❑ Ensure that expectations are clear when using subcontractors. (8.3, 8.4)

9. Do you consistently practice the highest ethical standards?

10. Are you professional in every respect?
    - ❑ Improve your skills.
    - ❑ Balance your life and your business. (10.1, 10.4)
    - ❑ Manage your time wisely. (10.2)
    - ❑ Mentor others.

11. Do you enjoy the profession as much as you thought you would?

Exhibit 11.3. Fast Fifty.

Instructions: List fifty things you can do to move closer to becoming a consultant.

1.	26.
2.	27.
3.	28.
4.	29.
5.	30.
6.	31.
7.	32.
8.	33.
9.	34.
10.	35.
11.	36.
12.	37.
13.	38.
14.	39.
15.	40.
16.	41.
17.	42.
18.	43.
19.	44.
20.	45.
21.	46.
22.	47.
23.	48.
24.	49.
25.	50.

READING LIST

Bacal, R. (2002). *The complete idiot's guide to consulting.* Madison, WI: CWL Publishing Enterprises.

Bell, C. R., & Nadler, L. (1979). *The client-consultant handbook.* Houston, TX: Gulf.

Bellman, G. M. (2002). *The consultant's calling* (2nd ed.). San Francisco: Jossey-Bass.

Bellman, G. M., Block, P., & Boehm, B. (1986). Find the right consultant. *Infoline,* 8610. Alexandria, VA: ASTD.

Biech, E. (1995, Summer). Ten mistakes CEOs make about training. *William & Mary Business Review,* pp. 13–16.

Biech, E. (2000). *The consultant's legal guide.* San Francisco: Pfeiffer.

Biech, E. (2001). *The consultant's quick start guide: An action plan for your first year in business.* San Francisco: Pfeiffer.

Biech, E. (Ed.). (2001). *The Pfeiffer book of successful team-building tools.* San Francisco: Pfeiffer.

Biech, E. (2003). *Marketing your consulting services.* San Francisco: Pfeiffer.

Biech, E. (Ed.). (2007). *90 world-class activities by 90 world-class trainers.* San Francisco: Pfeiffer.

Biech, E. (Ed.). (2007). *Thriving through change: A practical guide to change.* Alexandria, VA: ASTD Press.

Biswas, S., & Twitchelle, D. (2001). *Management consulting: A complete guide to the industry* (2nd ed.). Hoboken, NJ: Wiley.

Block, P. (2000). *Flawless consulting* (2nd ed.). San Francisco: Pfeiffer.

Bond, W. J. (1997). *Going solo.* New York: McGraw-Hill.

Carucci, R. A., & Tetenbaum, T. J. (2000). *The value-creating consultant: How to build and sustain lasting client relationships.* New York: AMACOM.

Chung, E. (2002). *Vault career guide to consulting: An indispensable guide to landing a consulting position and succeeding in a consulting career.* Boulder, CO: Vault.

Cohen, W. A. (1985). *How to make it big as a consultant.* New York: AMACOM.

Florzak, D. (1999). *Successful independent consulting: Turn your career experience into a consulting business.* Brookfield, IL: Logical Directions.

Fox, J. (2000). *How to become a rainmaker.* New York: Hyperion.

Freedman, R. (2000). *The IT consultant: A commonsense framework for managing the client relationship.* San Francisco: Pfeiffer.

Gendelman, J. (1995). *Consulting 101.* Alexandria, VA: ASTD.

Holtz, H. (1994). *The business plan guide for independent consultants.* Hoboken, NJ: Wiley.

Kintler, D., & Adams, B. (1998). *Streetwise independent consulting.* Holbrook, MA: Adams Media.

Koestenbaum, P. (2003). *The philosophic consultant: Revolutionizing organizations with ideas.* San Francisco: Pfeiffer.

Lewin, M. D. (1995). *The overnight consultant.* Hoboken, NJ: Wiley.

Lewin, M. D. (1997). *The consultant's survival guide.* Hoboken, NJ: Wiley.

Lewis, L. (2000). *What to charge: Pricing strategies for freelancers and consultants.* Putnam Valley, NY: Aletheia.

Moss, W. (2005). *Starting from scratch: Secrets from 21 ordinary people who made the entrepreneurial leap.* Chicago: Dearborn Trade.

Nelson, B., & Economy, P. (1997). *Consulting for dummies.* Hoboken, NJ: Wiley.

Peters, T. (1997, August-September). The brand called you. *Fast Company,* pp. 83–94.

Phillips, J. (2000). *The consultant's scorecard: Tracking results and bottom-line impact of consulting projects.* New York: McGraw-Hill.

Riddle, J. (2001). *Consulting business.* Irvine, CA: Entrepreneur Press.

Shefsky, L. E. (1994). *Entrepreneurs are made, not born.* New York: McGraw-Hill.

Stein, C. (1994, November 15). Millions for their thoughts: Management consulting finds big, profitable place in cutthroat economy. *Boston Globe.*

Stern, C. W., & Deimler, M. (2006). *The Boston Consulting Group on 2006 strategy: Classic concepts and new perspectives* (2nd ed.). Hoboken, NJ: Wiley.

Weinberg, G. M. (1985). *The secrets of consulting.* New York: Dorset House.

Weiss, A. (2002). *Million dollar consulting: The professional's guide to growing a practice* (3rd ed.). New York: McGraw-Hill.

Weiss, A. (2003). *Great consulting challenges: And how to surmount them.* San Francisco: Pfeiffer.

WetFeet. (2006). *Careers in management consulting: WetFeet insider guide.* San Francisco: Author.

Wharton MBA Consulting Club. (1997). *The Wharton MBA case interview study guide.* San Francisco: WetFeet.

Wong, L. (2001). *The Harvard Business School guide to careers in management consulting, 2001.* Cambridge, MA: Harvard Business School Press.

INDEX

ideas on, 229–230; collaboration with another consultant, 221–223; competency in developing and managing, 249–250; considering practice versus firm, 211; costs and trends in, 173, 175*e*, 176; expanding geographical market, 227–229; expanding into product market, 225–227; hiring graduate students, 218; hiring subcontractors, 211–218; joint ventures or "virtual partners," 220–221; offering other services, 223–224; using temporary services for, 219

Business image, 88–93

business logo, 89–90

Business names: adding "tag line" to your business, 64; Doing Business As (DBA) certificate, 65; reserving website domain, 96, 98, 107; selecting your business, 64–66; website resources on naming process, 65, 66

Business niche, 87–88

Business plan format: business description, 73*e*; competitive analysis, 74*e*–75*e*; financial plan, 76*e*–77*e*, 78*e*; management plan, 76*e*; market analysis, 74*e*; marketing plan, 75*e*

Business plans: benefits of developing, 69–70; budget format, 81*e*; first-year cash-flow projection, 82*e*; format for, 71*e*–78*e*; personal financial statement, 84*e*; printing your, 83; scheduling reviews of your, 85; start-up expenses, 79*e*–80*e*; three-year projection, 83*e*; using your, 84–85; website resources for, 70, 85; worst-case scenario included as part of, 148

Business structures: corporation, 68–69; limited liability company (LLC), 69; list of possible configurations, 203–204; partnership, 68; sole proprietorship, 67–68

BusinessWeek, 253

C

Capital investments, 176–177*e*

Card contacts, 259

CareerJournal, 12, 13

Careers in Business website, 32

Cash flow issues: bill immediately, 149; clients' reputation for prompt payment, 150–151; comparing actual expenses to budget, 156; comparing leasing and purchase rates, 154; late payments, 154–155; making your money work for you, 152; monitoring accounts receivable, 150; obtaining line of credit, 153; offering prepayment discounts, 151; pay bills when due and not before, 155; project initiation fees in proposals, 151; refraining from paying client expenses, 152; using reliable delivery system to send invoices, 149–150; selecting good bank and bankers, 152–153. *See also* Invoices

Cash stash, 260

Certification resources, 248

Certified Electrical Engineer (CEE), 248

Certified Management Consultant (CMC), 248

Certified Professional in Learning and Performance (CPLP) [ASTD], 114, 248, 269

Certified Public Accountant (CPA), 248

Certified Speaking Professional (CSP), 248

Chat rooms, 108

Client base: marketing plan to create, 100–107; 113 tactics for low-budget marketing, 114–121; practical thoughts on marketing for, 108–114; using website to build, 107–108

Client Contact Log, 130*e*

Client expenses: determining and billing for, 170; refraining from paying, 152; repaying costs related to consultant errors, 235

Client-consultant relationship: communication aspects of, 196; considering number of clients and, 200; continuous improvement of, 194–196; decisions facilitating, 196; ensuring successful, 200–202; ethical issues related to, 232–238; first meeting, 181–182; four phases of building, 182–184, 186–193*e*; maintaining post-project, 197–198; people element of, 197; professional competency in building, 250;

repeat business through good, 180; value produced through, 198–199. *See also* Consultants; Projects

Client-consultant relationship phases: 1: finding the right match, 183–184, 186, 190*e*, 192*e*; 2: getting to know one another, 186–187, 190*e*–191*e*, 192*e*–193*e*; 3: being productive, 187–188, 191*e*, 193*e*; 4: creating independence, 189, 191*e*, 193*e*; Client Checklist for, 192*e*–193*e*; Consultant Checklist for, 190*e*–191*e*; overview of, 182–183

Clients: acquiring new, 113; Company Profiles for, 123*e*; contracts with potential, 122–132; definition of, 2; determining how much they will pay, 48–49, 50*e*; discussing money/fees with, 60–61; electronic newsletters to, 117; ethical issues related to behavior of, 242–243; first meeting with, 181–182; getting map directions when driving to, 271; giving money-back guarantees to, 61–62; how to refuse assignment with, 145–146; number and management of multiple, 200; questions asked/ issues to cover with, 131–132, 183–184, 186; refraining from paying expenses of, 152; reputation for prompt payment by, 150–151; sending personal messages to, 112–113; why they need consultants, 10–11; word of mouth marketing by, 114. *See also* Consulting fees; Contracts; Projects

CMC (Certified Management Consultant), 114

Code of Ethics, 243–244

Cold call warm-ups, 122, 124

Cold calls, 122

Collaborating consultants, 221–223, 239–240, 254

Communication: client-consultant relationship and, 196; email, 276–277; as professional competency, 248–249

Company Profile, 123*e*

Competencies. *See* Professionalism competencies

Competitive analysis, 74*e*–75*e*

Conditional fees, 53–54

Confidential information, 143*e*, 161, 234

Conflict of interest, 234

Consultant partnerships, 5

Consultant subcontractors: advantages/disadvantages of hiring, 217–218; considerations when hiring, 95–96, 211; described, 5–6; ethical issues related to, 238–242; hiring yourself out as, 220; IRS criteria/tax issues for, 217; Subcontractor Agreement, 212*e*–215*e*; Subcontractor Expense Record, 216*e*

Consultants: business niche of, 87; collaborating with another, 221–223, 239–240, 254; consulting perspective of, 11–13; dozen questions to ask, 20*e*; entrepreneurial characteristics of, 35–38*e*; ethical issues regarding behavior of, 232–242; first meeting with clients, 181–182; mentoring by, 254–255; offering other services, 223–224; personal characteristics of successful, 29–30; personality traits required of, 21*e*–24; professional image of, 88–93; roles played by, 30–32; signs of a mediocre, 32; skills for success required of, 26–29; types of, 2–7; a week in the life of a, 268–278. *See also* Client-consultant relationship

The Consultant's Calling (Bellman), 48, 58, 253, 261

The Consultant's Quick Start Guide (Biech), 282

Consulting 101 (Gendelman), 256

Consulting: are you a match for the profession?, 21*e*–24; business trends affecting, 8–9; client perspective on, 10–11; consultant perspective on, 11–13; defining, 1–2; financing the business of, 32; growth as profession, 7–8; rewards and realities of, 18–19; trends in, 9–10

Consulting business: balancing your life and, 255–257; considering practice versus firm, 211; costs of doing, 79*e*–80*e*, 86–87, 147–177*e*; ensuring success of, 200–202; ethics of, 58–60, 231–244; growth of, 173, 175*e*, 176, 203–230; high failure rate of, 35; line of credit for, 153;

Double dipping, 237
Double trips, 261
Dues/subscriptions, 161
DVD language program, 228

E

e-Ideas: accounting software, 156; ASTD Ask a Consulting Expert website, 57; banking electronically, 153; blogging, 225; careerjournal.com for consulting information, 13; Careers in Business website on consulting information, 32; certification information, 248; consulting job listings, 7; cultural business etiquette and customs, 229; electronic billing, 150, 259; *Entrepreneur* magazine website for articles, 36; executive coaching, 224; filing work electronically, 260; financial tracking forms, 166; IFTDO and IODA websites, 228; IMC's code of ethics, 243; invoice templates, 170; iPod and DVD language programs, 228; IRS criteria on subcontractor vs. employee status, 217; keeping spreadsheets on memory sticks, 176; Kennedy Consulting for information on trends, 10; map directions, 271; monitoring office email while traveling, 277; NACE Salary Survey Report, 3; online ethics newsletters, 244; online survey tools, 258; payscale.com for salary information, 49; permissions to copy anything, 236; podcasts, 225–226, 278; professional development resources, 254; programming cell phone with information, 262; purging confidential information from old computers, 161; selling "add-on" products/services via the Web, 223; small-scale research for clients, 198; taking pictures of participants/work for clients, 195, 196; webcasts or video taking, 226; WetFeet for consulting industry information, 5. *See also* Websites
Edison, T., 245
EDS, 4
Einstein, A., 1

Electronic billing, 150, 259
Electronic filing tips, 260
Electronic newsletters, 117
Email address, 93
Email communication, 276–277
End-of-the-year tickler file, 258–259
Entertainment expenses, 161
Entrepreneur magazine, 85, 90
Entrepreneurial characteristics: overview of, 35–36; self-testing your, 37*e*–38*e*
Ernst & Young, 4
Ethical issues: associated with fees, 58–60; of client-consultant relationship, 232–238; Code of Ethics, 243–244; consultant to consultant, 238–242; in the context of consulting, 231–232; double dipping, 237; related to subcontractors, 238–242
Ethics Today Online, 244
ExecuNet, 7
Executive coaching, 224
Experience. *See* Consulting experience

F

Facilitating Organizational Change Certificate program (ASTD), 268
Fast Company (journal), 14, 254, 270
Fast Fifty, 282, 285*e*
Fax cover page, 91, 92*e*
FedBizOpps.gov, 119
Federal government consulting, 119, 151
Fees. *See* Consulting fees
FEIN (federal employer ID number), 68
Filing system tips, 259–260
Financial plan, 76*e*–77*e*
Financial statements: budget format, 81*e*; first-year cash-flow projection, 82*e*; listed, 78*e*; personal financial statement, 84*e*; start-up costs, 79*e*–80*e*, 86–87; three-year projection, 83*e*. *See also* Business costs; Consulting fees
Firm versus practice, 211
First client meeting, 181–182

First-year cash-flow projection, 82*e*
Fixed-price projects, 52–53
Flawless Consulting (Block), 131, 184, 253
Ford, H., 25, 147
Fortune Magazine, 85, 253
4imprint, 116
Fox, J. J., 120

G

Gartner Group, 4
Gendelman, J., 256
Geographical market expansion, 227–229
Giving back, 265
Goldwyn, S., 41
Google Maps, 271
Government consulting, 119, 151
GPS systems, 271
Graduate student hires, 218
Gretzky, W., 7
Growth. *See* Business growth
Guarantees, 61–62

H

Half-day events, 54–55
Harris Interactive, 13
Harvard Business Review, 14, 85, 253, 270
Hay Group, 4
Hewitt Associates, 4
Home offices, 86
Hourly rates, 52
How Things Work, 113
How to Become a Rainmaker (Fox), 120
HP Technology, 4

I

Image (business), 88–93
Independent Consultant Association, 31
Initiation fees, 151
Institute of Management Consultants (IMC), 243, 247
Insurance expenses, 161
International Coach Federation (ICF), 248

International cross-cultural issues, 229
International expansion, 228
International Federation of Training Development Organizations (IFTDO), 228
International Organization Development Association (IODA), 228
Invoices: acting on late payments, 154–155; electronic billing of, 150, 259; include "small-business" status on, 154; Invoice Summary, 168*e*; monitoring accounts receivable, 150; professional image reflected in, 91; sample, 169*e*; sending out, 149–150; template for, 170, 259; what to include in, 167. *See also* Cash flow issues; Consulting fee charges
iPod language program, 228
IRS 1099 form, 217
IRS Publication 587, 86
ISA, 247

J

Jefferson, T., 231
Joint ventures, 220–221
Junk mail research, 111, 254

K

Keller, H., 267
Kennedy Consulting, 10
KPMG, 4

L

Land O'Lakes, 198
Language of Life, 228
Laptops, 277
Large firm consultants, 3–5
Late payments, 154–155
Learning events, 252–253
Leasing: comparing rates of purchase and, 154; tracking equipment and furniture, 161
Legal fees, 157, 159
Lewis, L., 155
Library Sign-Out Sheet, 176, 177*e*
Licenses, 162

ABOUT THE AUTHOR

Elaine Biech is president and managing principal of ebb associates inc, an organization development firm that helps organizations work through large-scale change. She has been in the training and consulting field for thirty years, and works with business, government, and nonprofit organizations.

Elaine specializes in helping people work as teams to maximize their effectiveness. Customizing all of her work for individual clients, she conducts strategic planning sessions and implements corporation-wide systems, such as quality improvement, reengineering of business processes, and mentoring programs. She facilitates such topics as coaching today's employee, fostering creativity, customer service, time management, stress management, speaking skills, training competence, conducting productive meetings, managing change, handling the difficult employee, organizational communication, conflict resolution, and effective listening.

Elaine has developed media presentations and training materials and has presented at dozens of national and international conferences. Known as the trainer's trainer, she custom designs training programs for managers, leaders, trainers, and consultants. Elaine has been featured in numerous publications, including the *Wall Street Journal, Harvard Management Update,* the *Washington Post,* and *Fortune.*

As a management and executive consultant, trainer, and designer, Elaine has provided services to Land O' Lakes, McDonald's, Lands' End, General Casualty Insurance, Chrysler, Johnson Wax, PricewaterhouseCoopers, American Family Insurance, Marathon Oil, Hershey Chocolate, Johnson Wax, Federal Reserve Bank, the U.S. Navy, NASA, Newport News Shipbuilding, Kohler Company, the FAA, American

Society for Training and Development (ASTD), American Red Cross, the Association of Independent Certified Public Accountants, the University of Wisconsin, the College of William and Mary, ODU, and hundreds of other public and private sector organizations to help them prepare for the challenges of the new millennium.

Elaine is the author and editor of over four dozen books and articles, including *90 World-Class Activities from 90 World-Class Trainers* (2007); ASTD's *Certification Study Guides* (2006), a nine-volume set; "12 Habits of Successful Trainers," ASTD *Infoline, 0509* (2005); "The ASTD Infoline Dictionary of Basic Trainer Terms," ASTD *Infoline, 0513* (2005); *Training for Dummies* (2005); *Marketing Your Consulting Services* (2003); *The Consultant's Quick Start Guide* (2001); *Successful Team-Building Tools* (2001); *The Consultant's Legal Guide* (2000); *Building High Performance* (1998); *Interpersonal Skills: Understanding Your Impact on Others* (1996); *The Pfeiffer Annual: Consulting* and *The Pfeiffer Annual: Training* (1998–2008, published annually); *The ASTD Sourcebook: Creativity and Innovation—Widen Your Spectrum* (1996); *The HR Handbook* (1996); *TQM for Training* (1994); *Managing Teamwork* (1994); *Process Improvement: Achieving Quality Together* (1994); *Business Communications* (1992); *Delegating for Results* (1992); "Diagnostic Tools for Total Quality," *Infoline, 9109* (1991); *Increased Productivity Through Effective Meetings* (1987); *Stress Management: Building Healthy Families* (1984). Her books have been translated into Chinese, German, and Dutch.

Elaine has a B.S. degree in business and education consulting and an M.S. degree in human resource development, both from the University of Wisconsin-Superior. She is active at the national level of the ASTD, serving on the 1990 national conference design committee, as a member of the national ASTD board of directors, and as the society's secretary from 1991 to 1994; initiating and chairing Consultant's Day for seven years; and serving as the international conference design chair in 2000. In addition to her work with ASTD, she has served on the advisory committee of the Independent Consultants Association (ICA) and on the board of directors of the Instructional Systems Association (ISA).

Elaine is the recipient of the 1992 National ASTD Torch Award and the 2004 ASTD Volunteer-Staff Partnership Award. She was selected for the 1995 Wisconsin Women Entrepreneur's Mentor Award. In 2001 she received ISA's highest award, the ISA Spirit Award. For the past ten years, she has been the consulting editor for the prestigious training and consulting annuals published by Pfeiffer.

Elaine can be reached at ebb associates inc, Box 8249, Norfolk, VA 23503 or by email at Elaine@ebbweb.com. Her website is www.ebbweb.com.

HOW TO USE THE CD-ROM

SYSTEM REQUIREMENTS

PC with Microsoft Windows 98SE or later
Mac with Apple OS version 8.6 or later

USING THE CD WITH WINDOWS

To view the items located on the CD, follow these steps:

1. Insert the CD into your computer's CD-ROM drive.
2. A window appears with the following options:

    Contents: Allows you to view the files included on the CD-ROM.

    Software: Allows you to install useful software from the CD-ROM.

    Links: Displays a hyperlinked page of websites.

    Author: Displays a page with information about the author(s).

    Contact Us: Displays a page with information on contacting the publisher or author.

    Help: Displays a page with information on using the CD.

    Exit: Closes the interface window.

If you do not have autorun enabled, or if the autorun window does not appear, follow these steps to access the CD:

1. Click Start -› Run.

2. In the dialog box that appears, type d:\start.exe, where d is the letter of your CD-ROM drive. This brings up the autorun window described in the preceding set of steps.

3. Choose the desired option from the menu. (See Step 2 in the preceding list for a description of these options.)

IN CASE OF TROUBLE

If you experience difficulty using the CD-ROM, please follow these steps:

1. Make sure your hardware and systems configurations conform to the systems requirements noted under "System Requirements" above.

2. Review the installation procedure for your type of hardware and operating system. It is possible to reinstall the software if necessary.

To speak with someone in Product Technical Support, call 800-762-2974 or 317-572-3994 Monday through Friday from 8:30 A.M. to 5 P.M. EST. You can also contact Product Technical Support and get support information through our website at www.wiley.com/techsupport.

Before calling or writing, please have the following information available:

- Type of computer and operating system.
- Any error messages displayed.
- Complete description of the problem.

It is best if you are sitting at your computer when making the call.

Pfeiffer Publications Guide

This guide is designed to familiarize you with the various types of Pfeiffer publications. The formats section describes the various types of products that we publish; the methodologies section describes the many different ways that content might be provided within a product. We also provide a list of the topic areas in which we publish.

FORMATS

In addition to its extensive book-publishing program, Pfeiffer offers content in an array of formats, from fieldbooks for the practitioner to complete, ready-to-use training packages that support group learning.

FIELDBOOK Designed to provide information and guidance to practitioners in the midst of action. Most fieldbooks are companions to another, sometimes earlier, work, from which its ideas are derived; the fieldbook makes practical what was theoretical in the original text. Fieldbooks can certainly be read from cover to cover. More likely, though, you'll find yourself bouncing around following a particular theme, or dipping in as the mood, and the situation, dictate.

HANDBOOK A contributed volume of work on a single topic, comprising an eclectic mix of ideas, case studies, and best practices sourced by practitioners and experts in the field.

An editor or team of editors usually is appointed to seek out contributors and to evaluate content for relevance to the topic. Think of a handbook not as a ready-to-eat meal, but as a cookbook of ingredients that enables you to create the most fitting experience for the occasion.

RESOURCE Materials designed to support group learning. They come in many forms: a complete, ready-to-use exercise (such as a game); a comprehensive resource on one topic (such as conflict management) containing a variety of methods and approaches; or a collection of like-minded activities (such as icebreakers) on multiple subjects and situations.

TRAINING PACKAGE An entire, ready-to-use learning program that focuses on a particular topic or skill. All packages comprise a guide for the facilitator/trainer and a workbook for the participants. Some packages are supported with additional media—such as video—or learning aids, instruments, or other devices to help participants understand concepts or practice and develop skills.

- *Facilitator/trainer's guide* Contains an introduction to the program, advice on how to organize and facilitate the learning event, and step-by-step instructor notes. The guide also contains copies of presentation materials—handouts, presentations, and overhead designs, for example—used in the program.

- *Participant's workbook* Contains exercises and reading materials that support the learning goal and serves as a valuable reference and support guide for participants in the weeks and months that follow the learning event. Typically, each participant will require his or her own workbook.

ELECTRONIC CD-ROMs and web-based products transform static Pfeiffer content into dynamic, interactive experiences. Designed to take advantage of the searchability, automation, and ease-of-use that technology provides, our e-products bring convenience and immediate accessibility to your workspace.

METHODOLOGIES

CASE STUDY A presentation, in narrative form, of an actual event that has occurred inside an organization. Case studies are not prescriptive, nor are they used to prove a point; they are designed to develop critical analysis and decision-making skills. A case study has a specific time frame, specifies a sequence of events, is narrative in structure, and contains a plot structure—an issue (what should be/have been done?). Use case studies when the goal is to enable participants to apply previously learned theories to the circumstances in the case, decide what is pertinent, identify the real issues, decide what should have been done, and develop a plan of action.

ENERGIZER A short activity that develops readiness for the next session or learning event. Energizers are most commonly used after a break or lunch to stimulate or refocus the group. Many involve some form of physical activity, so they are a useful way to counter post-lunch lethargy. Other uses include transitioning from one topic to another, where "mental" distancing is important.

EXPERIENTIAL LEARNING ACTIVITY (ELA) A facilitator-led intervention that moves participants through the learning cycle from experience to application (also known as a Structured Experience). ELAs are carefully thought-out designs in which there is a definite learning purpose and intended outcome. Each step—everything that participants do during the activity—facilitates the accomplishment of the stated goal. Each ELA includes complete instructions for facilitating the intervention and a clear statement of goals, suggested group size and timing, materials required, an explanation of the process, and, where appropriate, possible variations to the activity. (For more detail on Experiential Learning Activities, see the Introduction to the *Reference Guide to Handbooks and Annuals*, 1999 edition, Pfeiffer, San Francisco.)

GAME A group activity that has the purpose of fostering team spirit and togetherness in addition to the achievement of a pre-stated goal. Usually contrived—undertaking a desert expedition, for example—this type of learning method offers an engaging means for participants to demonstrate and practice business and interpersonal skills. Games are effective for team building and personal development mainly because the goal is subordinate to the process—the means through which participants reach decisions, collaborate, communicate, and generate trust and understanding. Games often engage teams in "friendly" competition.

ICEBREAKER A (usually) short activity designed to help participants overcome initial anxiety in a training session and/or to acquaint the participants with one another. An icebreaker can be a fun activity or can be tied to specific topics or training goals. While a useful tool in itself, the icebreaker comes into its own in situations where tension or resistance exists within a group.

INSTRUMENT A device used to assess, appraise, evaluate, describe, classify, and summarize various aspects of human behavior. The term used to describe an instrument depends primarily on its format and purpose. These terms include survey, questionnaire, inventory, diagnostic, survey, and poll. Some uses of instruments include providing instrumental feedback to group members, studying here-and-now processes or functioning within a group, manipulating group composition, and evaluating outcomes of training and other interventions.

Instruments are popular in the training and HR field because, in general, more growth can occur if an individual is provided with a method for focusing specifically on his or her own behavior. Instruments also are used to obtain information that will serve as a basis for change and to assist in workforce planning efforts.

Paper-and-pencil tests still dominate the instrument landscape with a typical package comprising a facilitator's guide, which offers advice on administering the instrument and interpreting the collected data, and an initial set of instruments. Additional instruments are available separately. Pfeiffer, though, is investing heavily in e-instruments. Electronic instrumentation provides effortless distribution and, for larger groups particularly, offers advantages over paper-and-pencil tests in the time it takes to analyze data and provide feedback.

LECTURETTE A short talk that provides an explanation of a principle, model, or process that is pertinent to the participants' current learning needs. A lecturette is intended to establish a common language bond between the trainer and the participants by providing a mutual frame of reference. Use a lecturette as an introduction to a group activity or event, as an interjection during an event, or as a handout.

MODEL A graphic depiction of a system or process and the relationship among its elements. Models provide a frame of reference and something more tangible, and more easily remembered, than a verbal explanation. They also give participants something to "go on," enabling them to track their own progress as they experience the dynamics, processes, and relationships being depicted in the model.

ROLE PLAY A technique in which people assume a role in a situation/scenario: a customer service rep in an angry-customer exchange, for example. The way in which the role is approached is then discussed and feedback is offered. The role play is often repeated using a different approach and/or incorporating changes made based on feedback received. In other words, role playing is a spontaneous interaction involving realistic behavior under artificial (and safe) conditions.

SIMULATION A methodology for understanding the interrelationships among components of a system or process. Simulations differ from games in that they test or use a model that depicts or mirrors some aspect of reality in form, if not necessarily in content. Learning occurs by studying the effects of change on one or more factors of the model. Simulations are commonly used to test hypotheses about what happens in a system—often referred to as "what if?" analysis—or to examine best-case/worst-case scenarios.

THEORY A presentation of an idea from a conjectural perspective. Theories are useful because they encourage us to examine behavior and phenomena through a different lens.

TOPICS

The twin goals of providing effective and practical solutions for workforce training and organization development and meeting the educational needs of training and human resource professionals shape Pfeiffer's publishing program. Core topics include the following:

Leadership & Management

Communication & Presentation

Coaching & Mentoring

Training & Development

E-Learning

Teams & Collaboration

OD & Strategic Planning

Human Resources

Consulting

What will you find on pfeiffer.com?

- The best in workplace performance solutions for training and HR professionals

- Downloadable training tools, exercises, and content

- Web-exclusive offers

- Training tips, articles, and news

- Seamless on-line ordering

- Author guidelines, information on becoming a Pfeiffer Affiliate, and much more

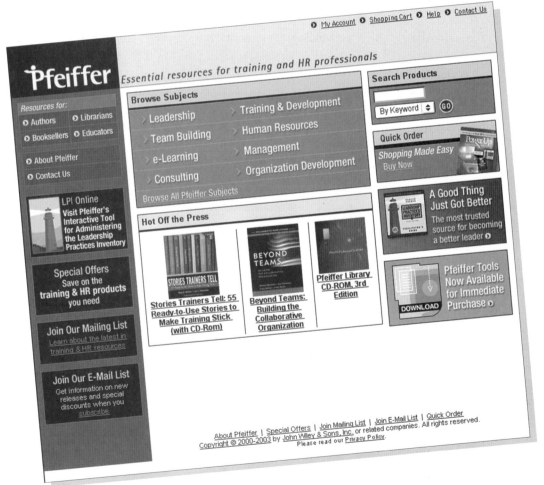

Discover more at www.pfeiffer.com